Dancing After TEN

Editors: Gary Groth & Conrad Groth
Designer: Chelsea Wirtz
Production: Christina Hwang
Project Manager: Kathleen Rea
Associate Publisher: Eric Reynolds
Publisher: Gary Groth

This edition of *Dancing After TEN* is copyright © 2020 Fantagraphics Books, Inc.
Art & text © Vivian Chong and Georgia Webber. All rights reserved.
Permission to reproduce content must be obtained from the publisher.

Fantagraphics Books, Inc.
7563 Lake City Way NE
Seattle, WA 98115

ISBN: 978-1-68396-316-5
Library of Congress Control Number: 2019953903
First Fantagraphics Books edition: May 2020
Printed in China

www.fantagraphics.com   @fantagraphics

I dedicate this book to my eyes.
You have gone through so much.

In the first half of my life you gave me
the opportunity to see all the colors,
patterns, and geometry in the world.
These were the building blocks for my
aesthetic sensibility.

'Eyes,' you still are beautiful.

— VIVIAN CHONG

One

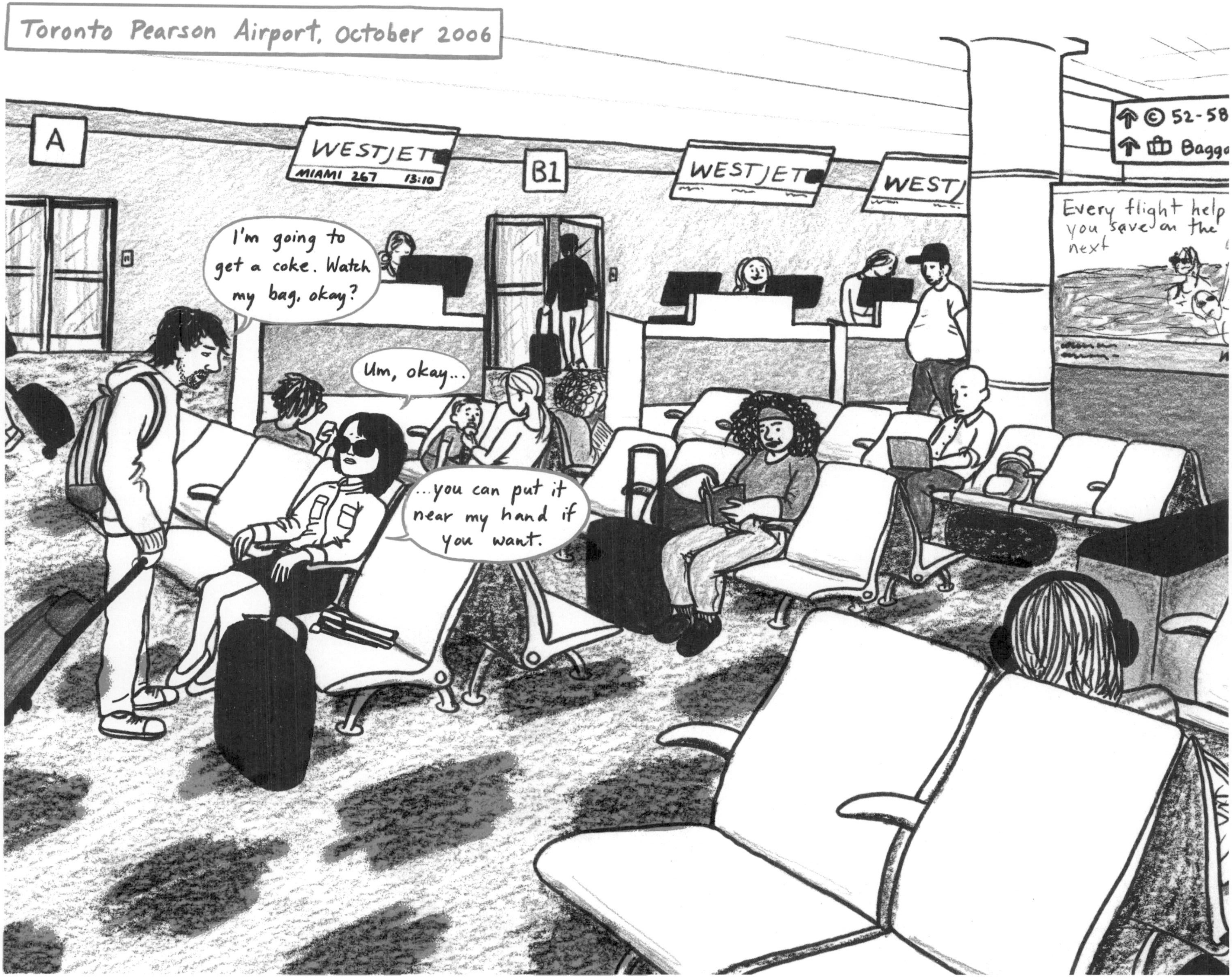
Toronto Pearson Airport, October 2006
A
WESTJET
MIAMI 267 13:10
B1
WESTJET
WEST
52-58
Bagg
Every flight help
you save on the
next
I'm going to get a coke. Watch my bag, okay?
Um, okay...
...you can put it near my hand if you want.

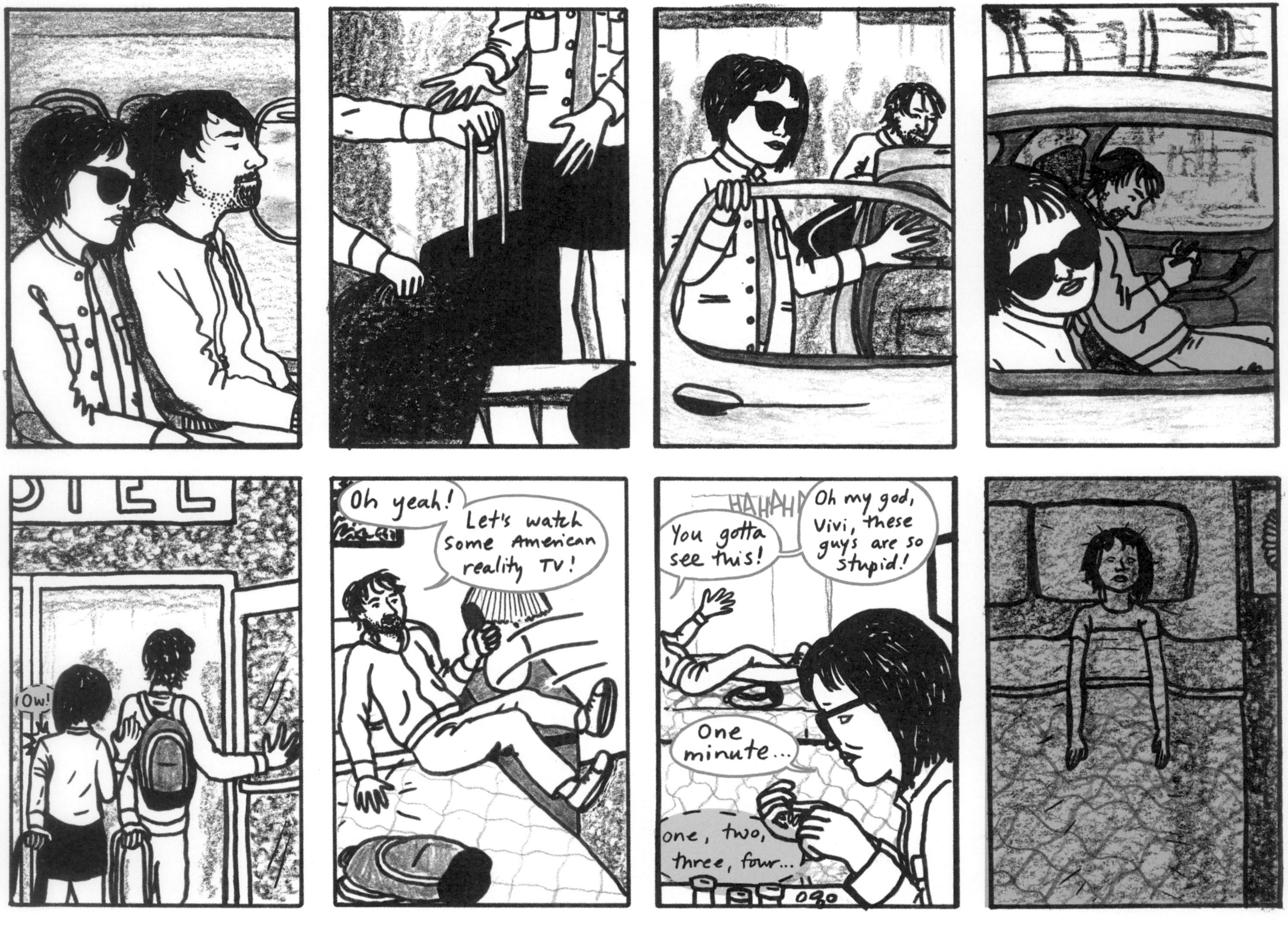

Ow!
Oh yeah!
Let's watch some American reality TV!
HAHAHA
You gotta see this!
Oh my god, Vivi, these guys are so stupid!
One minute...
one, two, three, four...

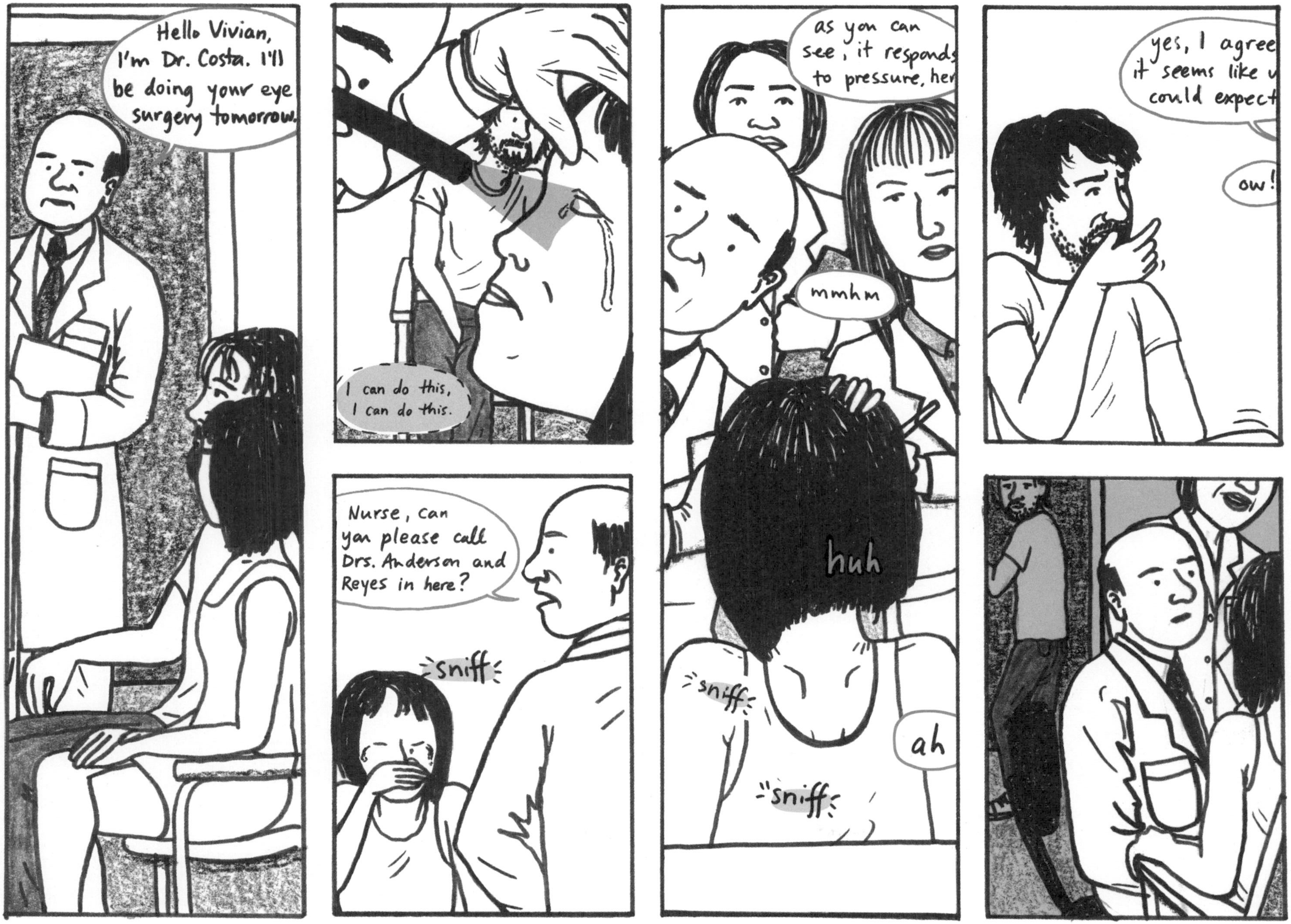
Hello Vivian, I'm Dr. Costa. I'll be doing your eye surgery tomorrow.
I can do this, I can do this.
Nurse, can you please call Drs. Anderson and Reyes in here?
sniff
as you can see, it responds to pressure, her
mmhm
huh
sniff
ah
sniff
yes, I agree it seems like could expect
ow!

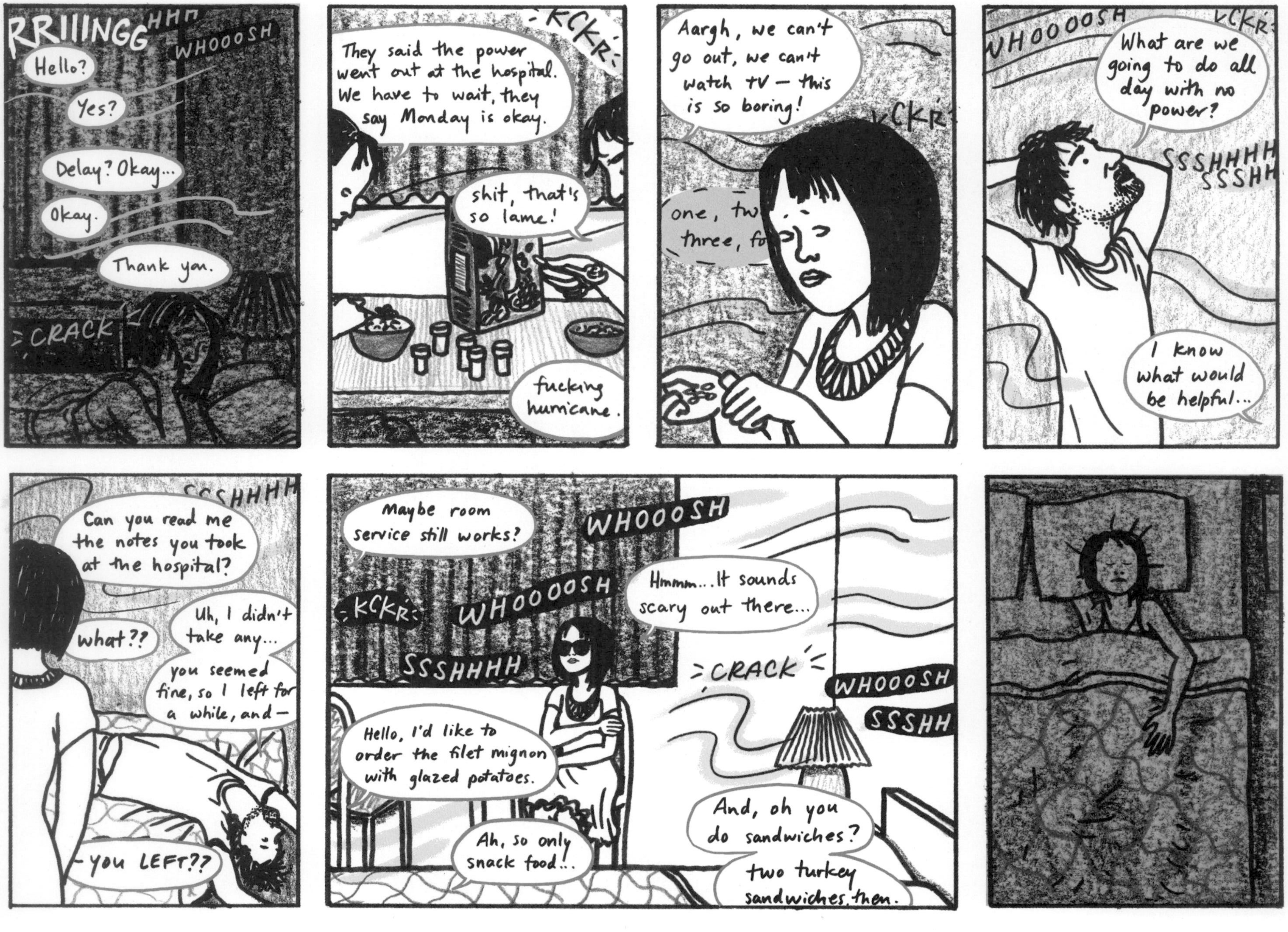
RRIIINGGHHH
WHOOOSH
Hello?
Yes?
Delay? Okay...
Okay.
Thank you.
CRACK
KCKR
They said the power went out at the hospital. We have to wait, they say Monday is okay.
shit, that's so lame!
fucking hurricane.
Aargh, we can't go out, we can't watch TV — this is so boring!
KCKR
one, two
three, fo
WHOOOOOSH
KCKR
What are we going to do all day with no power?
SSHHHH
SSSHH
I know what would be helpful...
SSSHHHH
Can you read me the notes you took at the hospital?
what??
Uh, I didn't take any...
you seemed fine, so I left for a while, and—
—you LEFT??
Maybe room service still works?
WHOOOSH
KCKR
WHOOOOOSH
SSSHHHH
Hmmm... It sounds scary out there...
CRACK
WHOOOSH
SSSHH
Hello, I'd like to order the filet mignon with glazed potatoes.
Ah, so only snack food!..
And, oh you do sandwiches?
two turkey sandwiches, then.

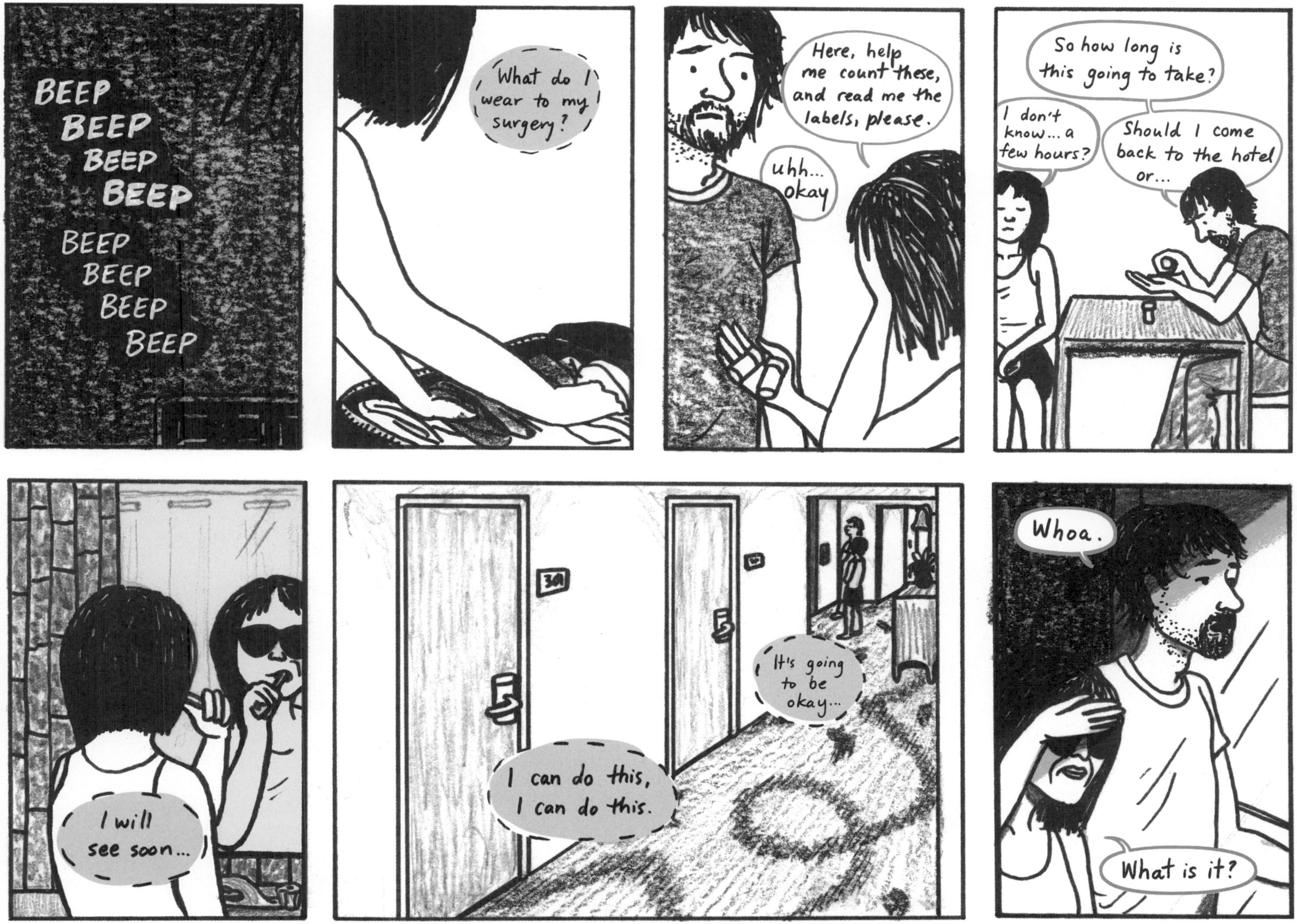
BEEP BEEP BEEP BEEP
BEEP BEEP BEEP BEEP
What do I wear to my surgery?
Here, help me count these, and read me the labels, please.
uhh... okay
So how long is this going to take?
I don't know... a few hours?
Should I come back to the hotel or...
I will see soon...
I can do this, I can do this.
It's going to be okay...
Whoa.
What is it?

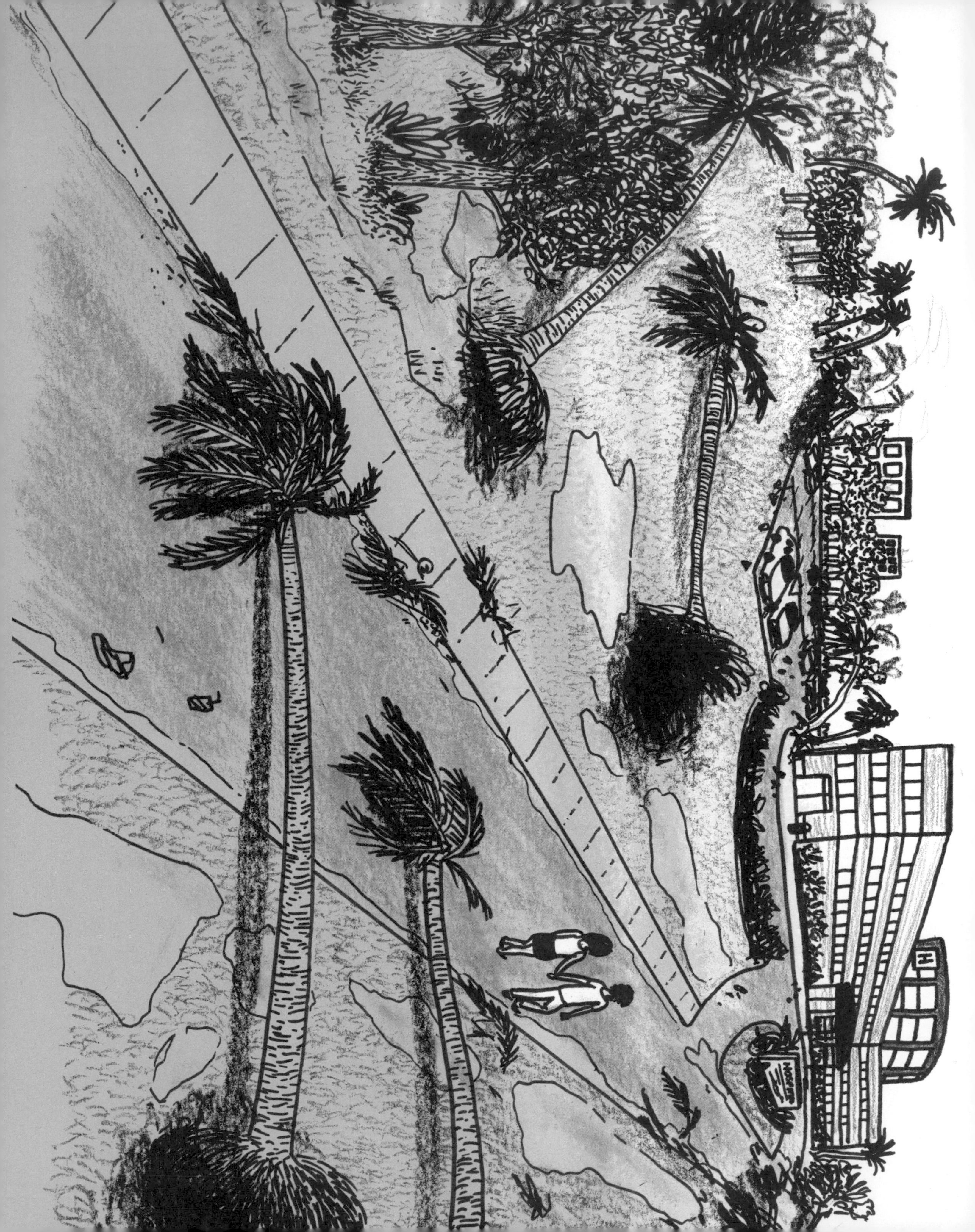

please shed
light on me

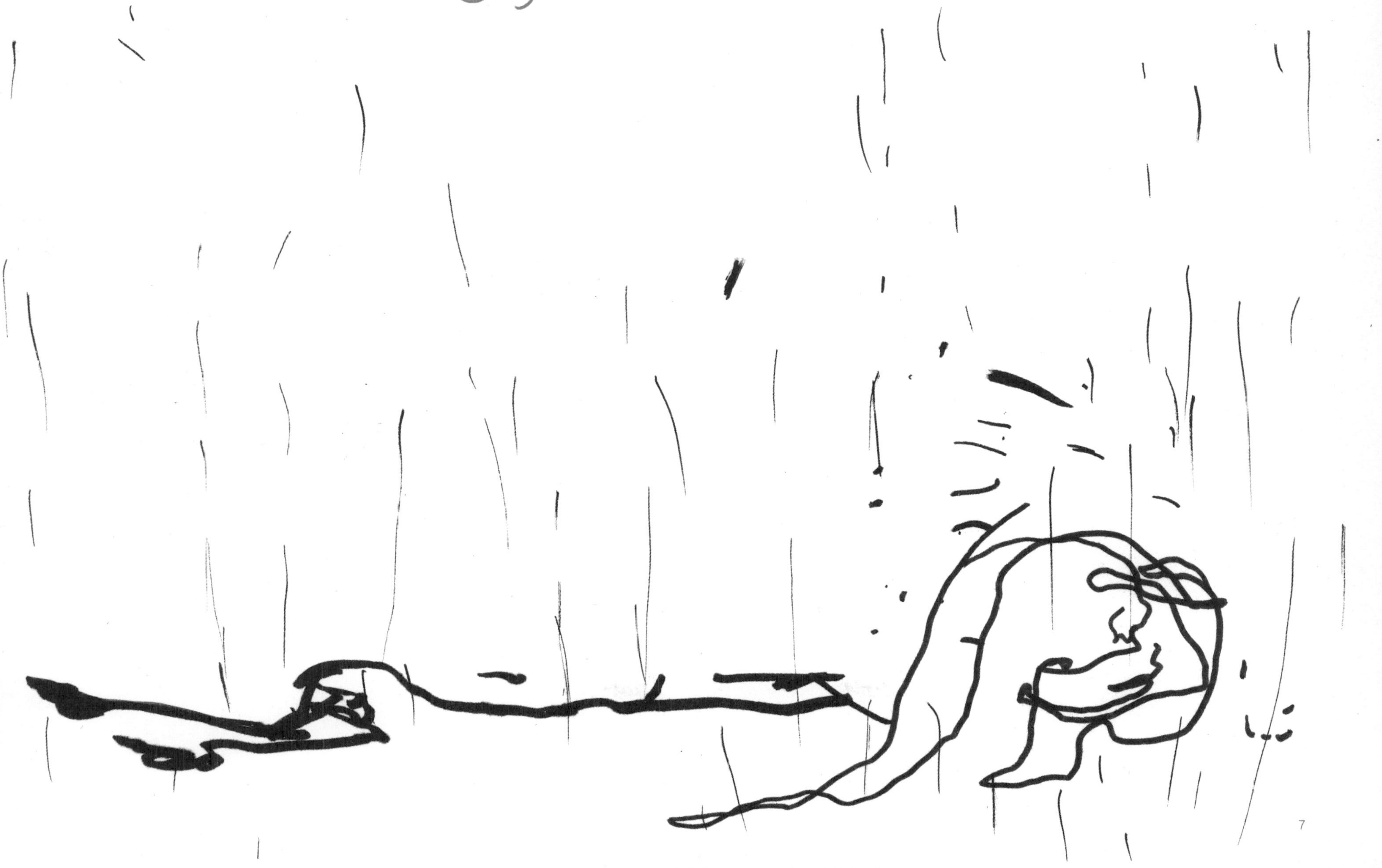

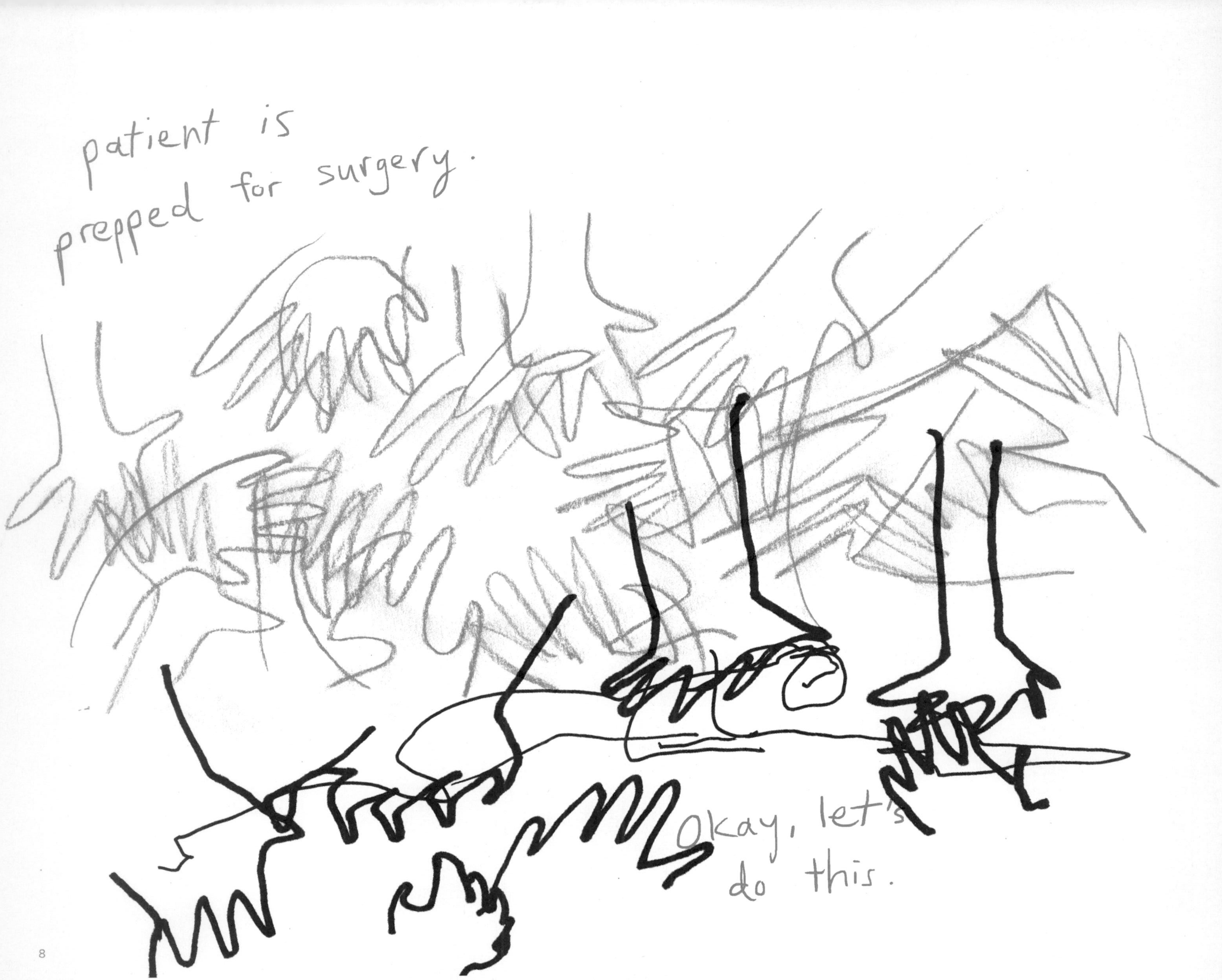
patient is prepped for surgery.
Okay, let's do this.

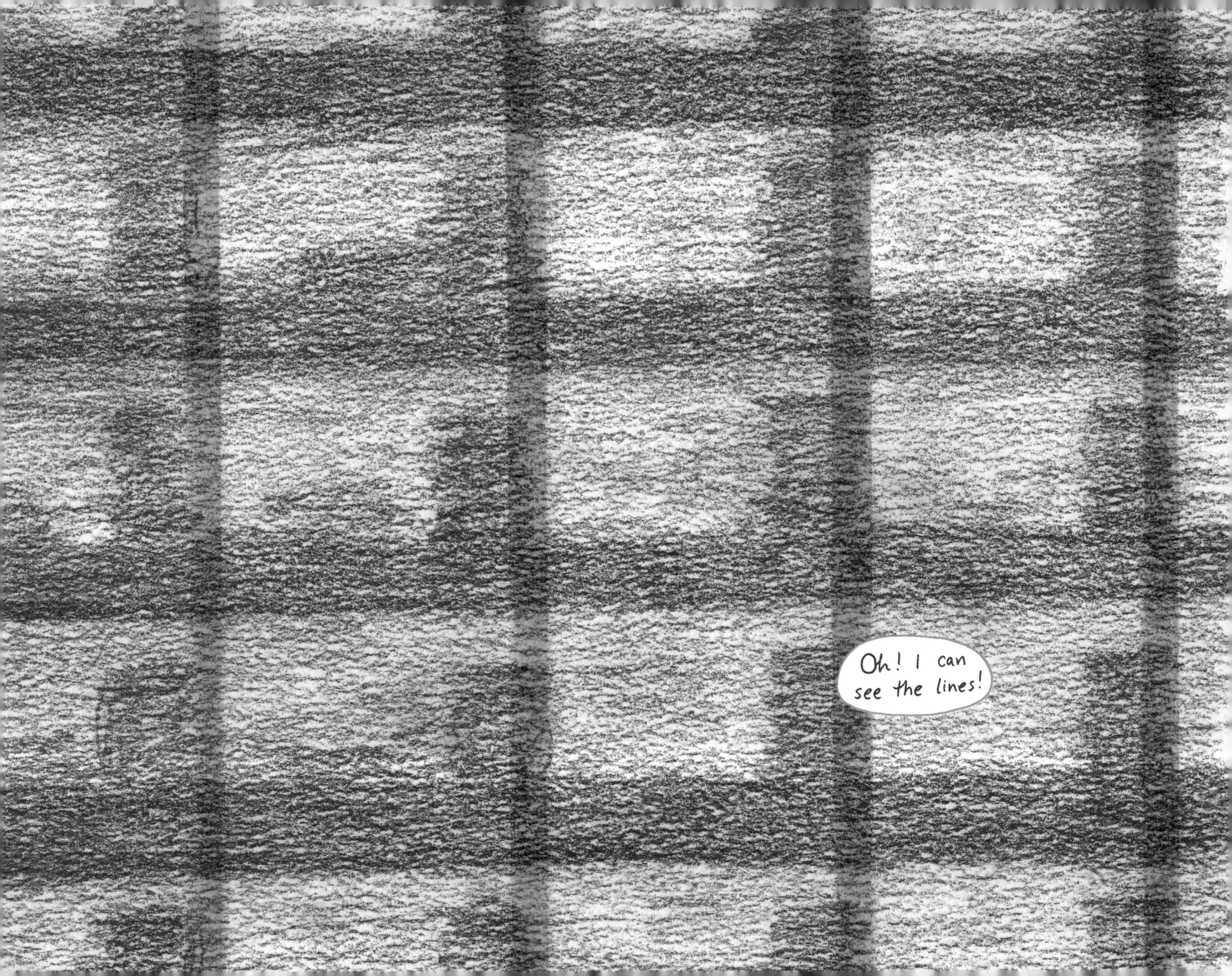
Oh! I can see the lines!

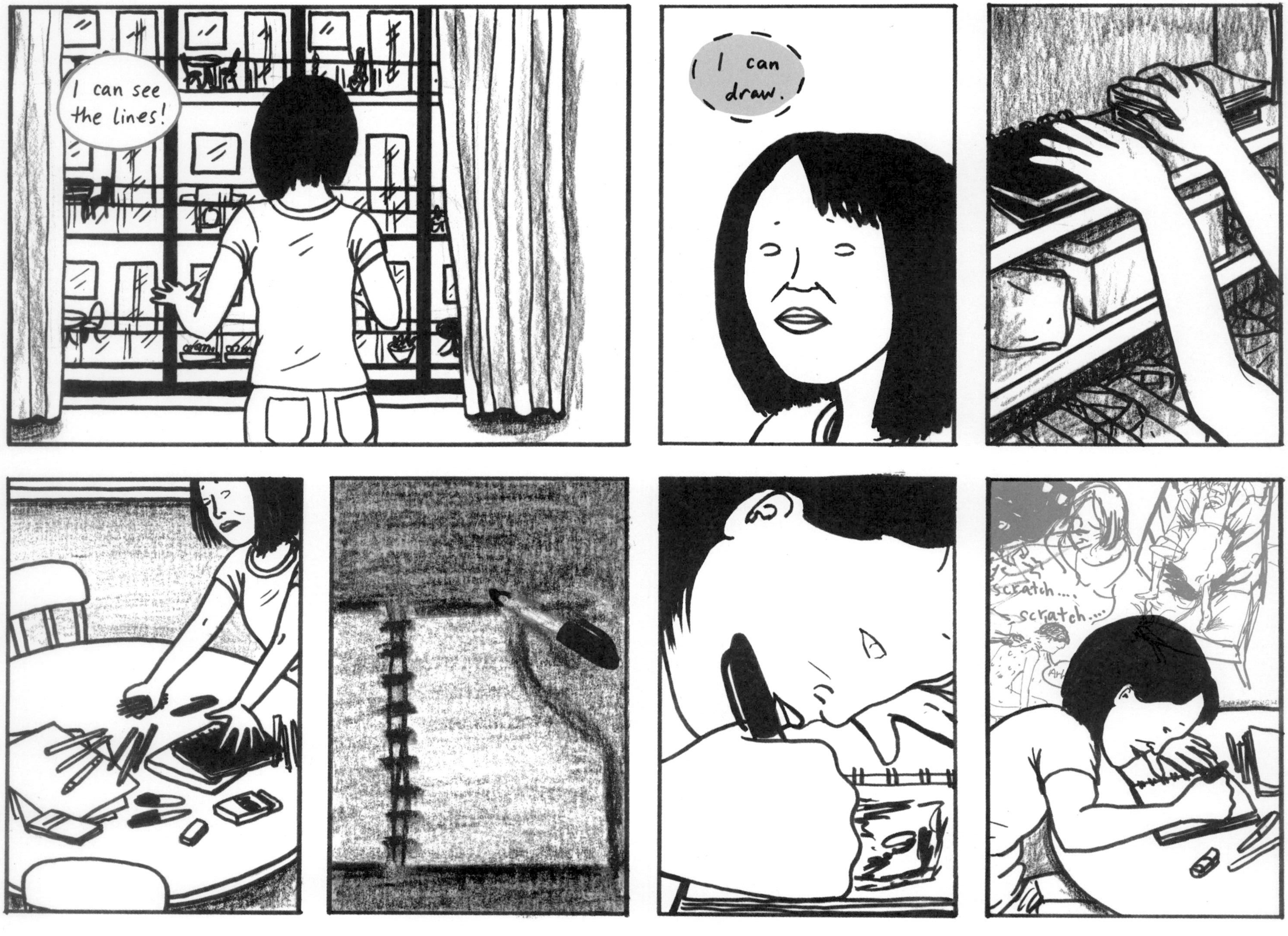
I can see the lines!
I can draw.
scratch....
scratch....
AH

Dancing After TEN

Two

St. Martin, 2004

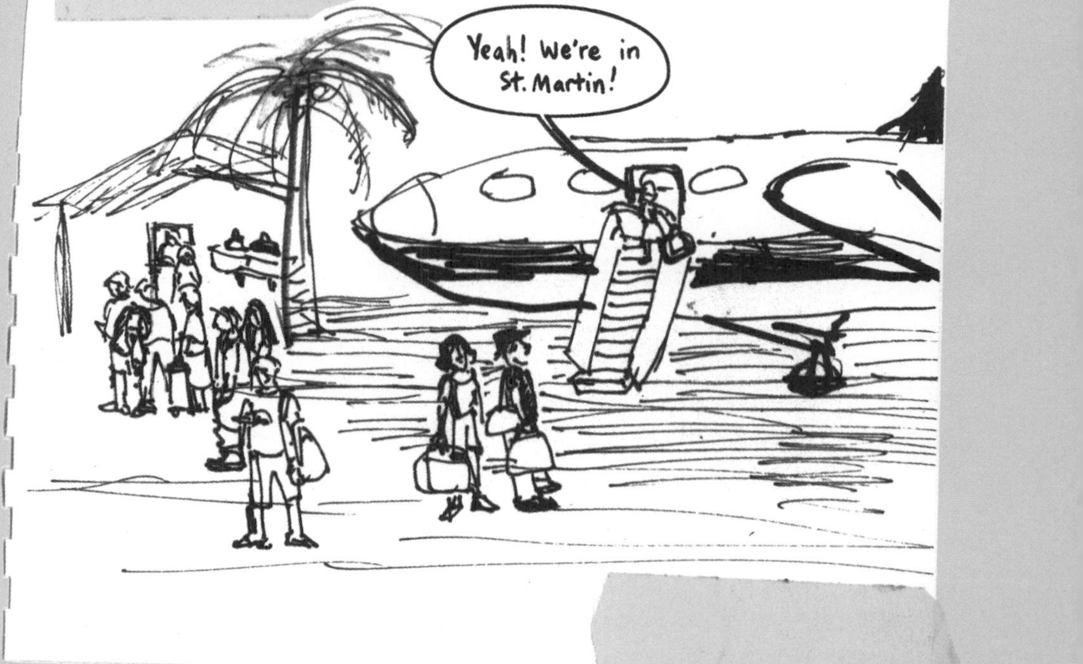
Yeah! We're in St. Martin!

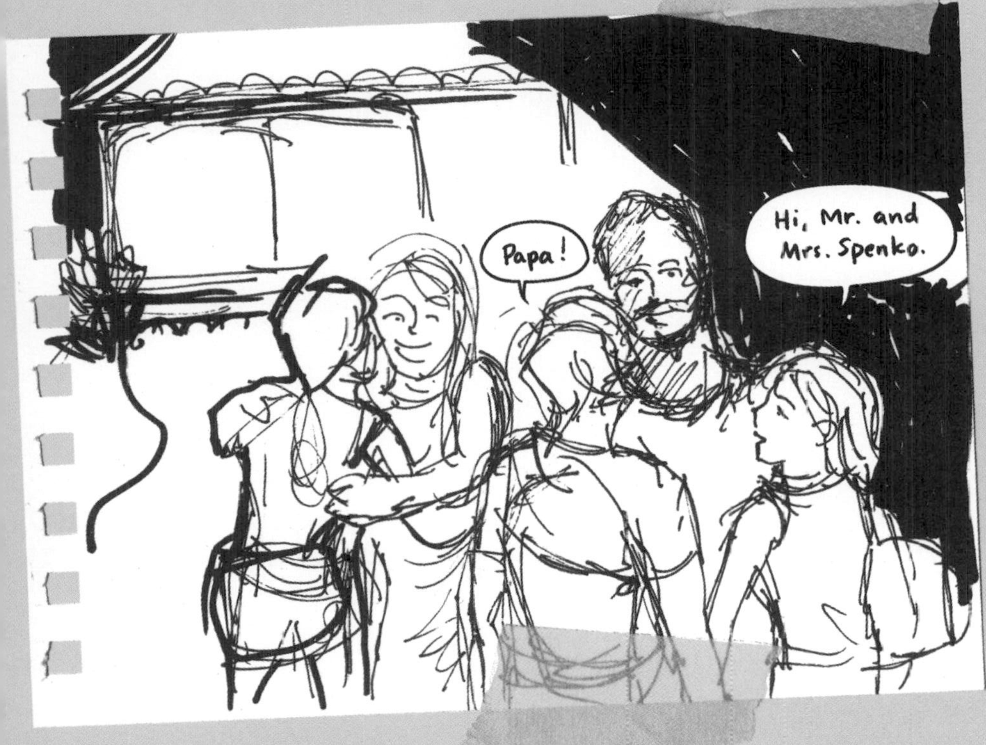
Papa!
Hi, Mr. and Mrs. Spenko.

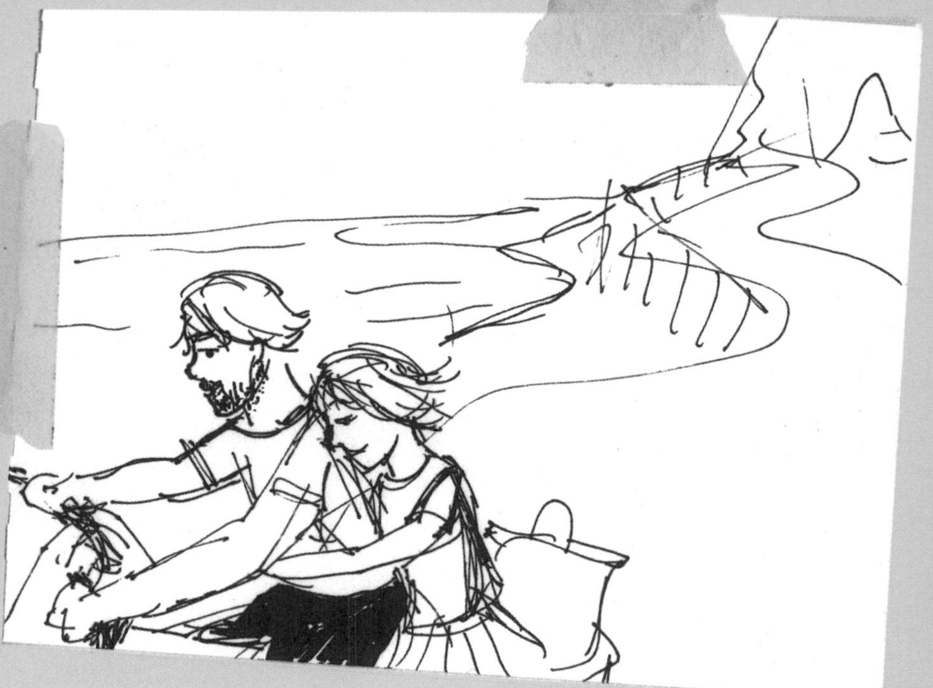

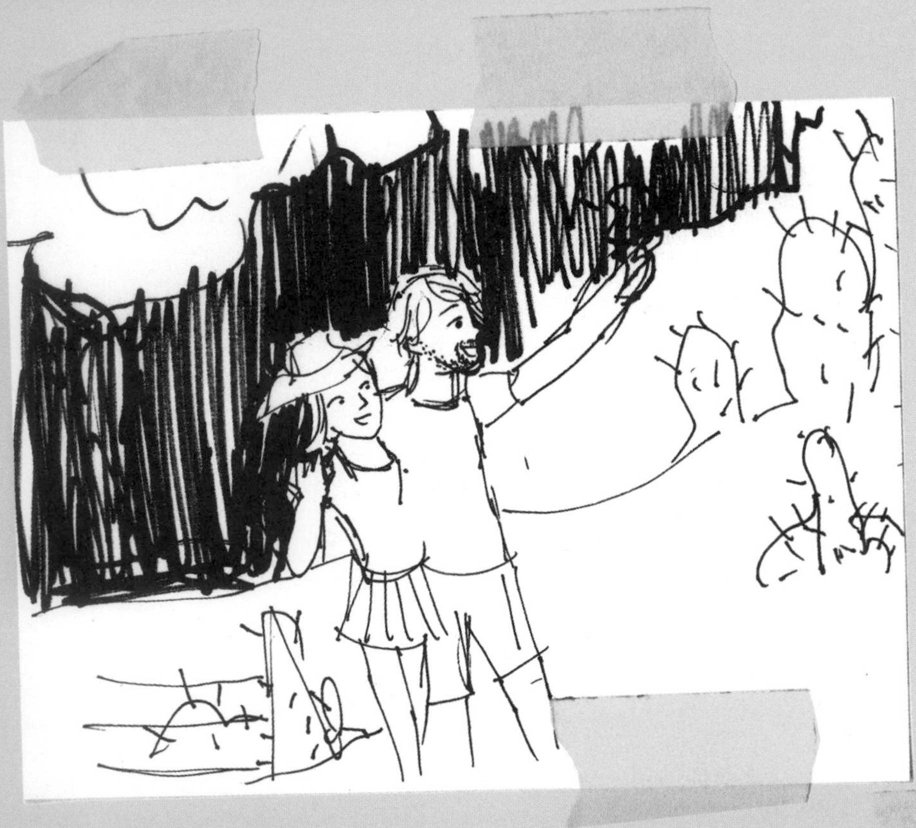

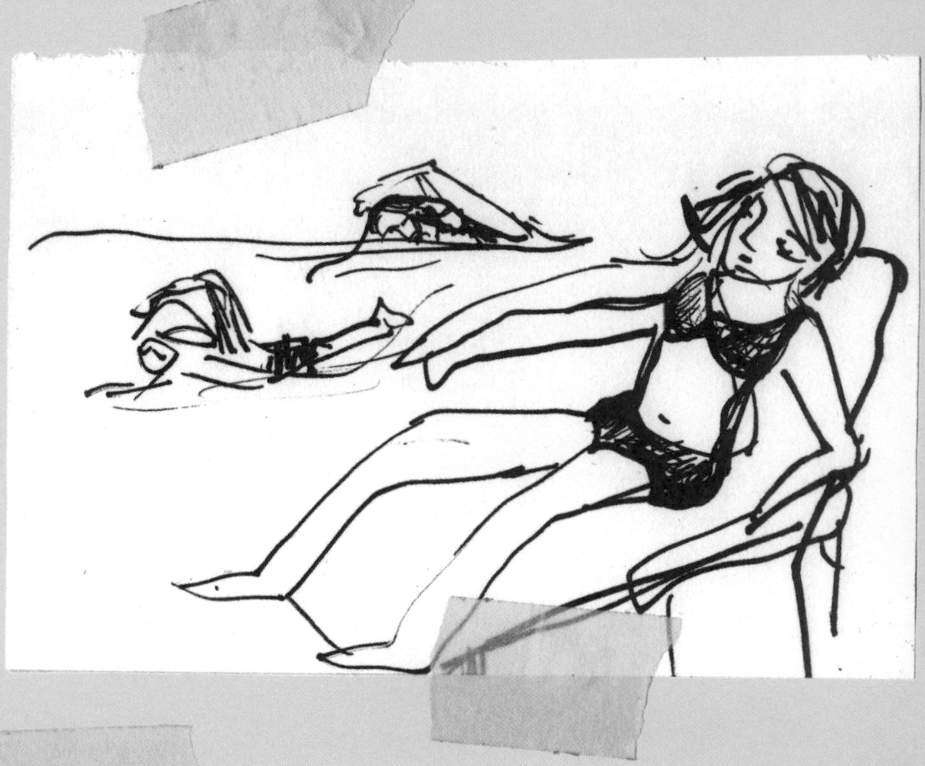

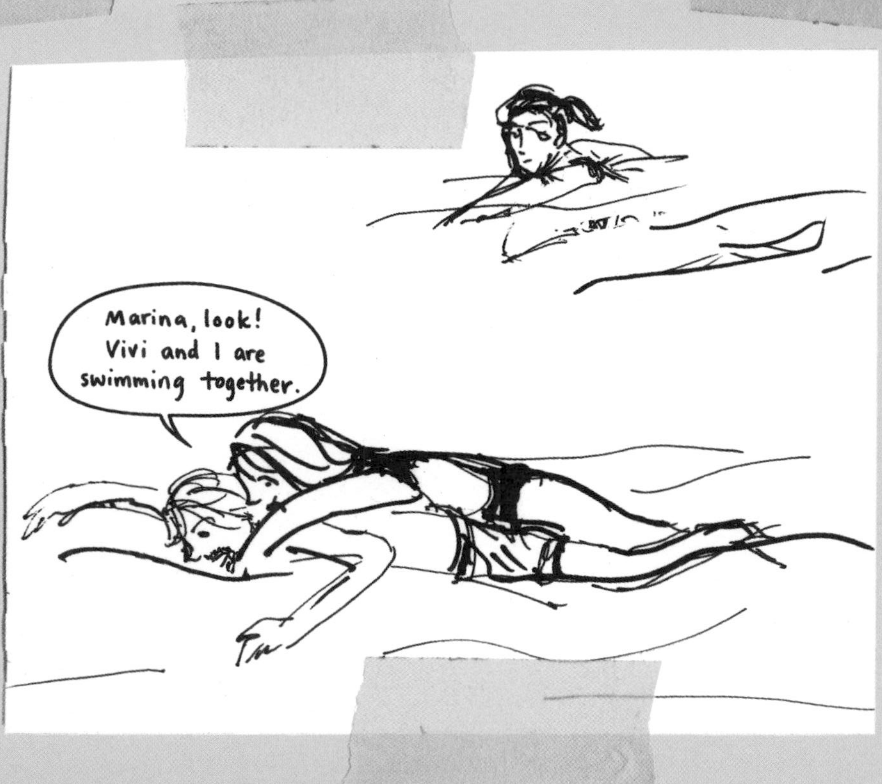
Marina, look! Vivi and I are swimming together.

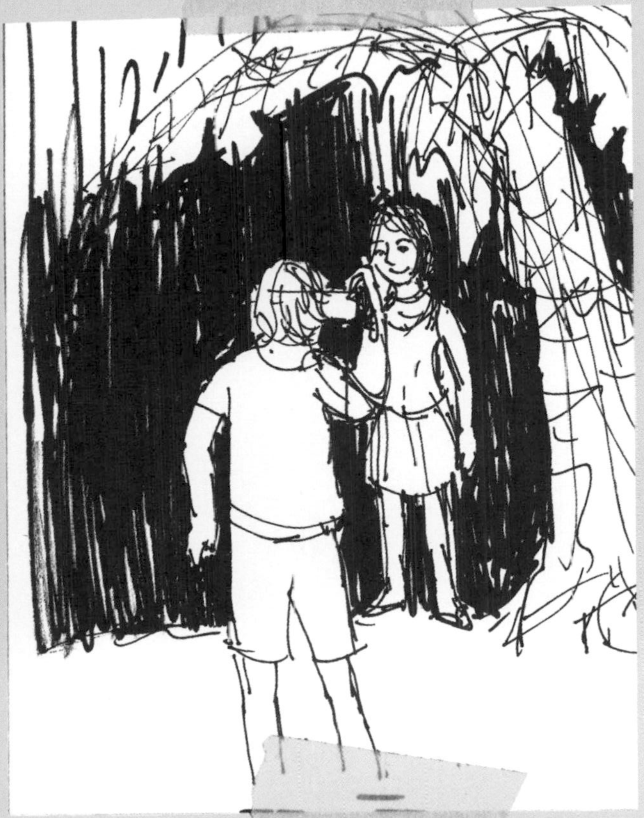

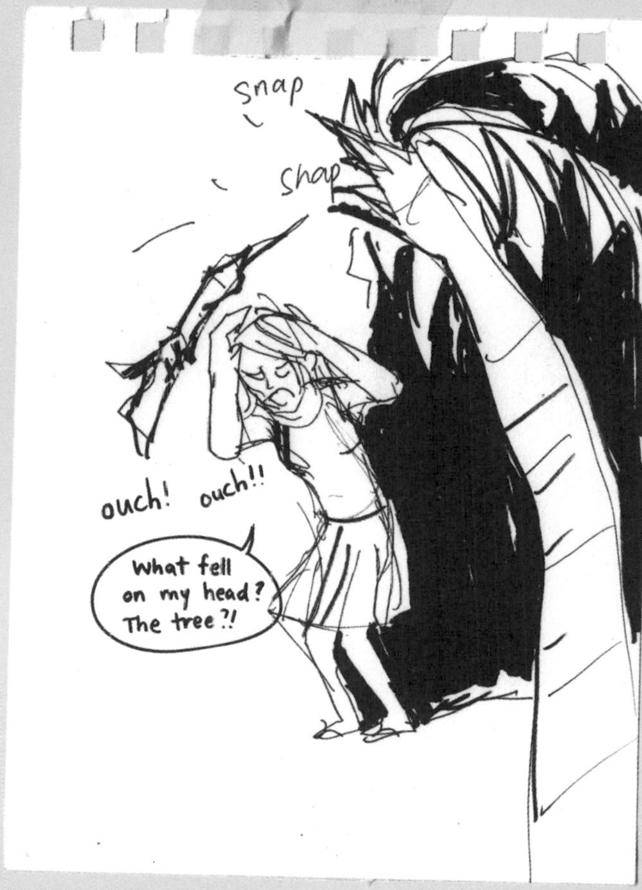
snap
snap
ouch! ouch!!
What fell on my head? The tree?!

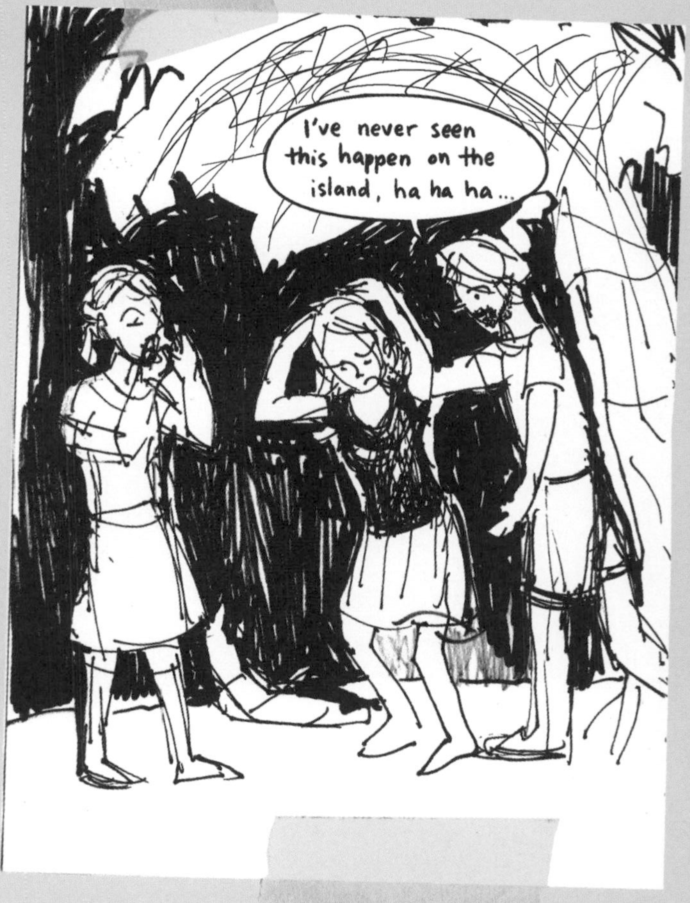
I've never seen this happen on the island, ha ha ha...

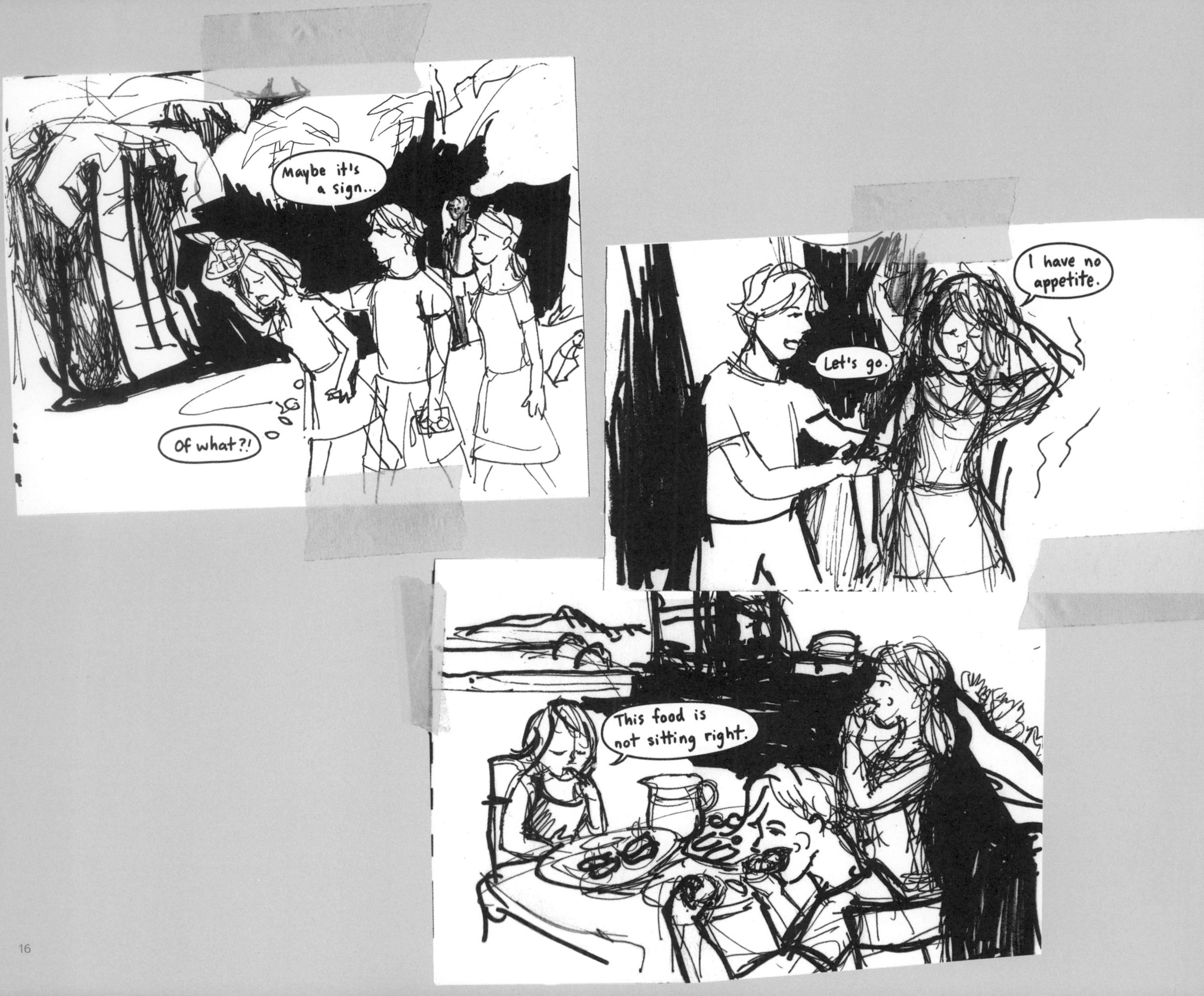
Maybe it's a sign...
Of what?!
I have no appetite.
Let's go.
This food is not sitting right.

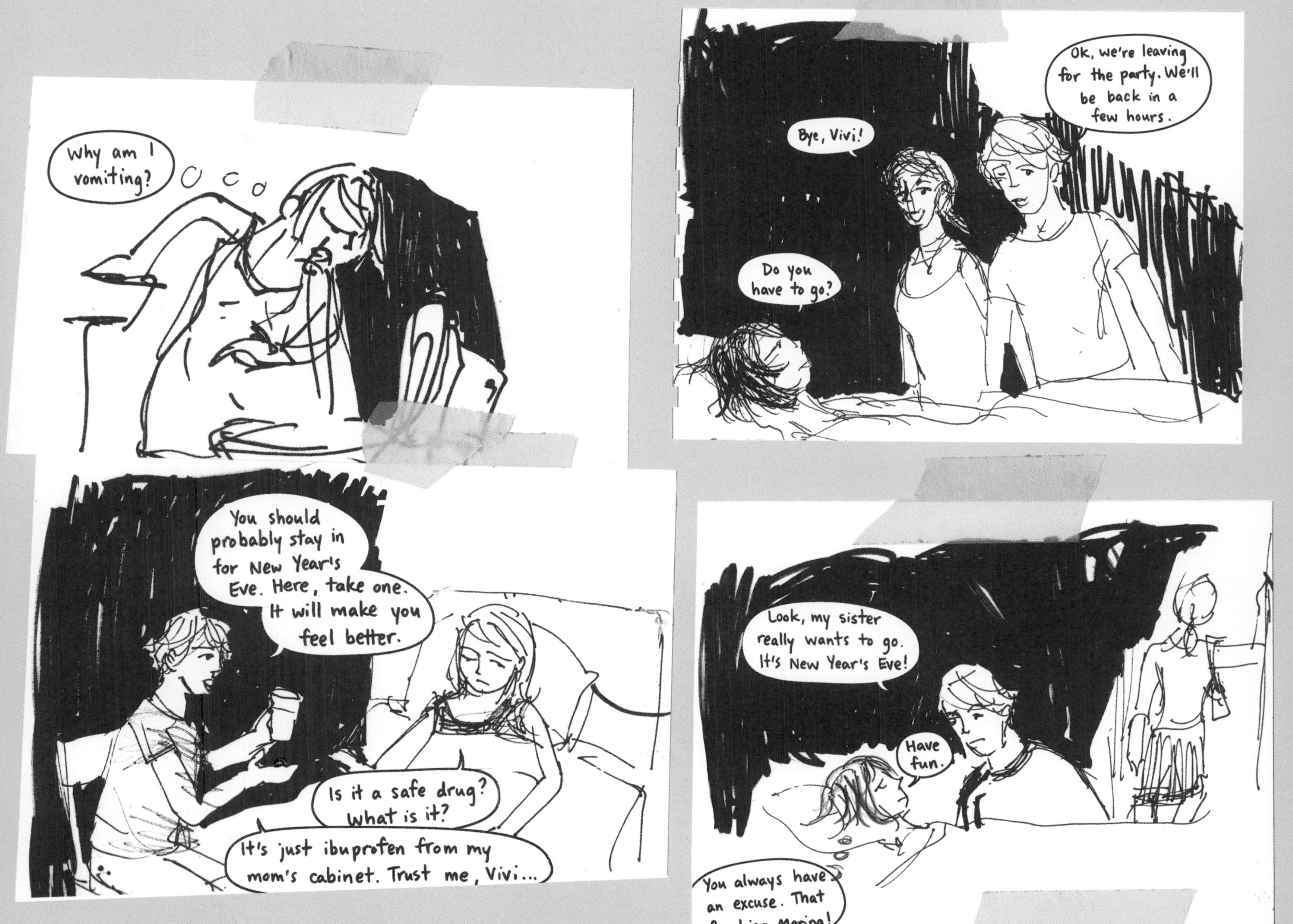

Why am I vomiting?
You should probably stay in for New Year's Eve. Here, take one. It will make you feel better.
Is it a safe drug? What is it?
It's just ibuprofen from my mom's cabinet. Trust me, Vivi...
Ok, we're leaving for the party. We'll be back in a few hours.
Bye, Vivi!
Do you have to go?
Look, my sister really wants to go. It's New Year's Eve!
Have fun.
You always have an excuse. That freaking Marina!

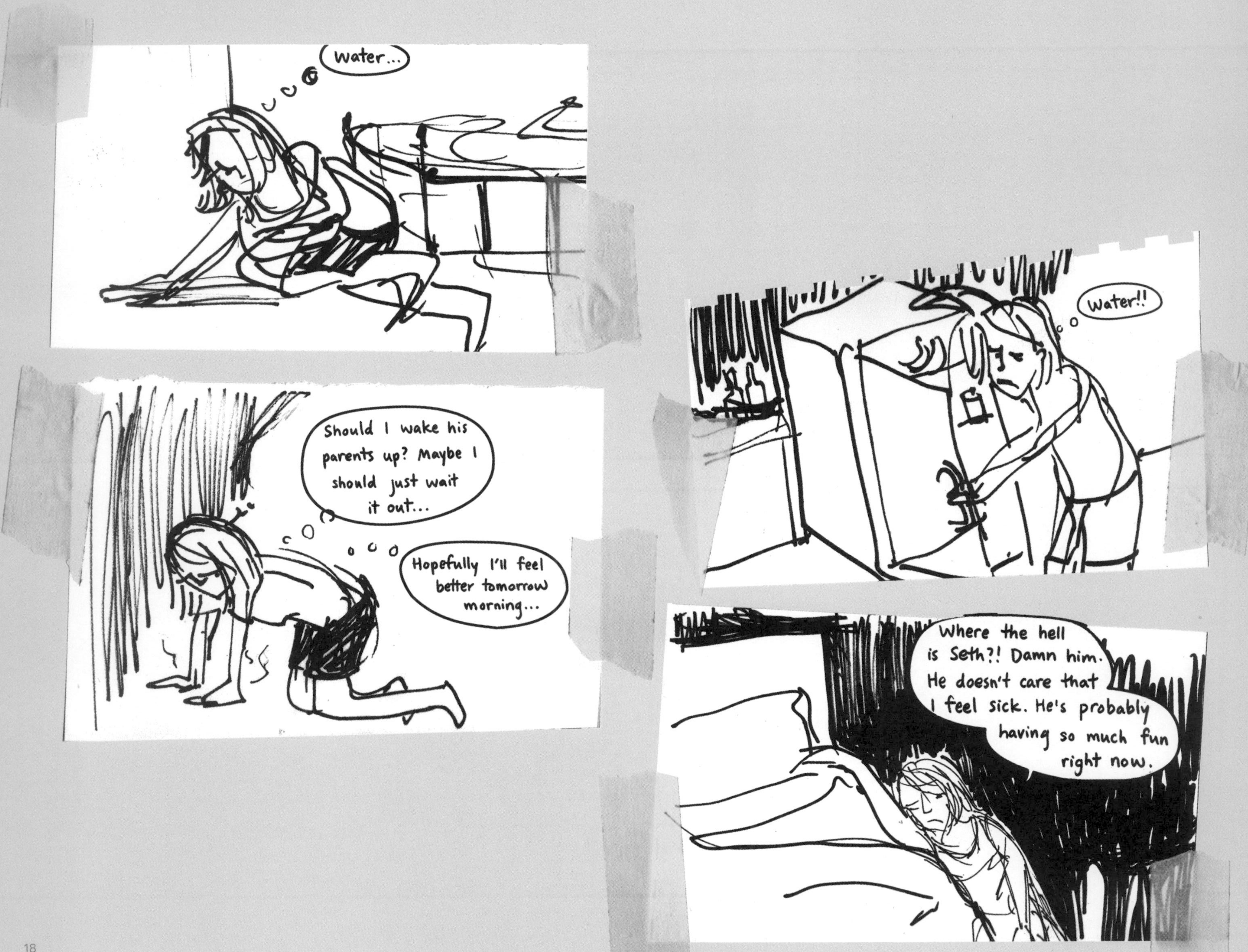
Water...
Should I wake his parents up? Maybe I should just wait it out...
Hopefully I'll feel better tomorrow morning...
Water!!
Where the hell is Seth?! Damn him. He doesn't care that I feel sick. He's probably having so much fun right now.

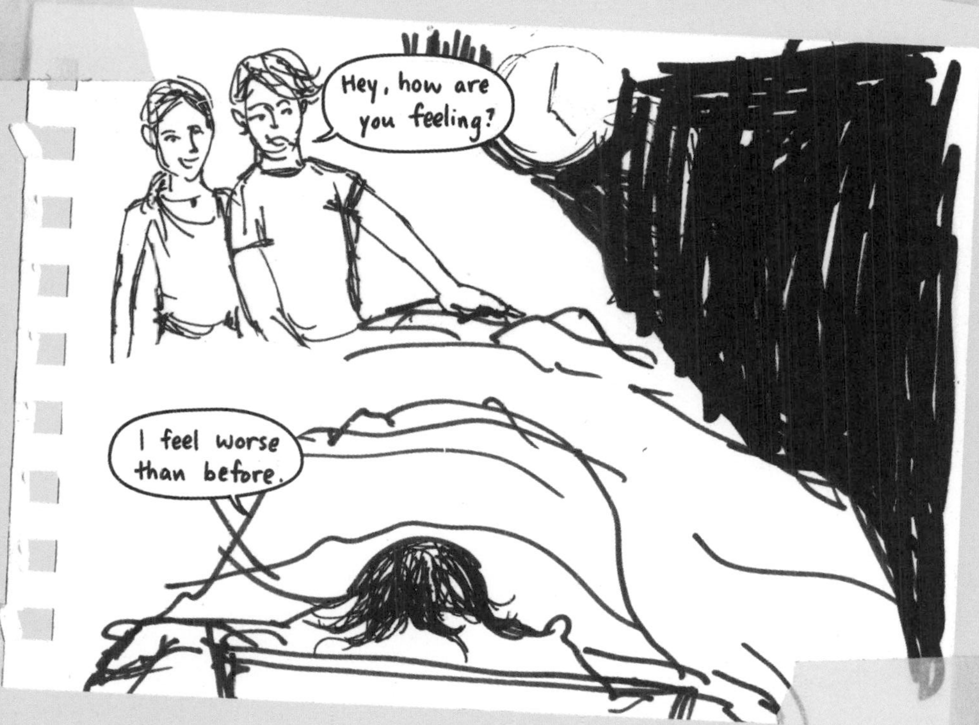
Hey, how are you feeling?
I feel worse than before.

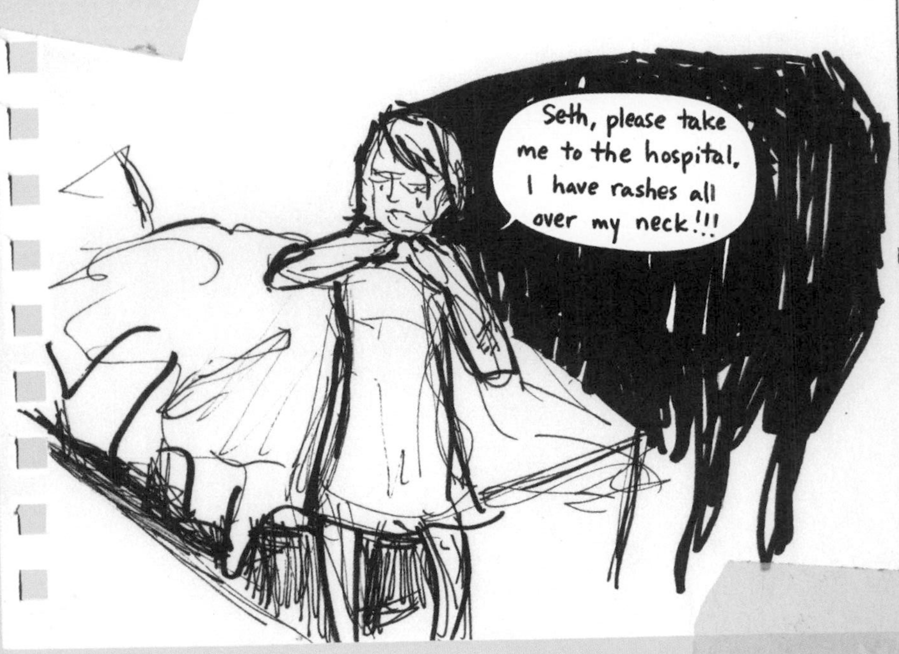
Seth, please take me to the hospital, I have rashes all over my neck!!!

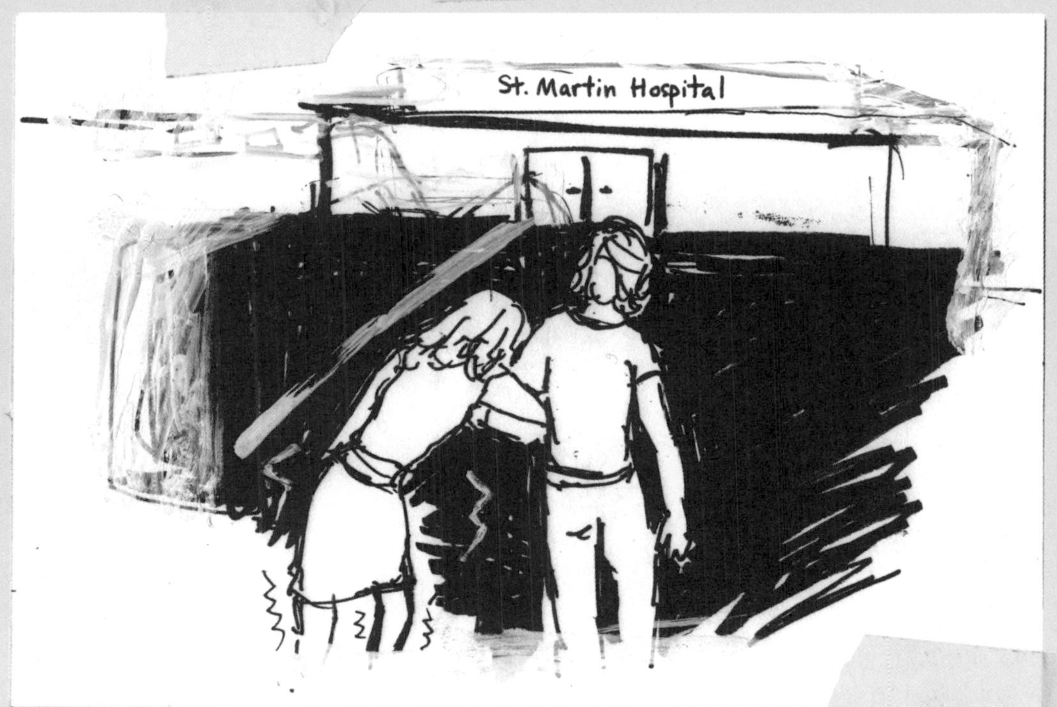
St. Martin Hospital

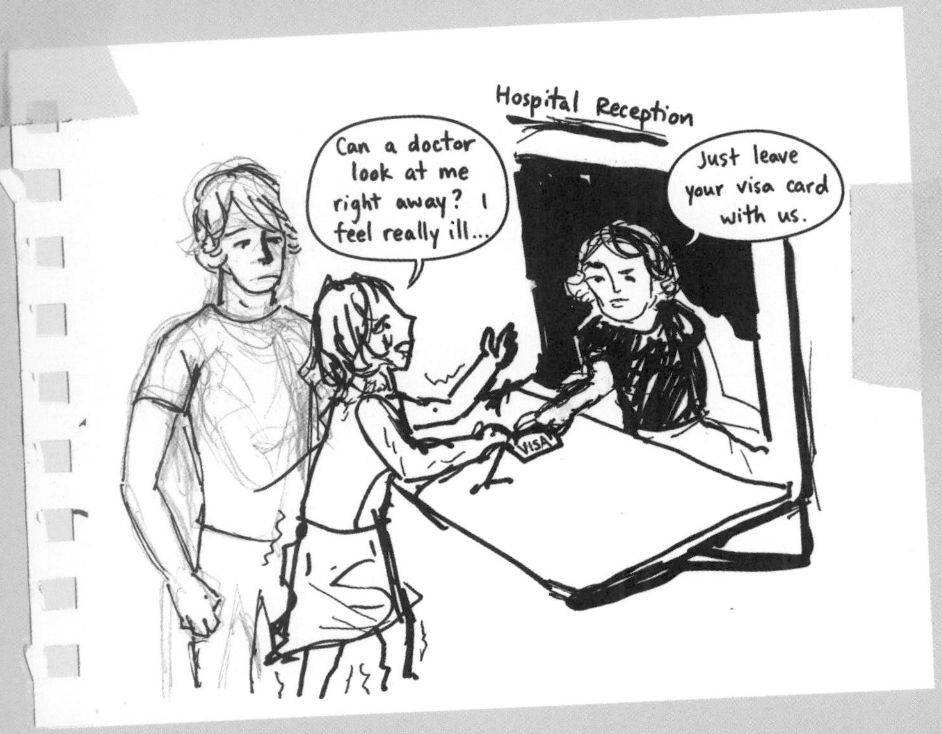
Hospital Reception
Can a doctor look at me right away? I feel really ill...
Just leave your visa card with us.
VISA

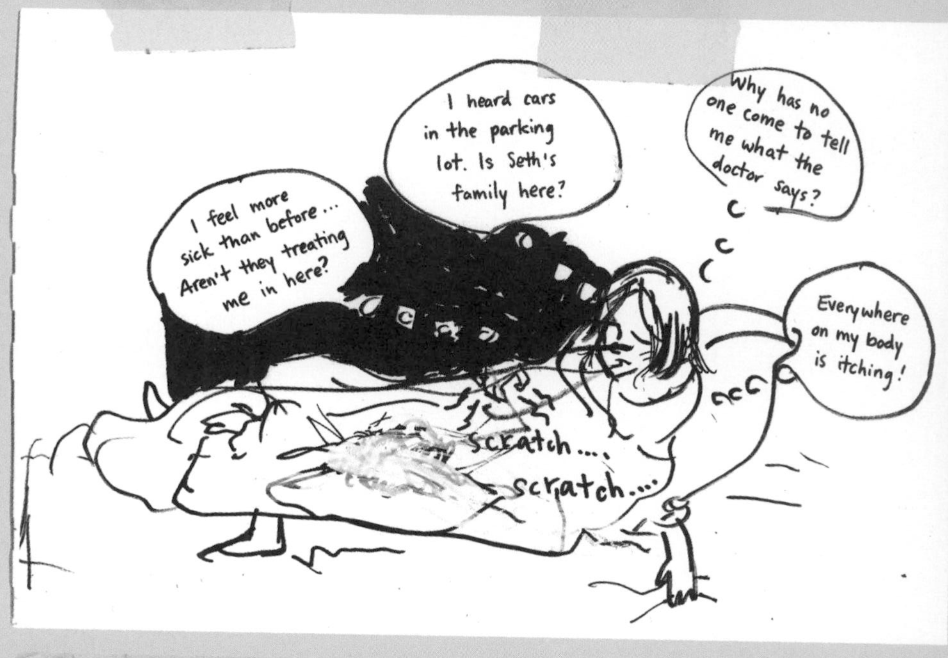
I feel more sick than before... Aren't they treating me in here?
I heard cars in the parking lot. Is Seth's family here?
Why has no one come to tell me what the doctor says?
Everywhere on my body is itching!
scratch....
scratch....

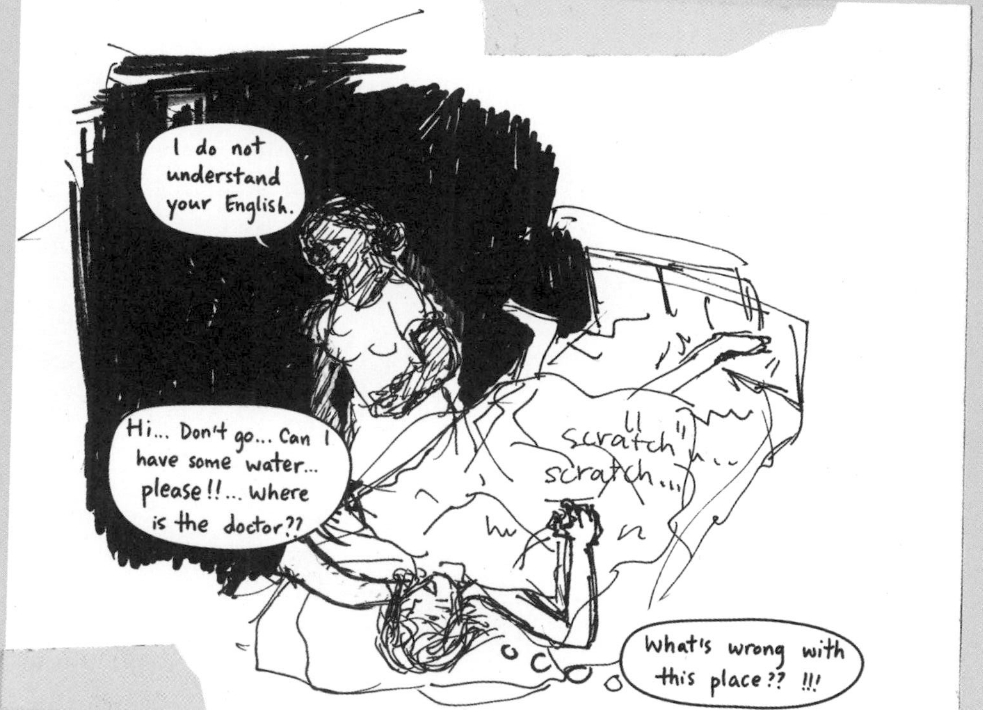
I do not understand your English.
Hi... Don't go... Can I have some water... please!!... where is the doctor??
scratch!!
scratch...!
What's wrong with this place?? !!!

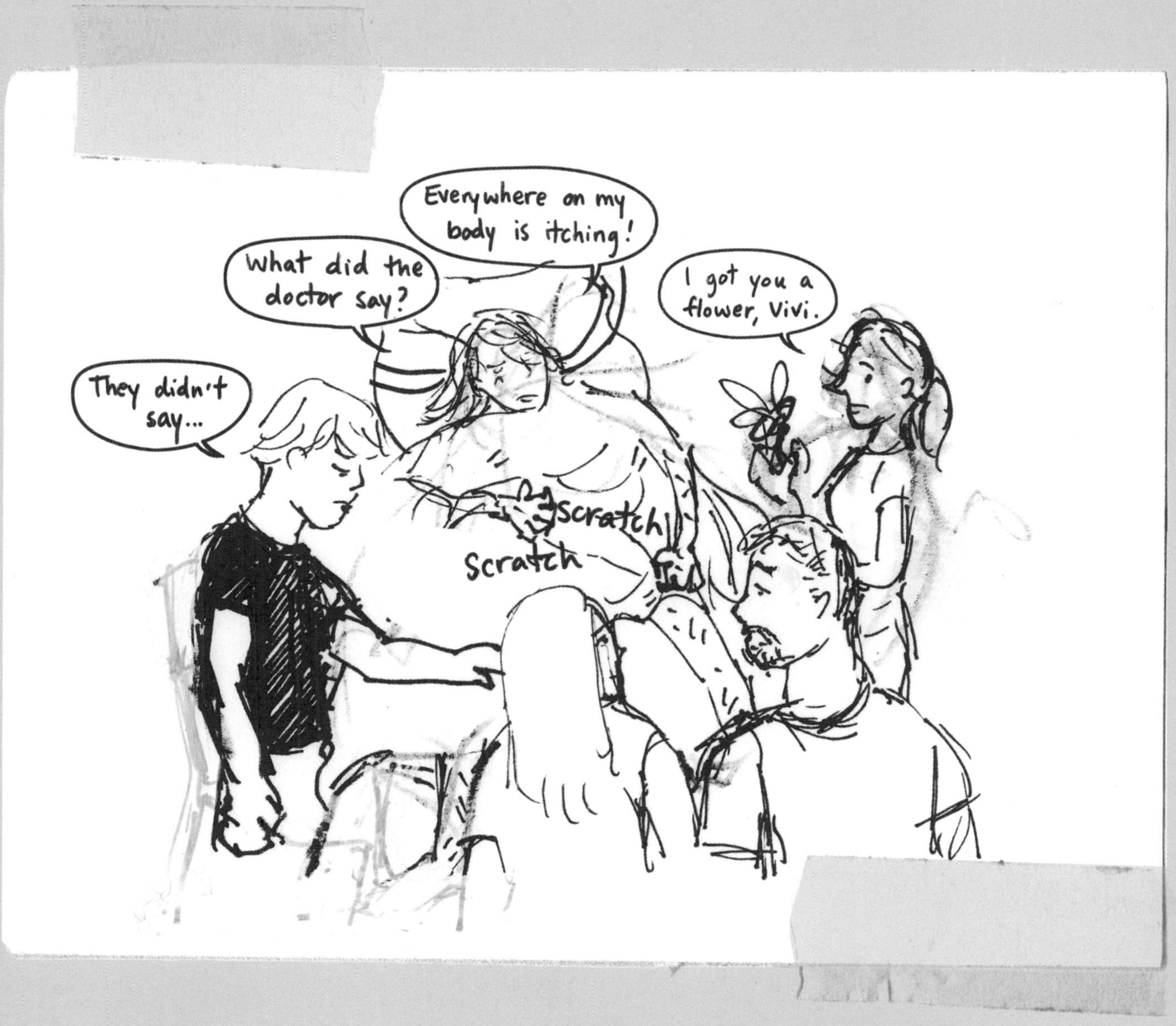
What did the doctor say?
They didn't say...
Everywhere on my body is itching!
I got you a flower, Vivi.
Scratch
Scratch

Three

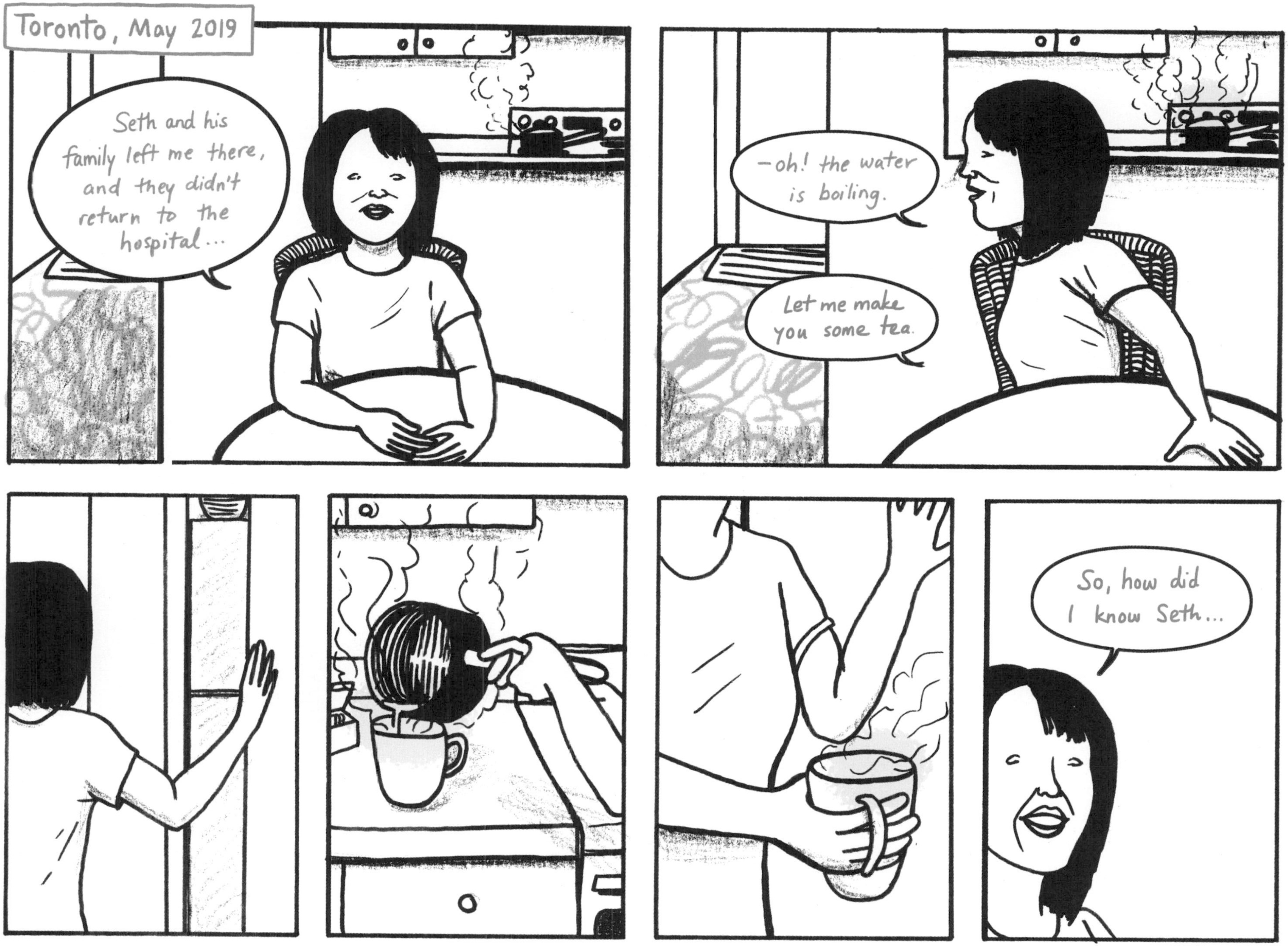
Toronto, May 2019
Seth and his family left me there, and they didn't return to the hospital...
-oh! the water is boiling.
Let me make you some tea.
So, how did I know Seth...

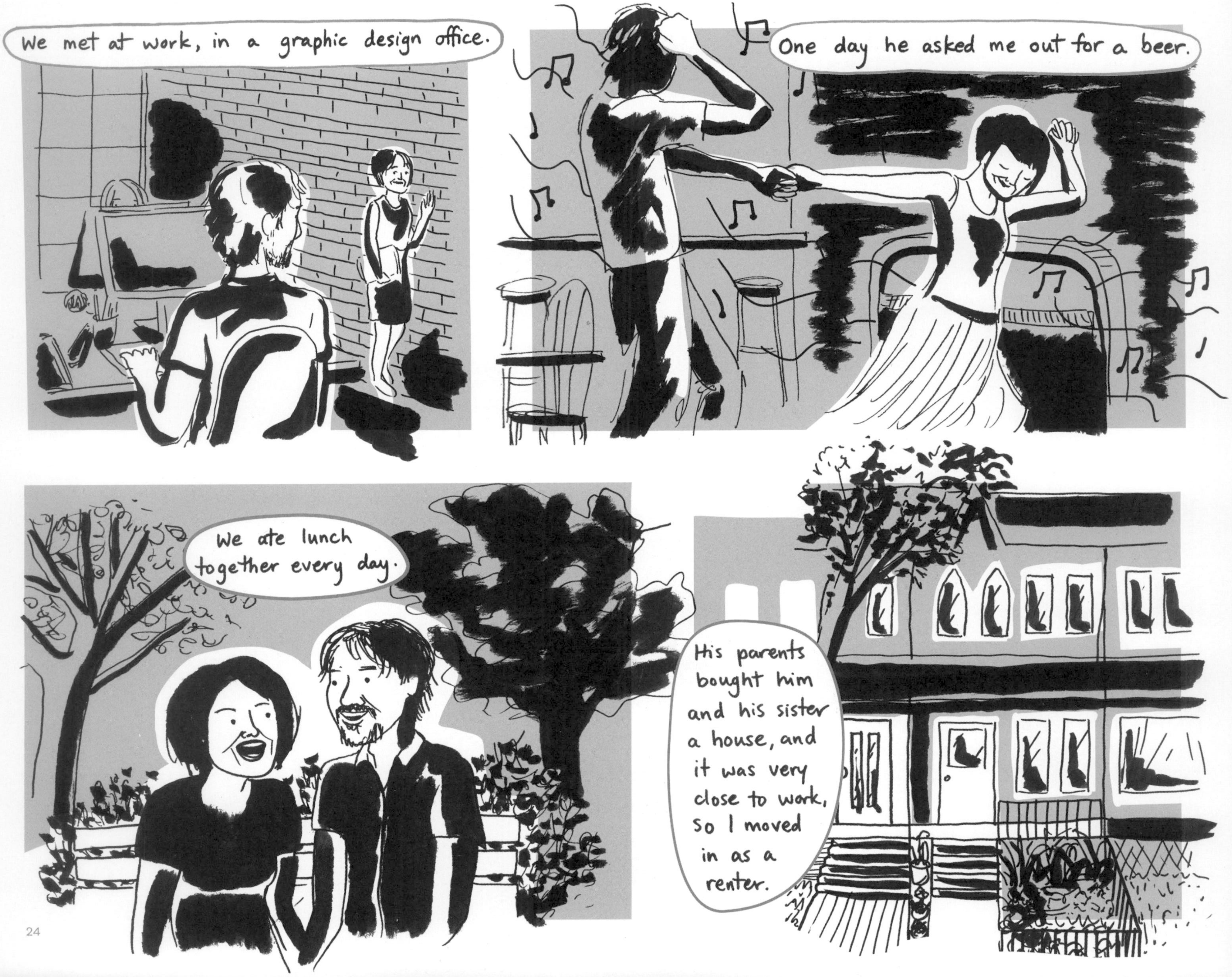
We met at work, in a graphic design office.
One day he asked me out for a beer.
We ate lunch together every day.
His parents bought him and his sister a house, and it was very close to work, so I moved in as a renter.

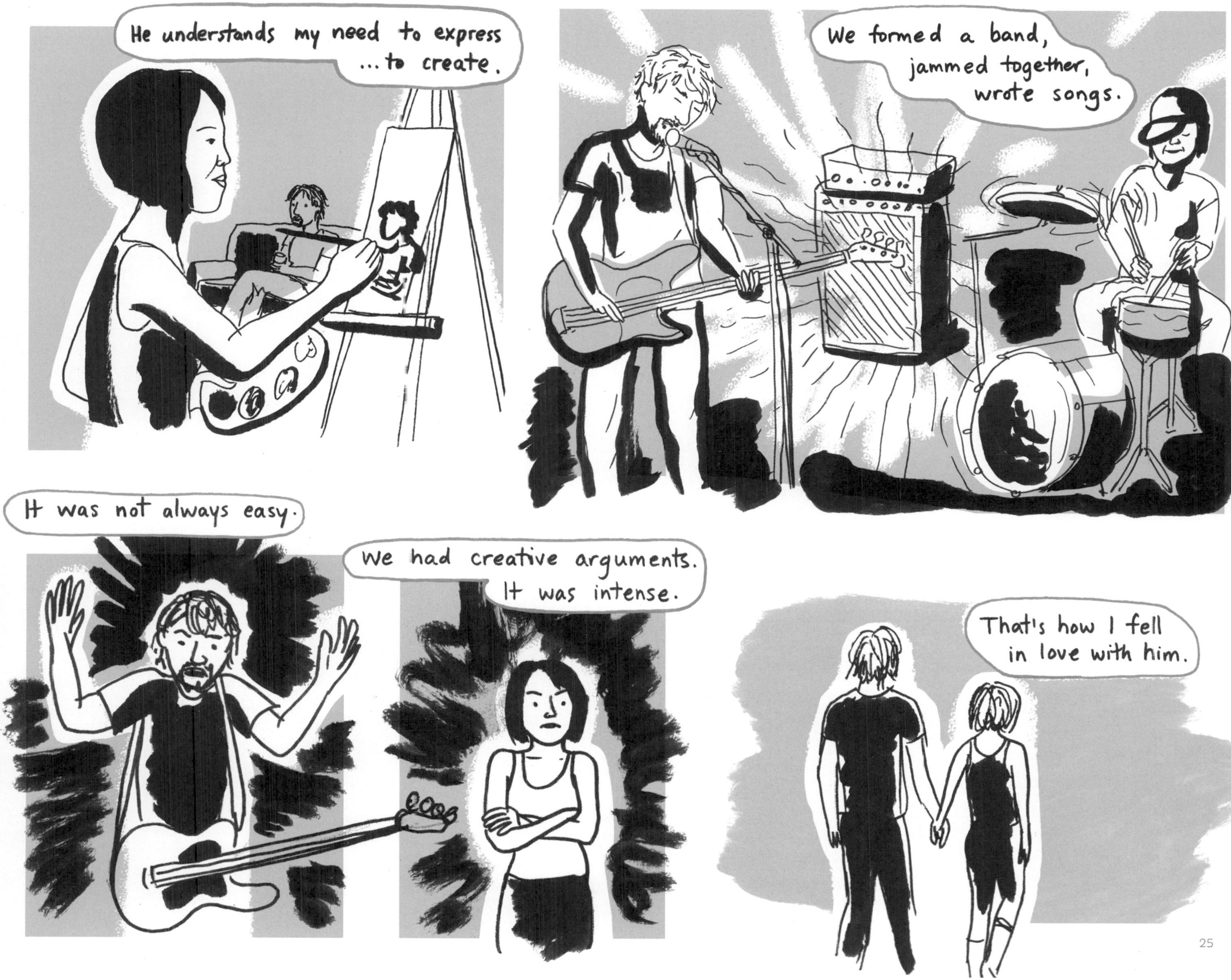
He understands my need to express ...to create.
We formed a band, jammed together, wrote songs.
It was not always easy.
We had creative arguments.
It was intense.
That's how I fell in love with him.

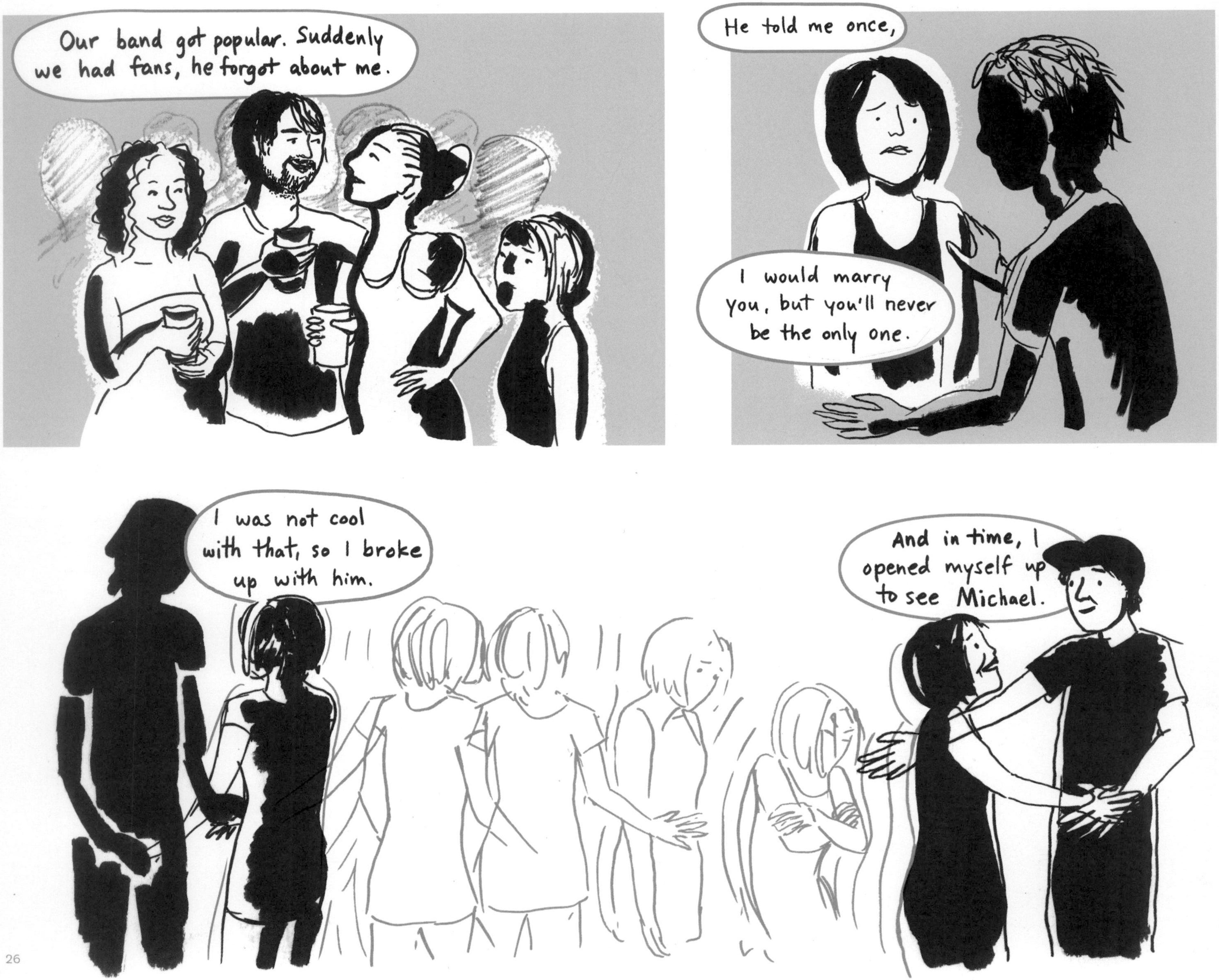
Our band got popular. Suddenly we had fans, he forgot about me.
He told me once,
I would marry you, but you'll never be the only one.
I was not cool with that, so I broke up with him.
And in time, I opened myself up to see Michael.

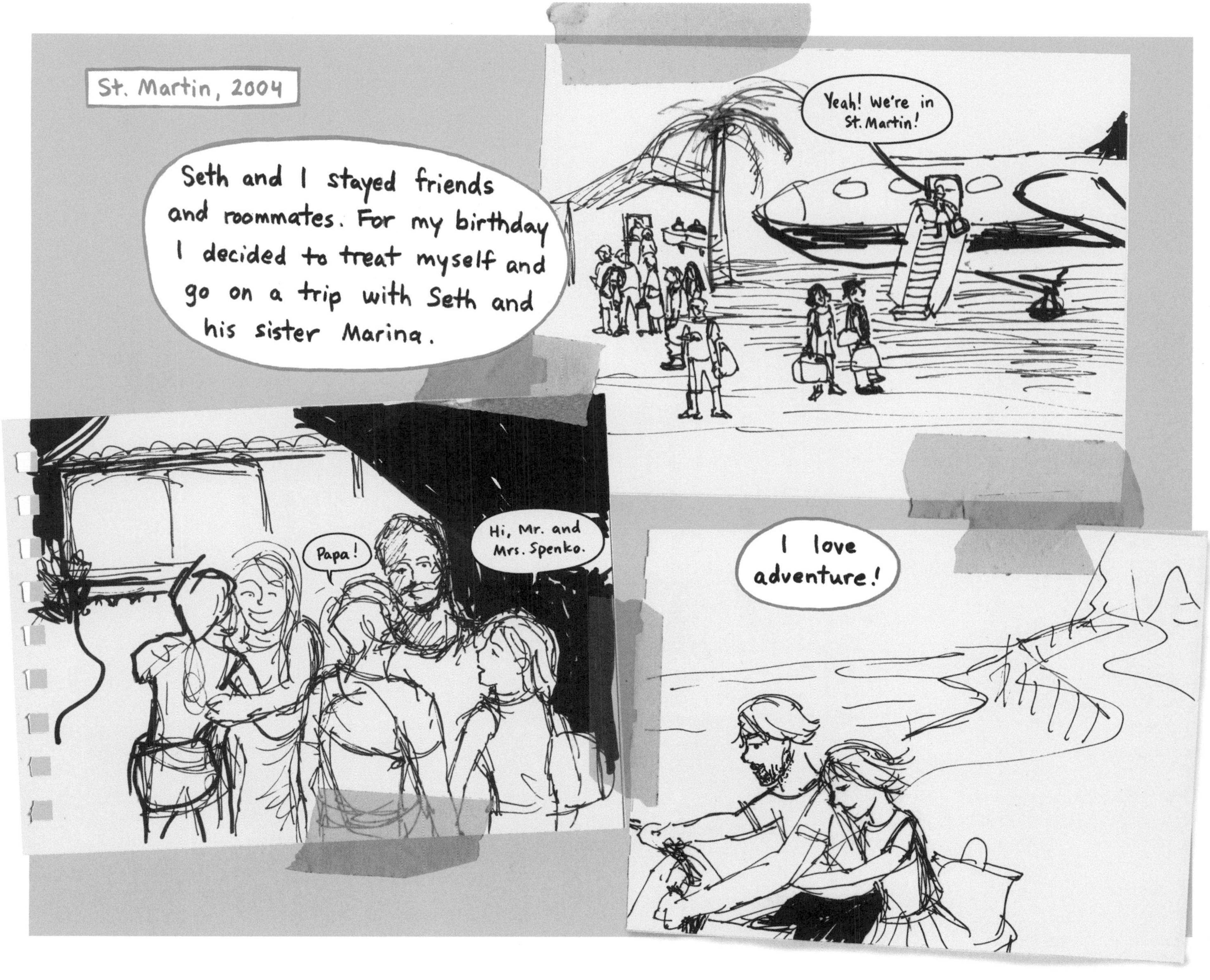
St. Martin, 2004
Seth and I stayed friends and roommates. For my birthday I decided to treat myself and go on a trip with Seth and his sister Marina.
Yeah! We're in St. Martin!
Papa!
Hi, Mr. and Mrs. Spenko.
I love adventure!

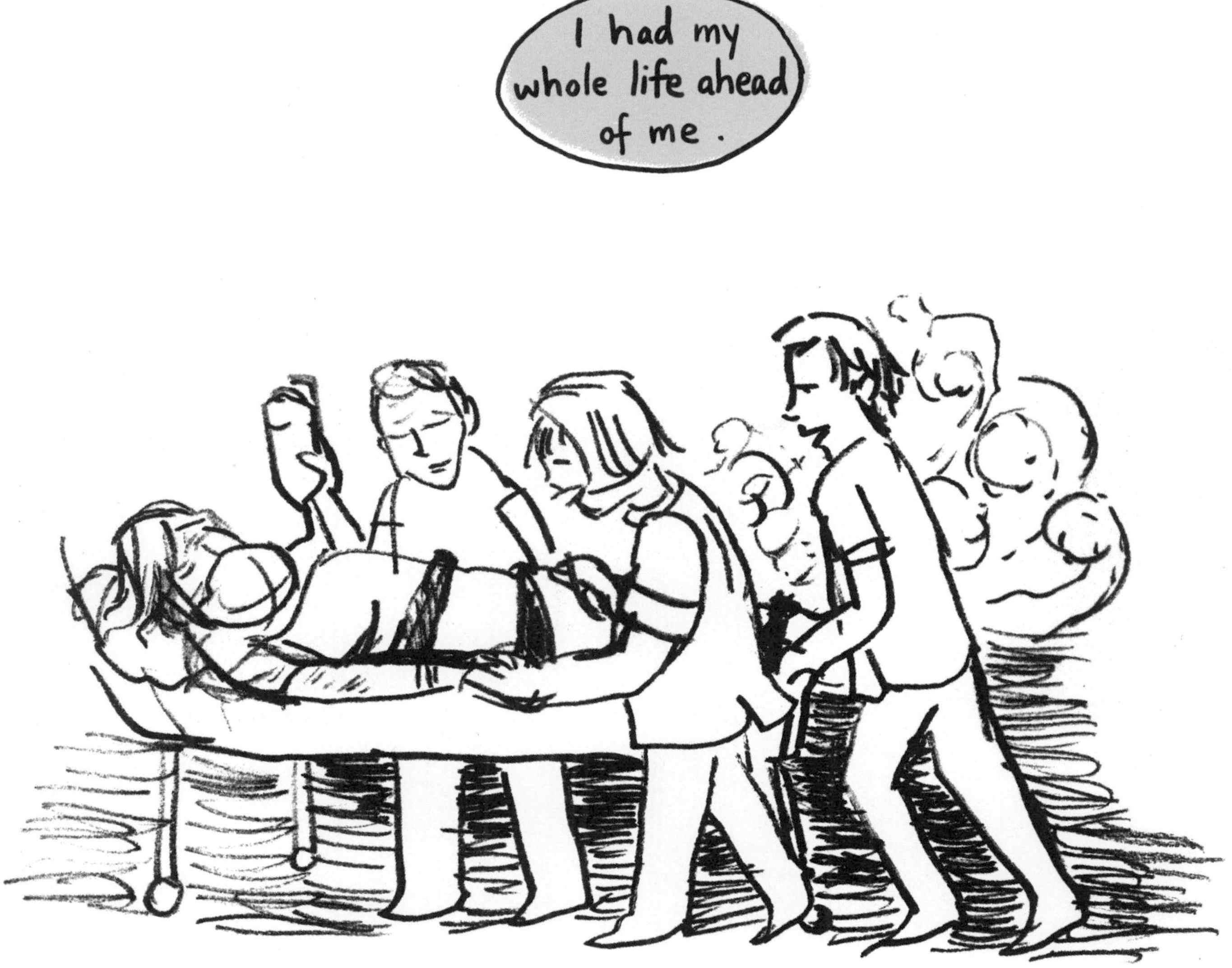
I had my whole life ahead of me.

Four

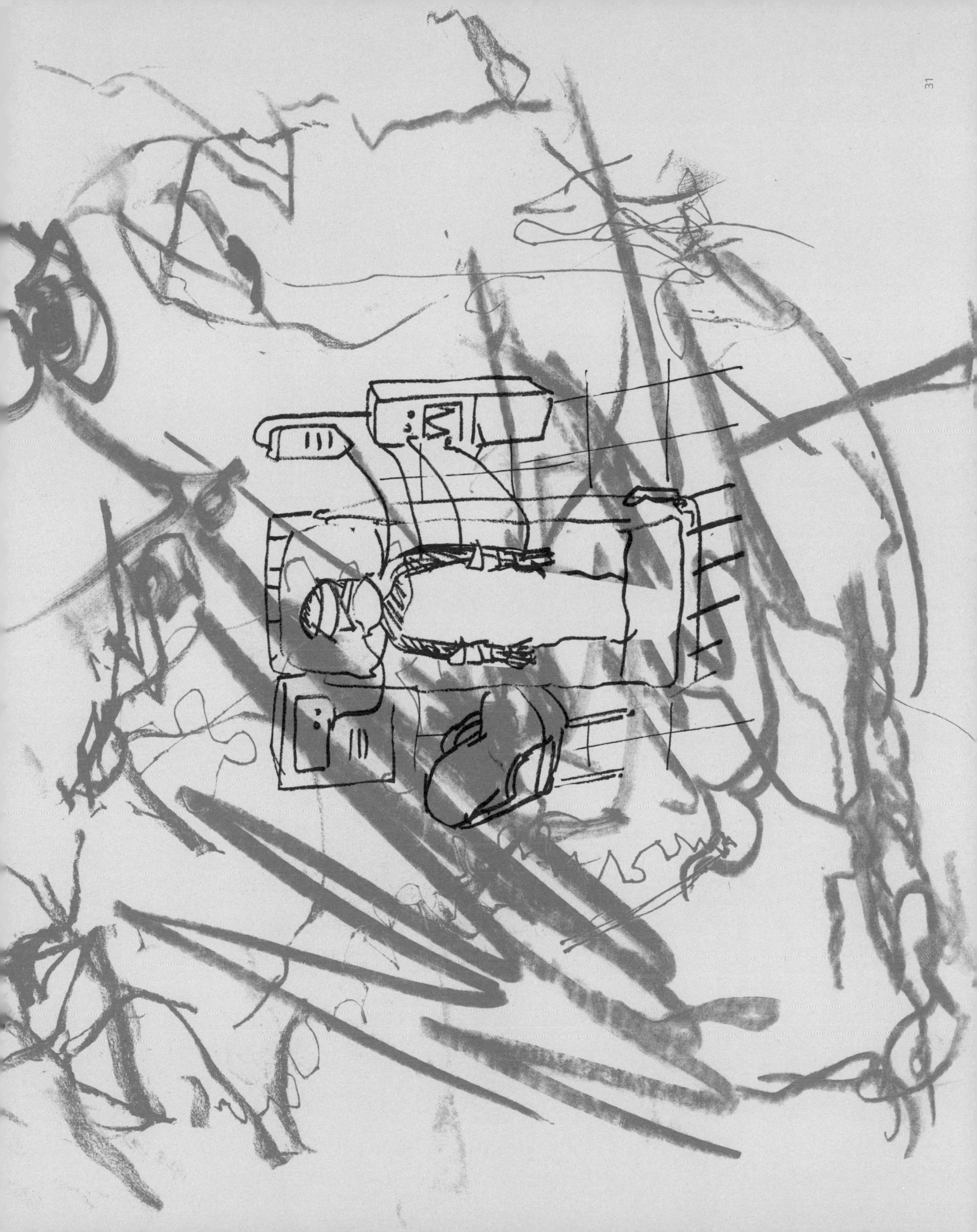

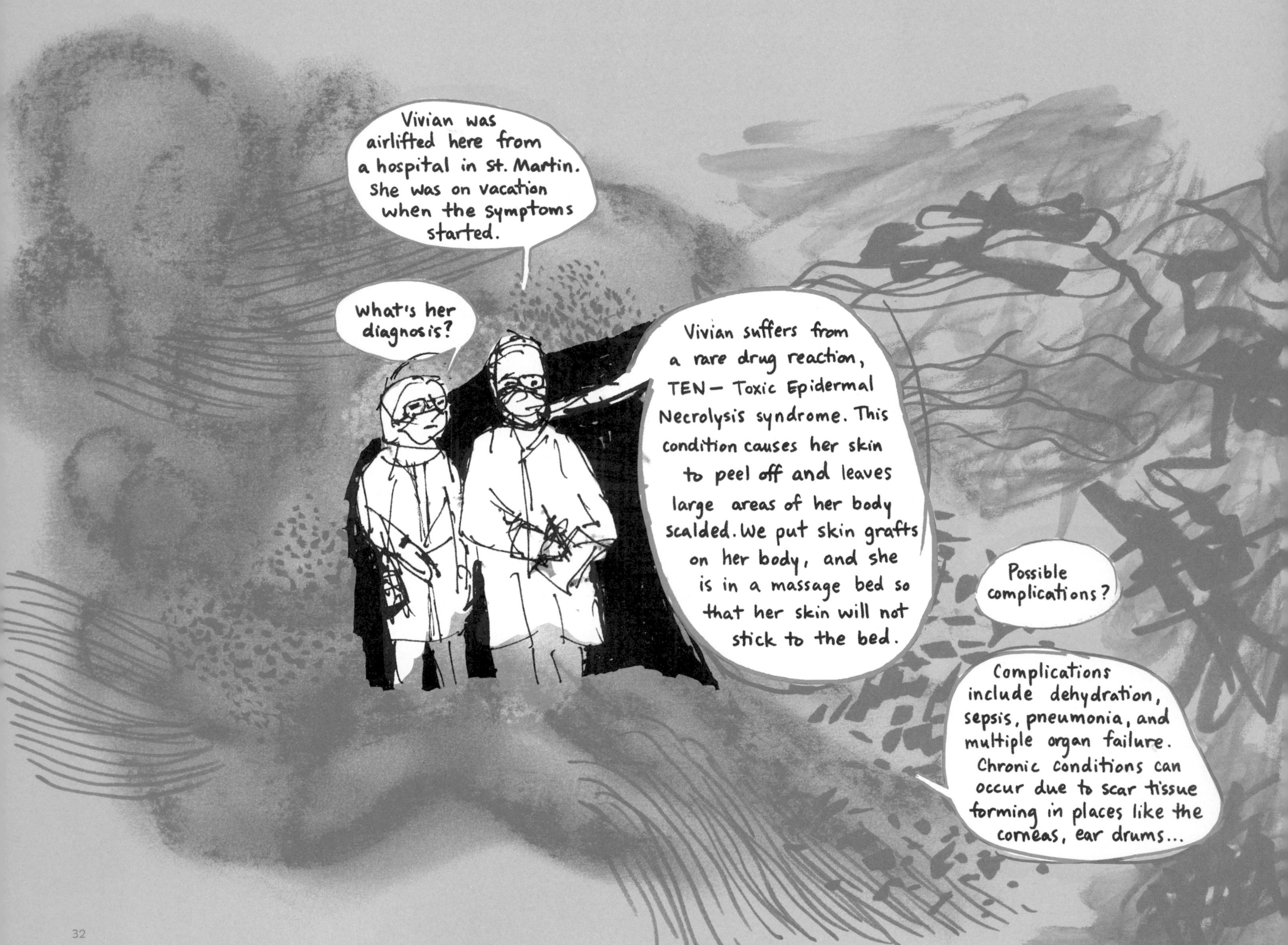
Vivian was airlifted here from a hospital in St. Martin. She was on vacation when the symptoms started.
What's her diagnosis?
Vivian suffers from a rare drug reaction, TEN— Toxic Epidermal Necrolysis syndrome. This condition causes her skin to peel off and leaves large areas of her body scalded. We put skin grafts on her body, and she is in a massage bed so that her skin will not stick to the bed.
Possible complications?
Complications include dehydration, sepsis, pneumonia, and multiple organ failure. Chronic conditions can occur due to scar tissue forming in places like the corneas, ear drums...

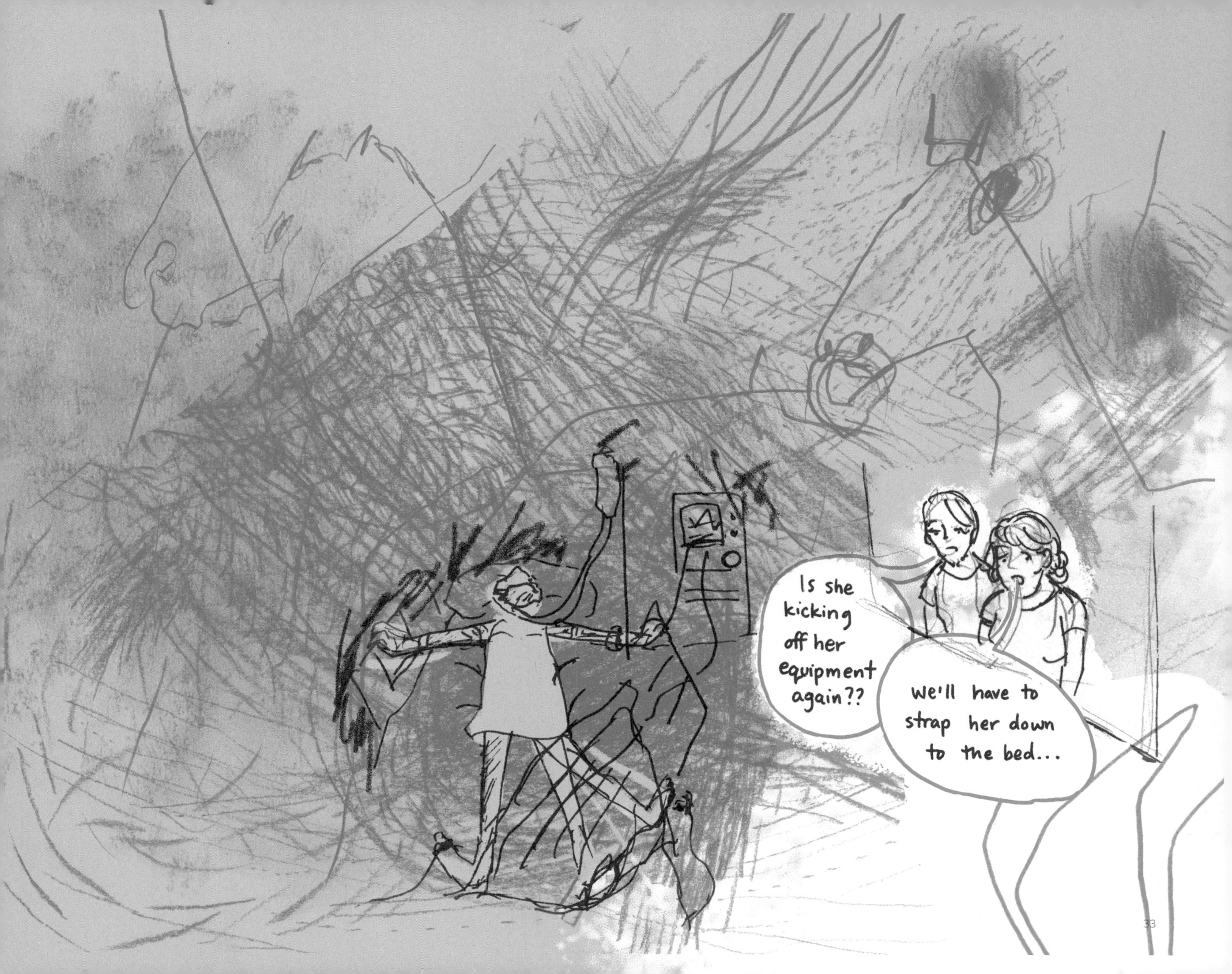
Is she kicking off her equipment again??
We'll have to strap her down to the bed...

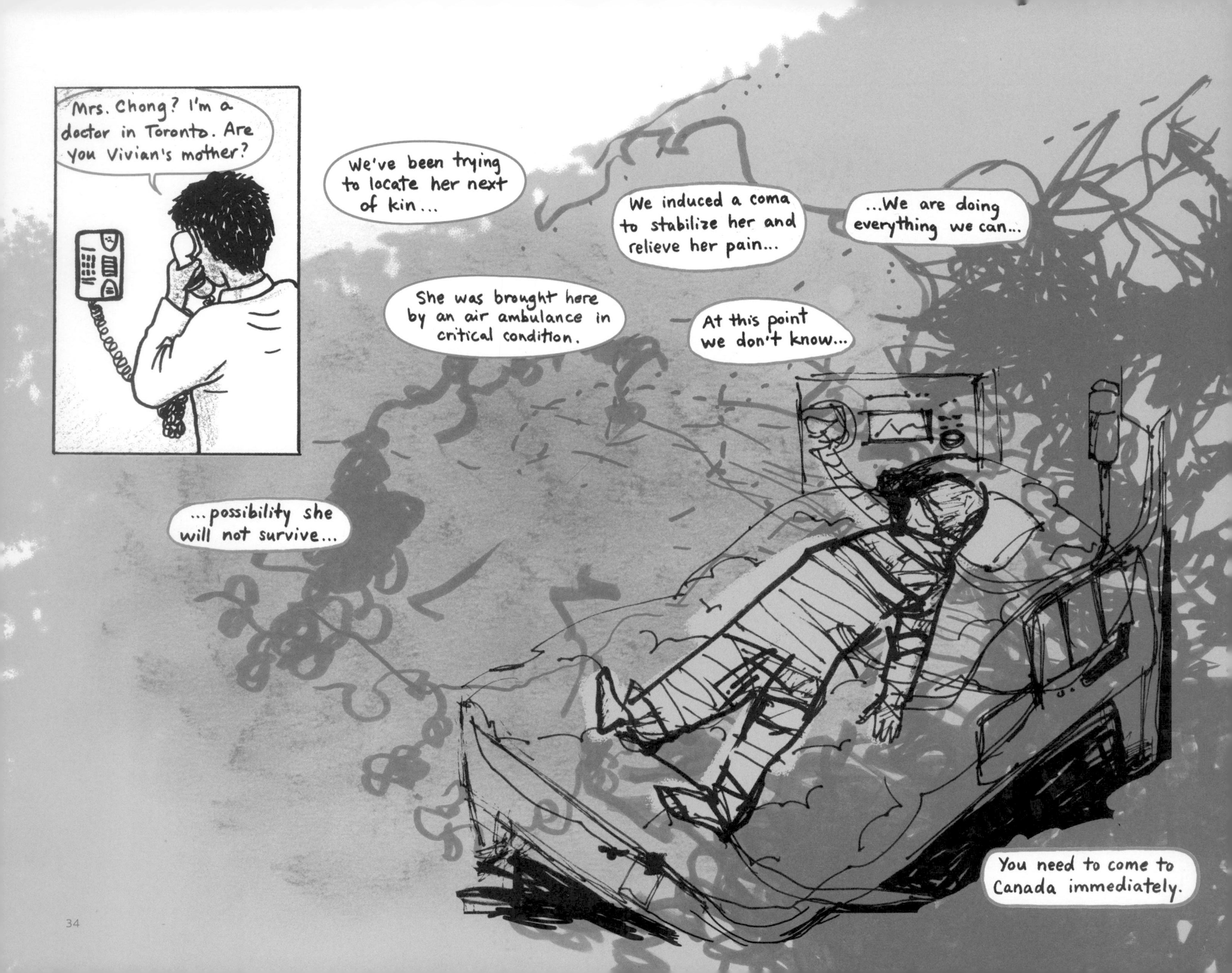
Mrs. Chong? I'm a doctor in Toronto. Are you Vivian's mother?
We've been trying to locate her next of kin...
She was brought here by an air ambulance in critical condition.
We induced a coma to stabilize her and relieve her pain...
...We are doing everything we can...
At this point we don't know...
...possibility she will not survive...
You need to come to Canada immediately.

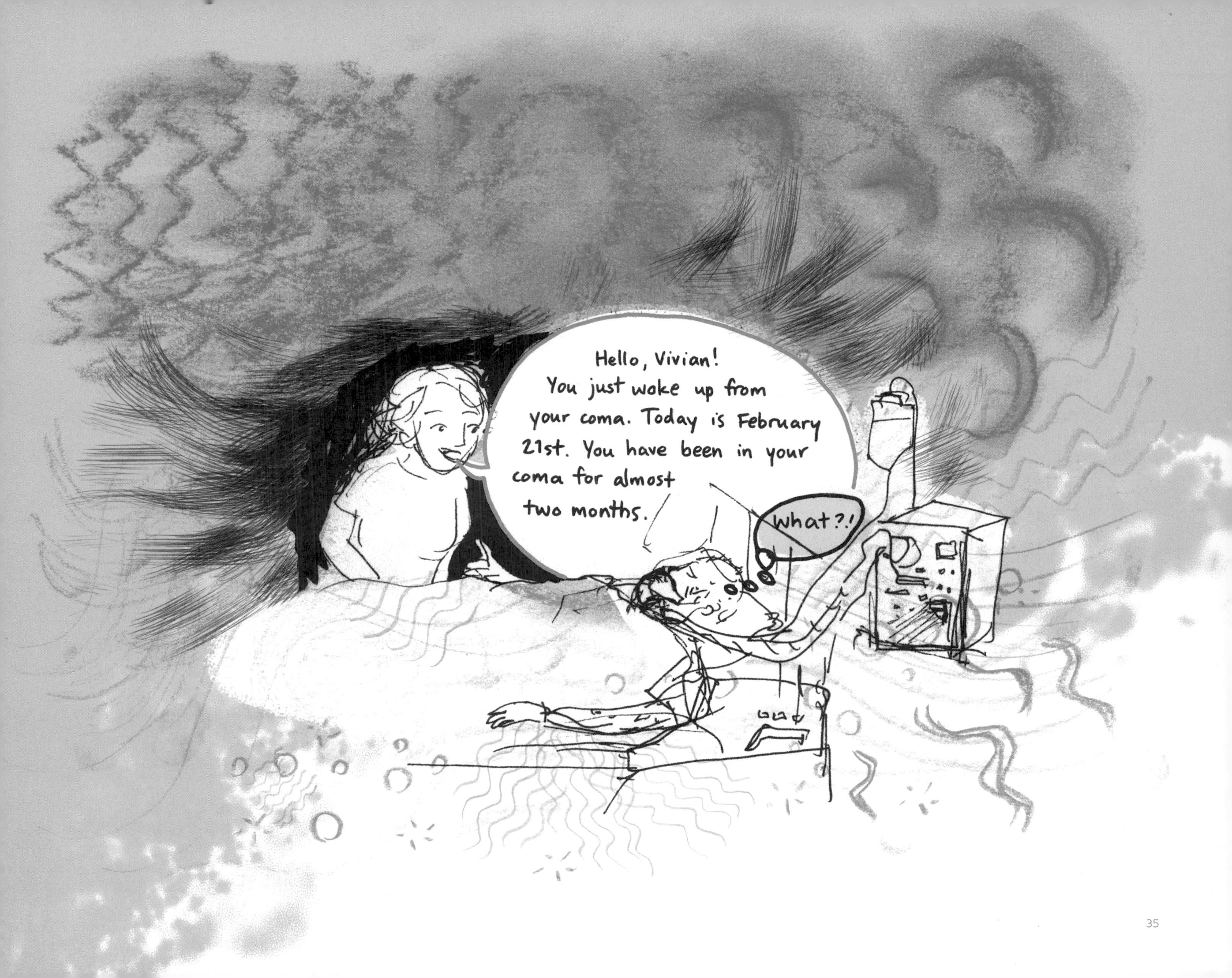
Hello, Vivian! You just woke up from your coma. Today is February 21st. You have been in your coma for almost two months.
What?!

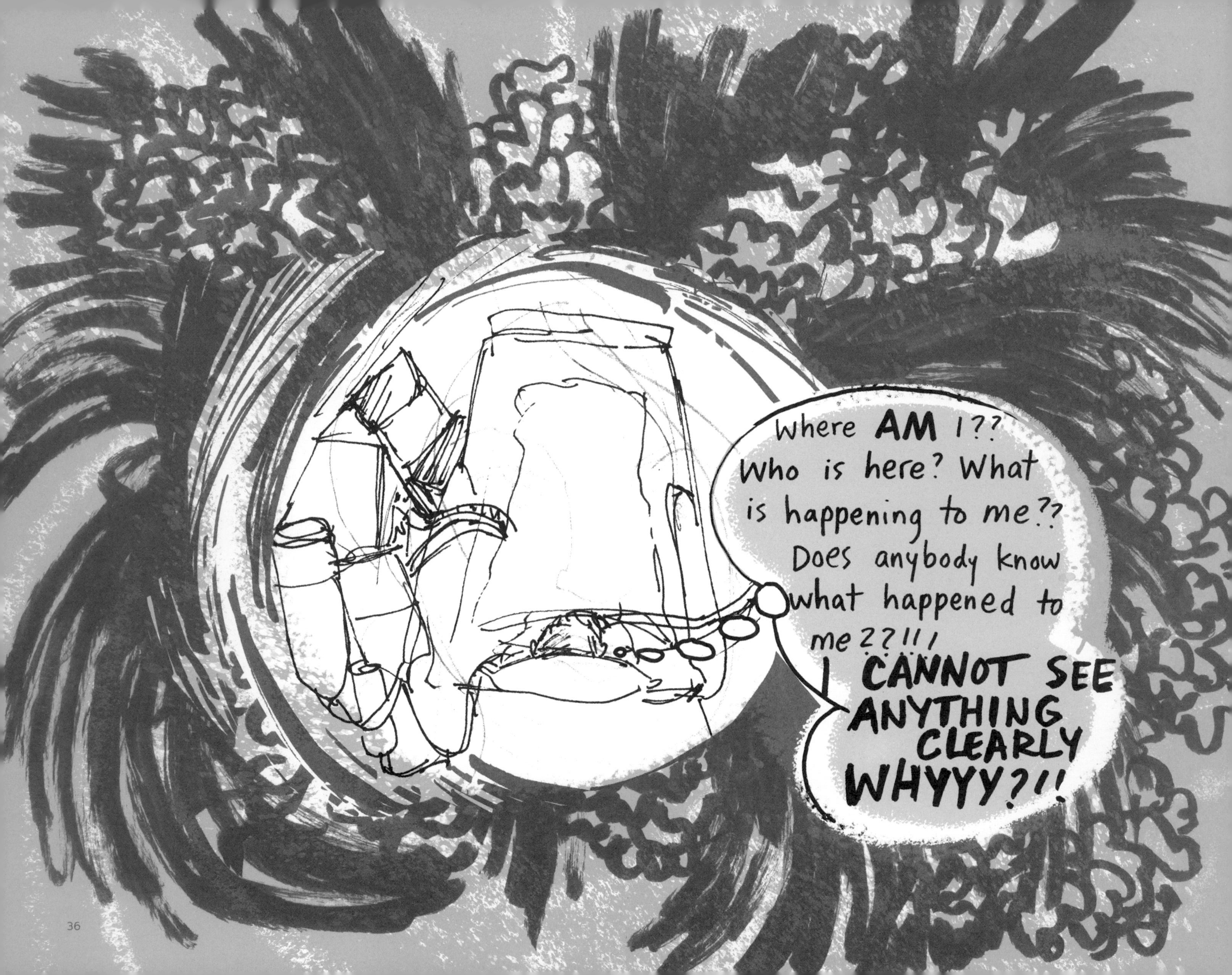
Where AM I??
Who is here? What is happening to me?? Does anybody know what happened to me??!!!
I CANNOT SEE ANYTHING CLEARLY WHYYY?!!

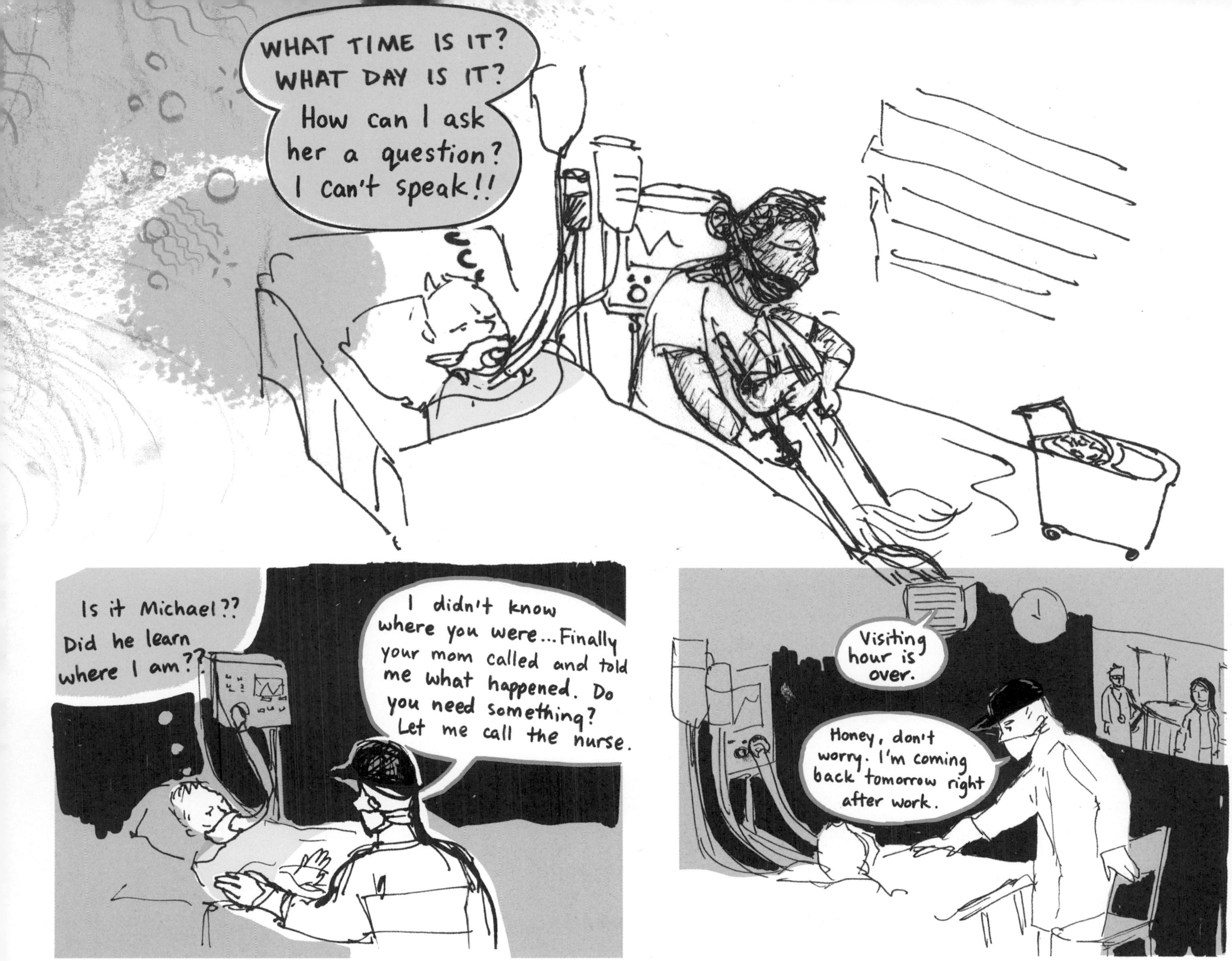
WHAT TIME IS IT? WHAT DAY IS IT? How can I ask her a question? I can't speak!!
Is it Michael?? Did he learn where I am??
I didn't know where you were... Finally your mom called and told me what happened. Do you need something? Let me call the nurse.
Visiting hour is over.
Honey, don't worry. I'm coming back tomorrow right after work.

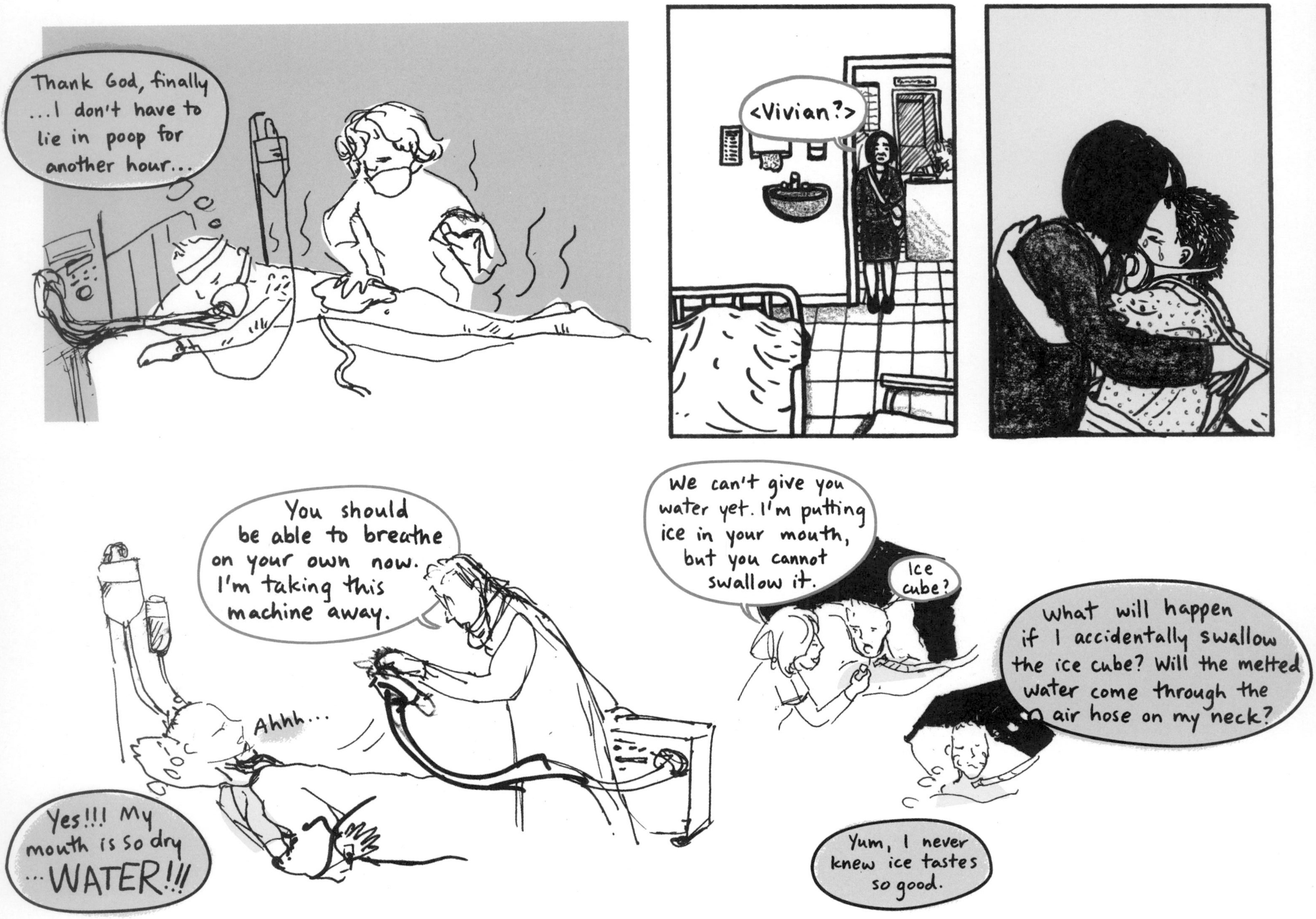
Thank God, finally ...I don't have to lie in poop for another hour...
<Vivian?>
You should be able to breathe on your own now. I'm taking this machine away.
Ahhh...
Yes!!! My mouth is so dry ...WATER!!!
We can't give you water yet. I'm putting ice in your mouth, but you cannot swallow it.
Ice cube?
What will happen if I accidentally swallow the ice cube? Will the melted water come through the air hose on my neck?
Yum, I never knew ice tastes so good.

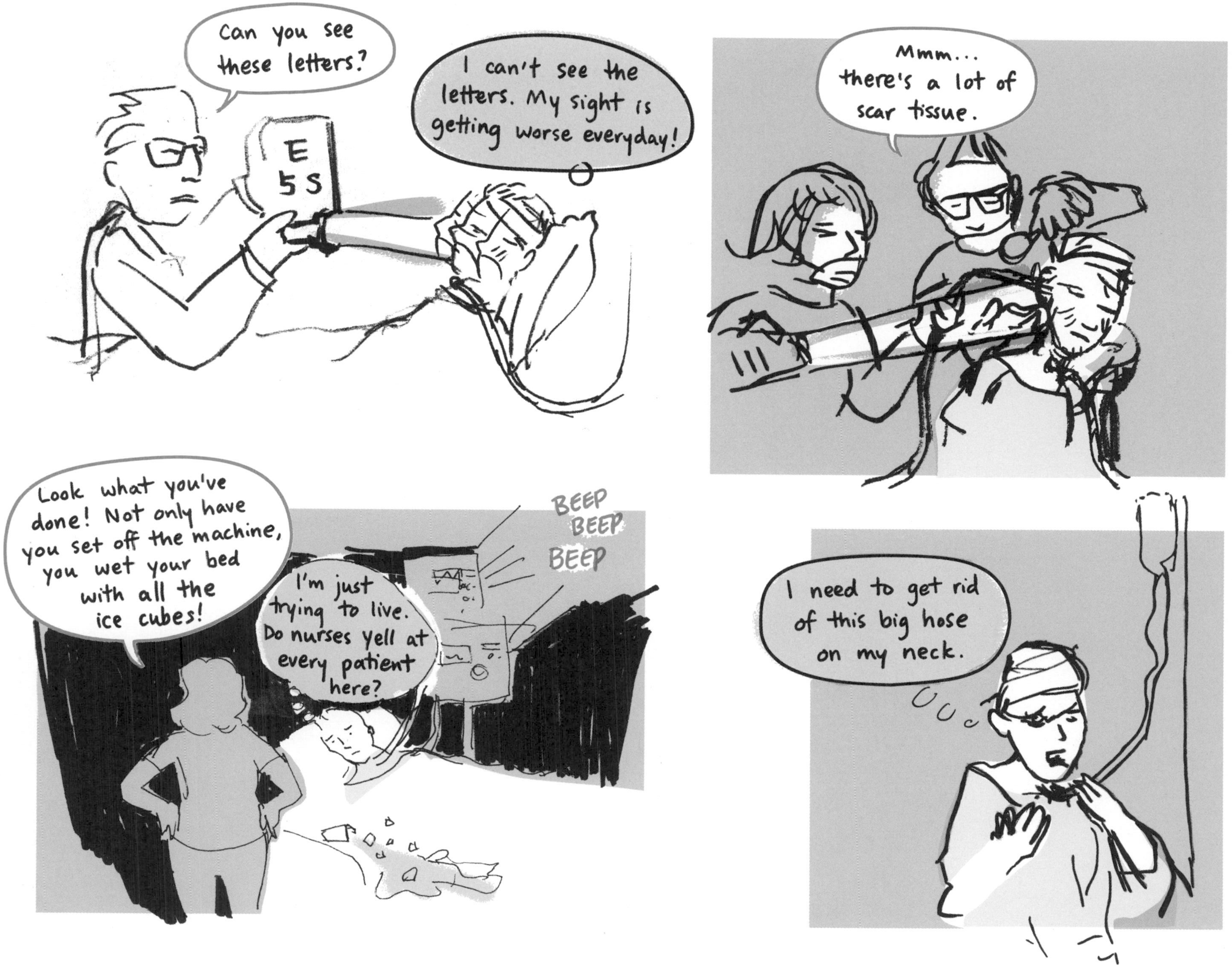
Can you see these letters?
E
5S
I can't see the letters. My sight is getting worse everyday!
Mmm... there's a lot of scar tissue.
Look what you've done! Not only have you set off the machine, you wet your bed with all the ice cubes!
I'm just trying to live. Do nurses yell at every patient here?
BEEP
BEEP
BEEP
I need to get rid of this big hose on my neck.

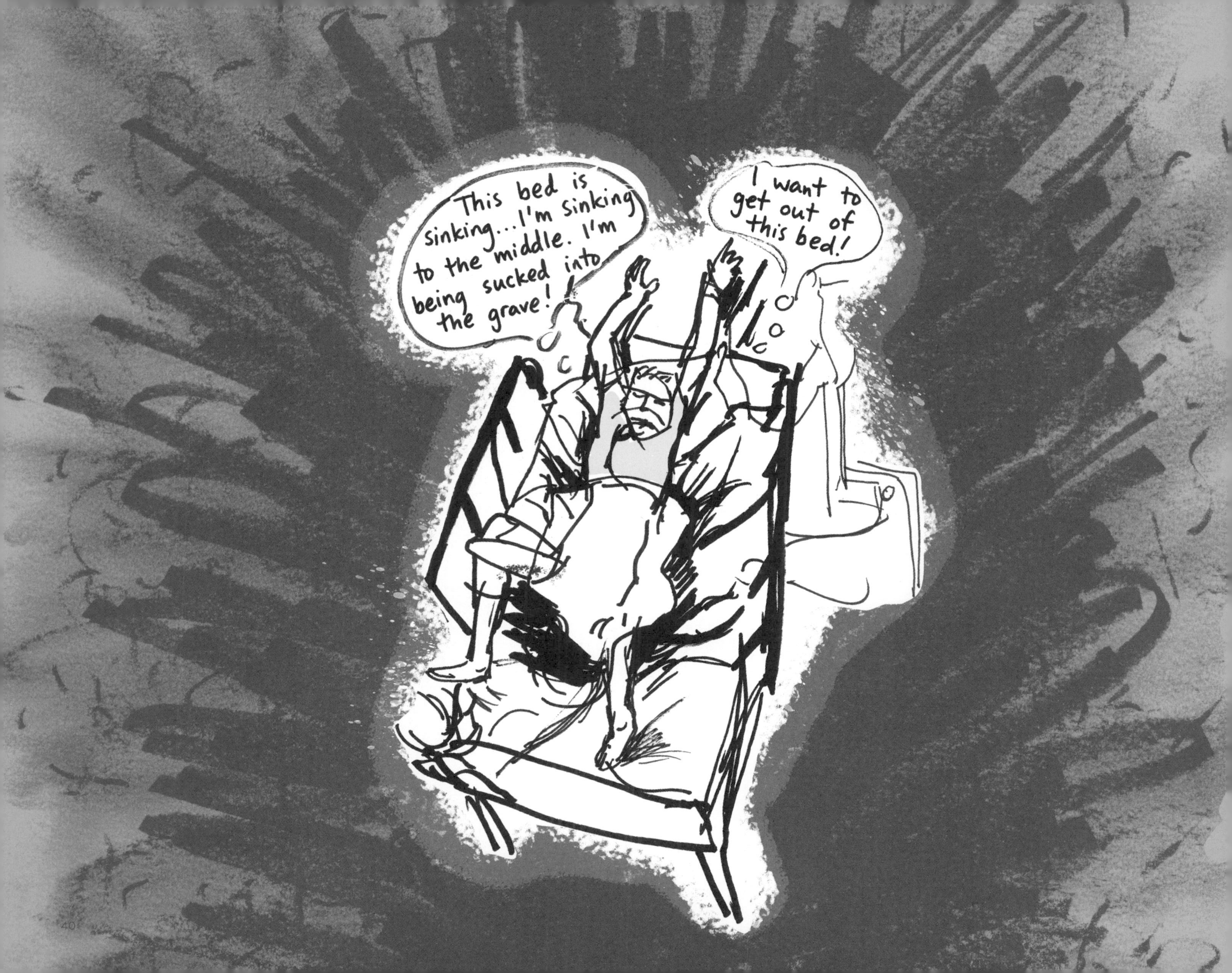
This bed is sinking...I'm sinking to the middle. I'm being sucked into the grave!
I want to get out of this bed!

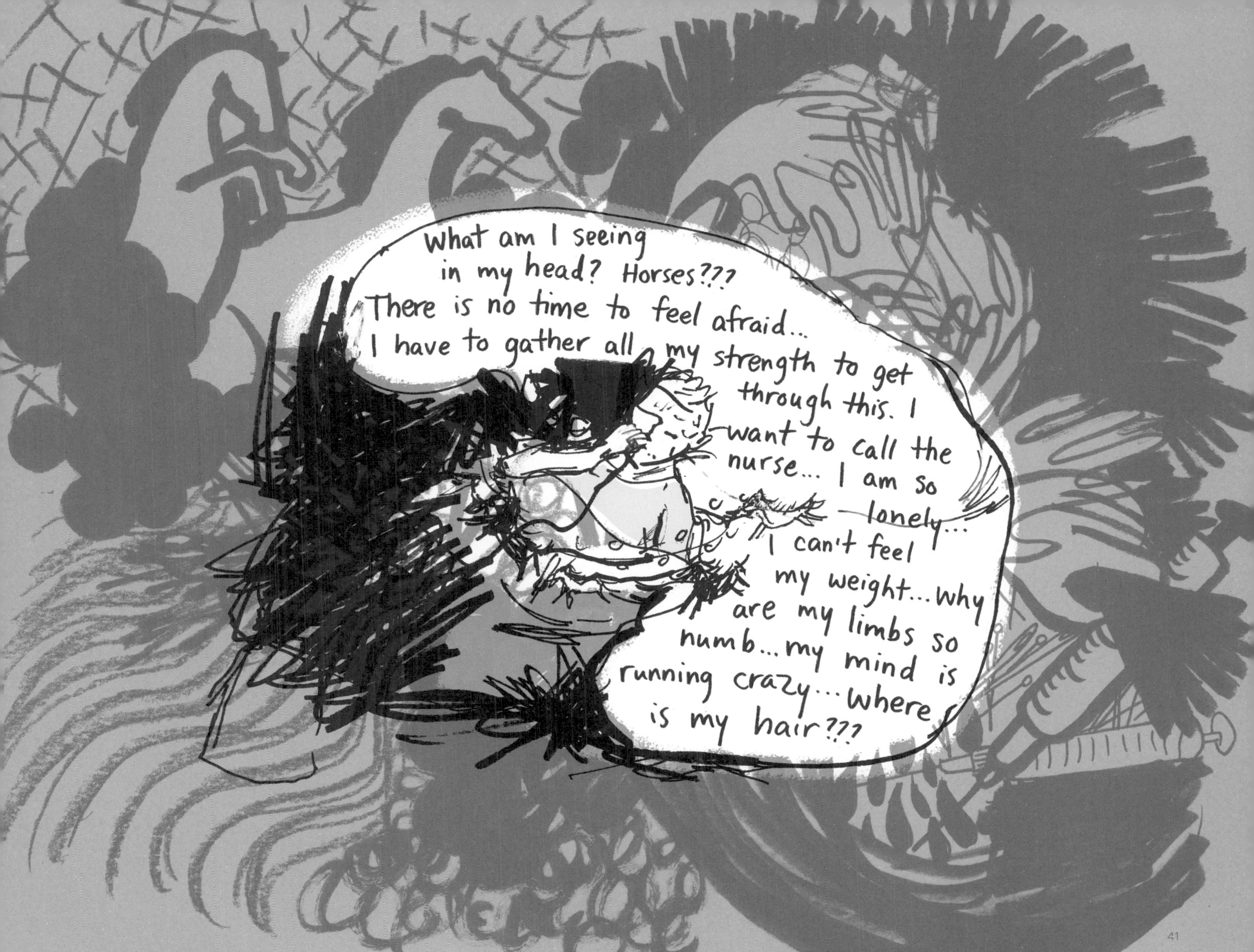
What am I seeing in my head? Horses??? There is no time to feel afraid... I have to gather all my strength to get through this. I want to call the nurse... I am so lonely... I can't feel my weight...why are my limbs so numb...my mind is running crazy...where is my hair???

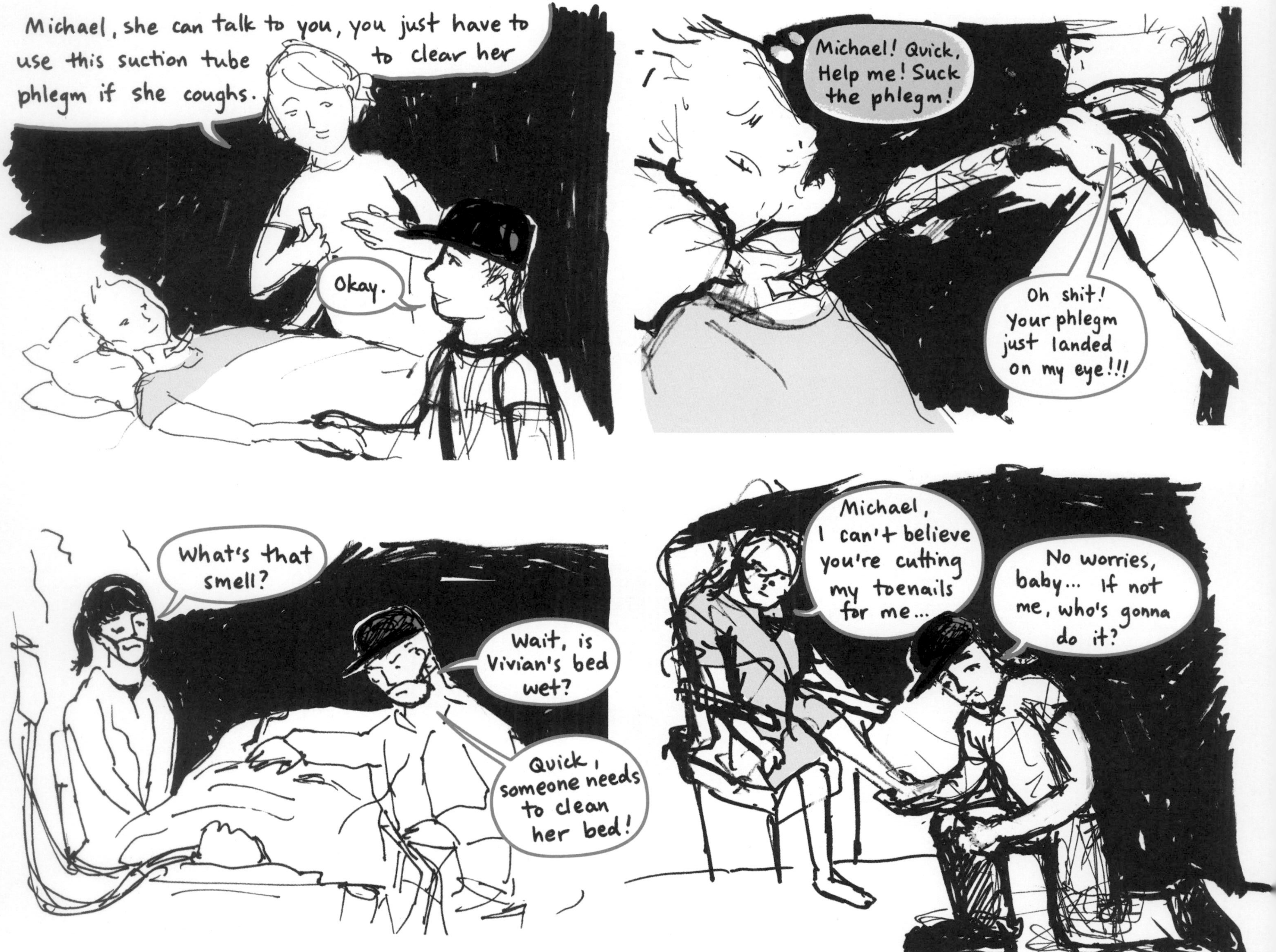
Michael, she can talk to you, you just have to use this suction tube to clear her phlegm if she coughs.
Okay.
Michael! Quick, Help me! Suck the phlegm!
Oh shit! Your phlegm just landed on my eye!!!
What's that smell?
Wait, is Vivian's bed wet?
Quick, someone needs to clean her bed!
Michael, I can't believe you're cutting my toenails for me...
No worries, baby... If not me, who's gonna do it?

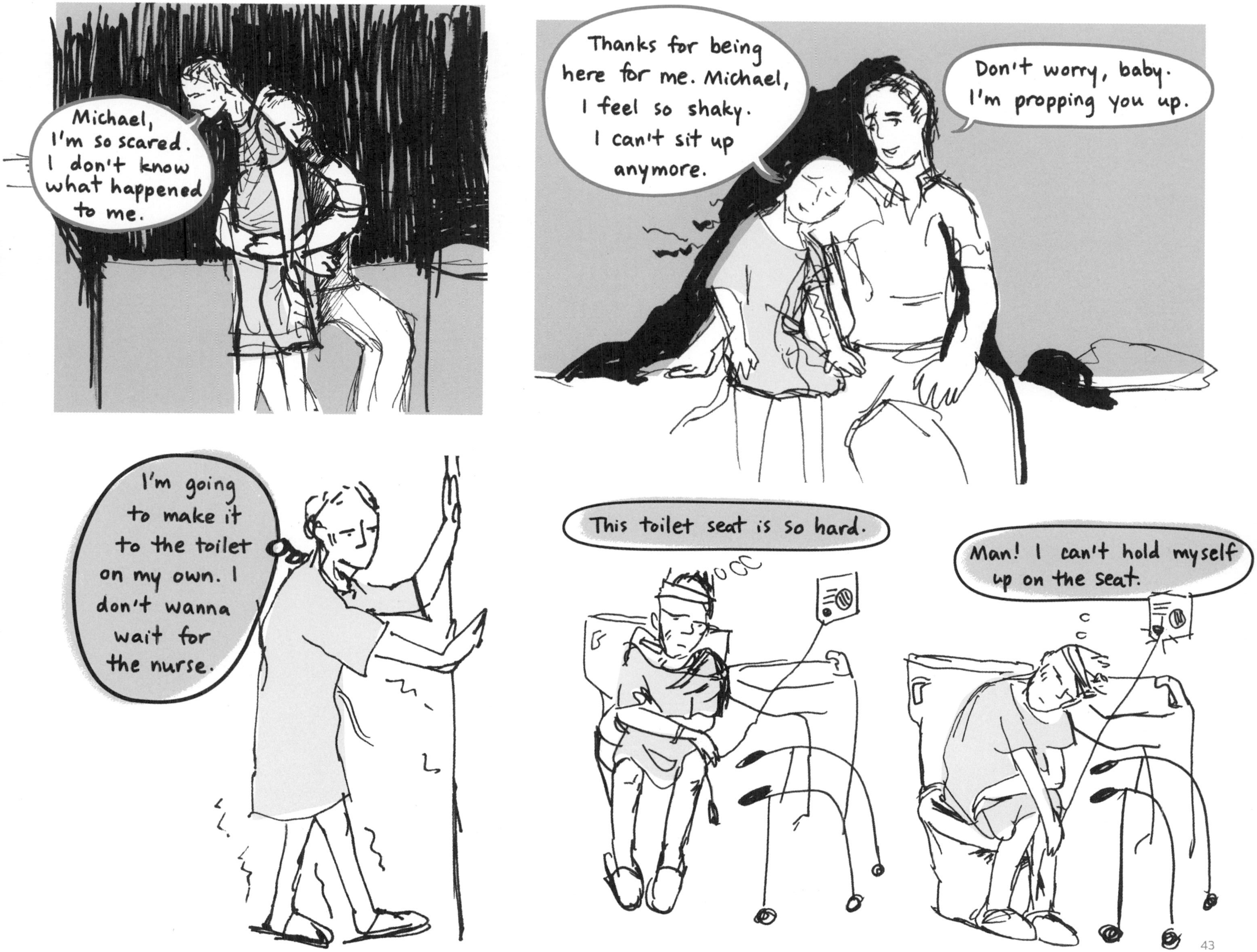
Michael, I'm so scared. I don't know what happened to me.
Thanks for being here for me. Michael, I feel so shaky. I can't sit up anymore.
Don't worry, baby. I'm propping you up.
I'm going to make it to the toilet on my own. I don't wanna wait for the nurse.
This toilet seat is so hard.
Man! I can't hold myself up on the seat.

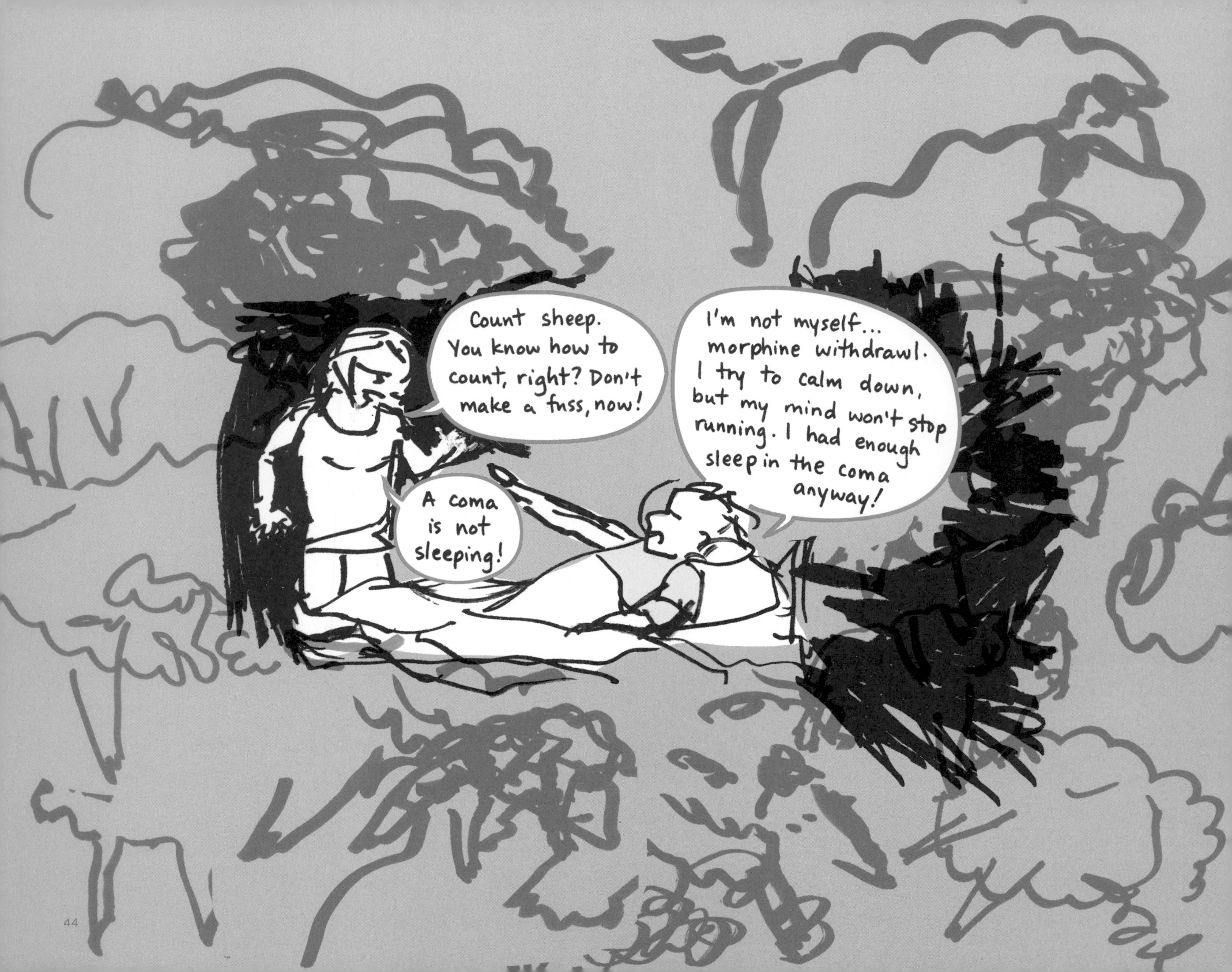
Count sheep. You know how to count, right? Don't make a fuss, now!
A coma is not sleeping!
I'm not myself... morphine withdrawl. I try to calm down, but my mind won't stop running. I had enough sleep in the coma anyway!

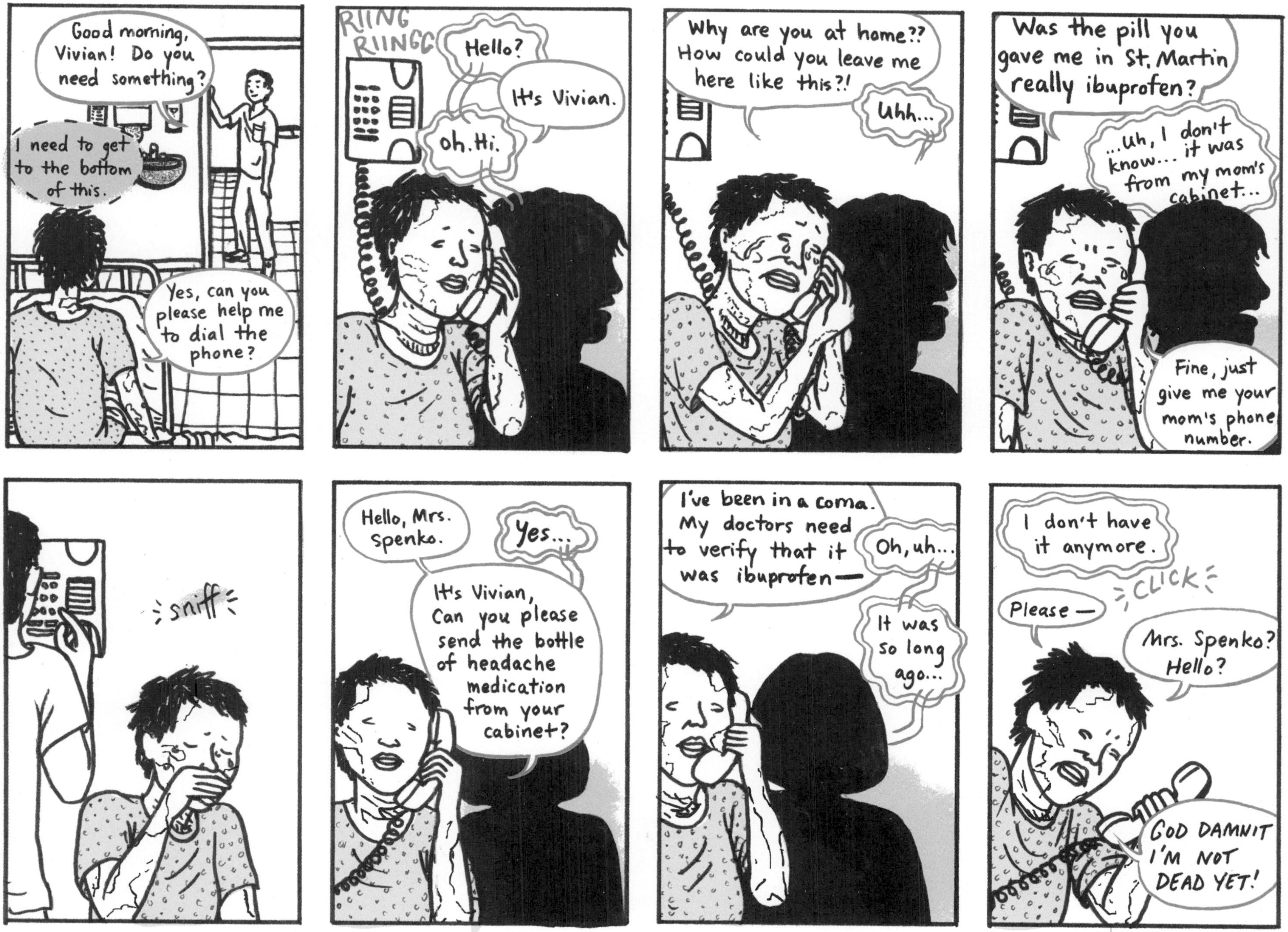
Good morning, Vivian! Do you need something?
I need to get to the bottom of this.
Yes, can you please help me to dial the phone?
RIING RIINGG
Hello?
It's Vivian.
Oh. Hi.
Why are you at home?? How could you leave me here like this?!
Uhh...
Was the pill you gave me in St. Martin really ibuprofen?
...uh, I don't know... it was from my mom's cabinet...
Fine, just give me your mom's phone number.
sniff
Hello, Mrs. Spenko.
Yes...
It's Vivian, Can you please send the bottle of headache medication from your cabinet?
I've been in a coma. My doctors need to verify that it was ibuprofen—
Oh, uh...
It was so long ago...
I don't have it anymore.
Please—
CLICK
Mrs. Spenko? Hello?
GOD DAMNIT I'M NOT DEAD YET!

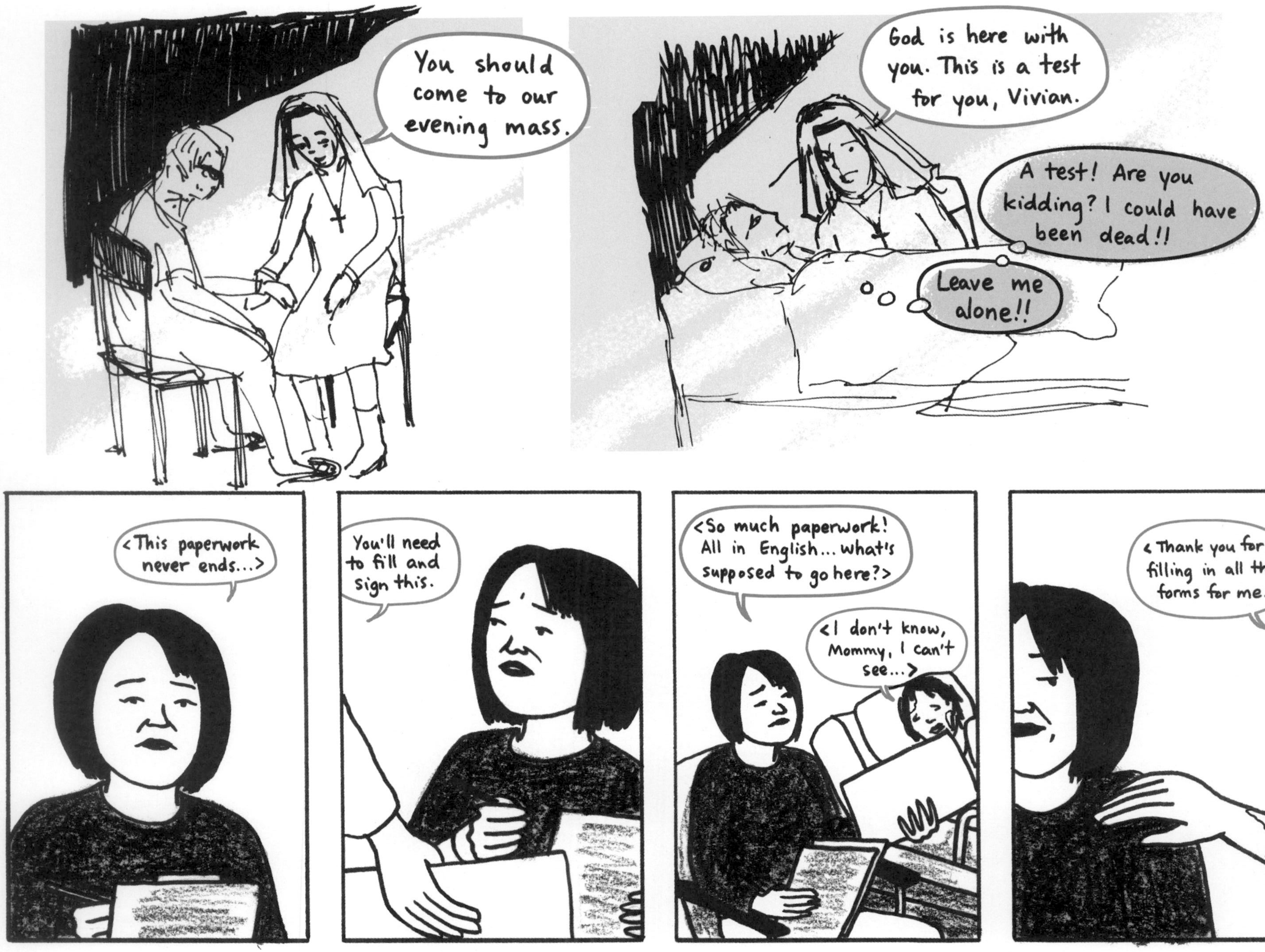
You should come to our evening mass.
God is here with you. This is a test for you, Vivian.
A test! Are you kidding? I could have been dead!!
Leave me alone!!
<This paperwork never ends...>
You'll need to fill and sign this.
<So much paperwork! All in English... what's supposed to go here?>
<I don't know, Mommy, I can't see...>
<Thank you for filling in all the forms for me.>

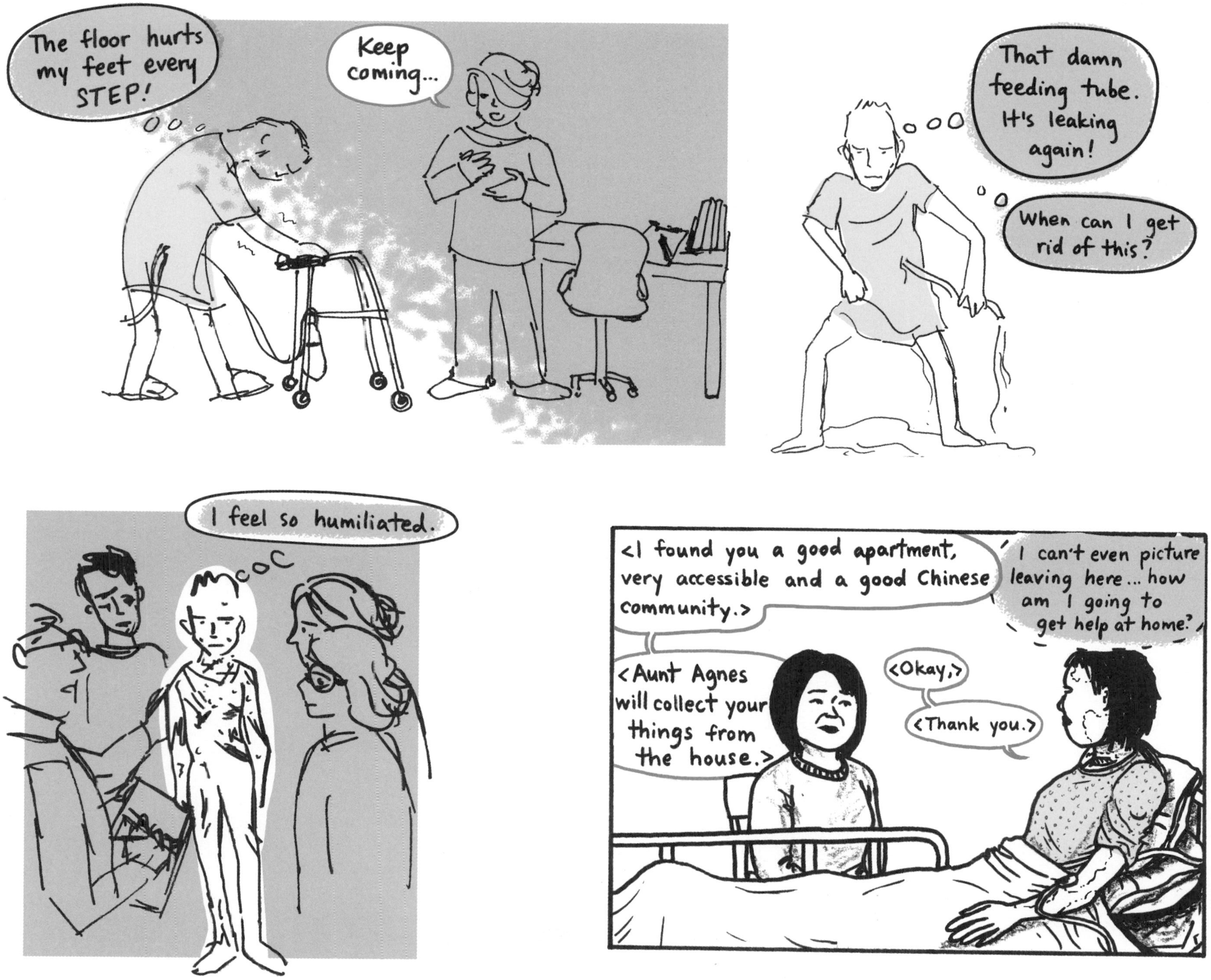
The floor hurts my feet every STEP!
Keep coming...
That damn feeding tube. It's leaking again!
When can I get rid of this?
I feel so humiliated.
<I found you a good apartment, very accessible and a good Chinese community.>
I can't even picture leaving here... how am I going to get help at home?
<Aunt Agnes will collect your things from the house.>
<Okay,>
<Thank you.>

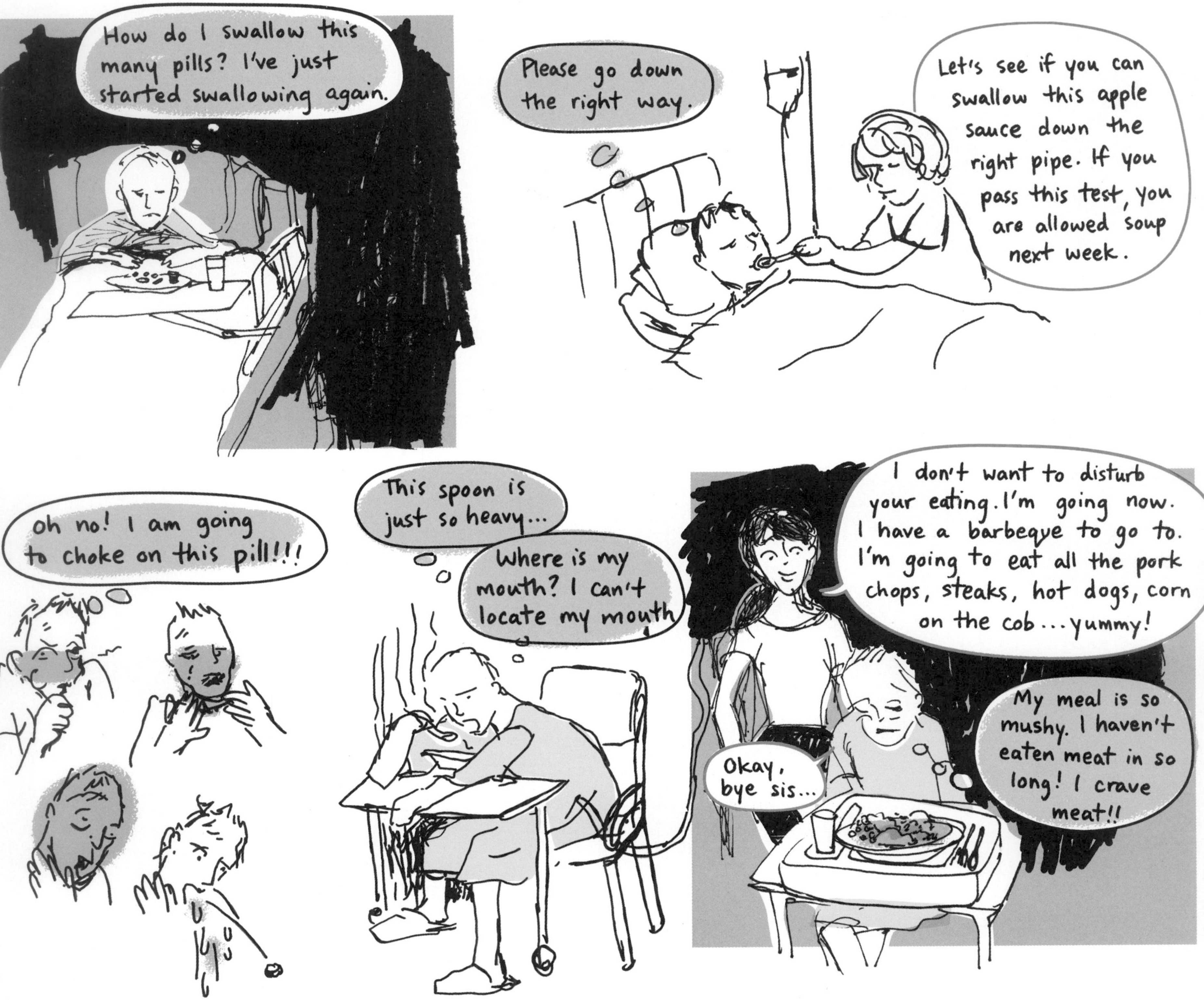
How do I swallow this many pills? I've just started swallowing again.
Please go down the right way.
Let's see if you can swallow this apple sauce down the right pipe. If you pass this test, you are allowed soup next week.
oh no! I am going to choke on this pill!!!
This spoon is just so heavy...
Where is my mouth? I can't locate my mouth
I don't want to disturb your eating. I'm going now. I have a barbeque to go to. I'm going to eat all the pork chops, steaks, hot dogs, corn on the cob...yummy!
Okay, bye sis...
My meal is so mushy. I haven't eaten meat in so long! I crave meat!!

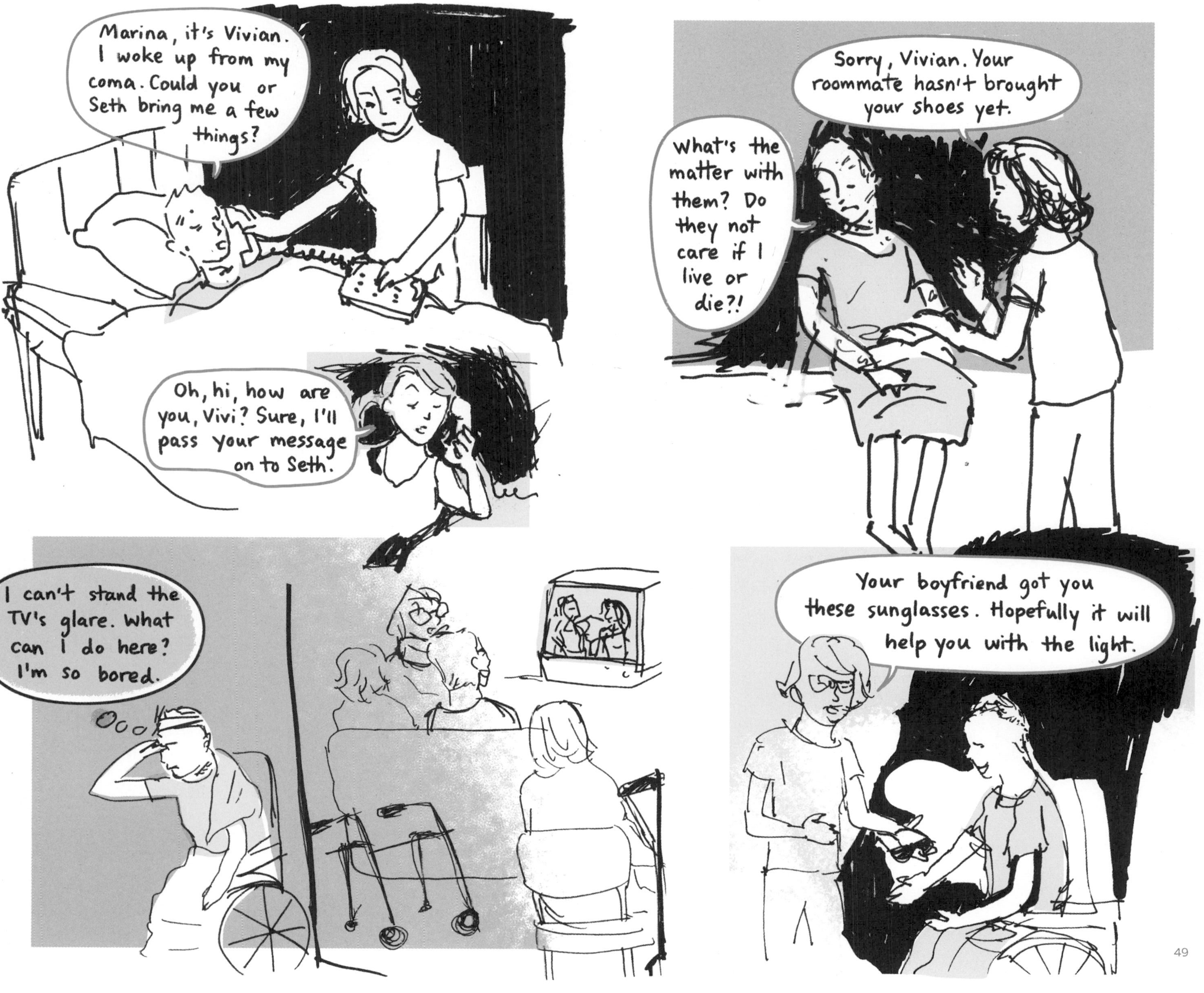
Marina, it's Vivian. I woke up from my coma. Could you or Seth bring me a few things?
Oh, hi, how are you, Vivi? Sure, I'll pass your message on to Seth.
I can't stand the TV's glare. What can I do here? I'm so bored.
Ooo
What's the matter with them? Do they not care if I live or die?!
Sorry, Vivian. Your roommate hasn't brought your shoes yet.
Your boyfriend got you these sunglasses. Hopefully it will help you with the light.

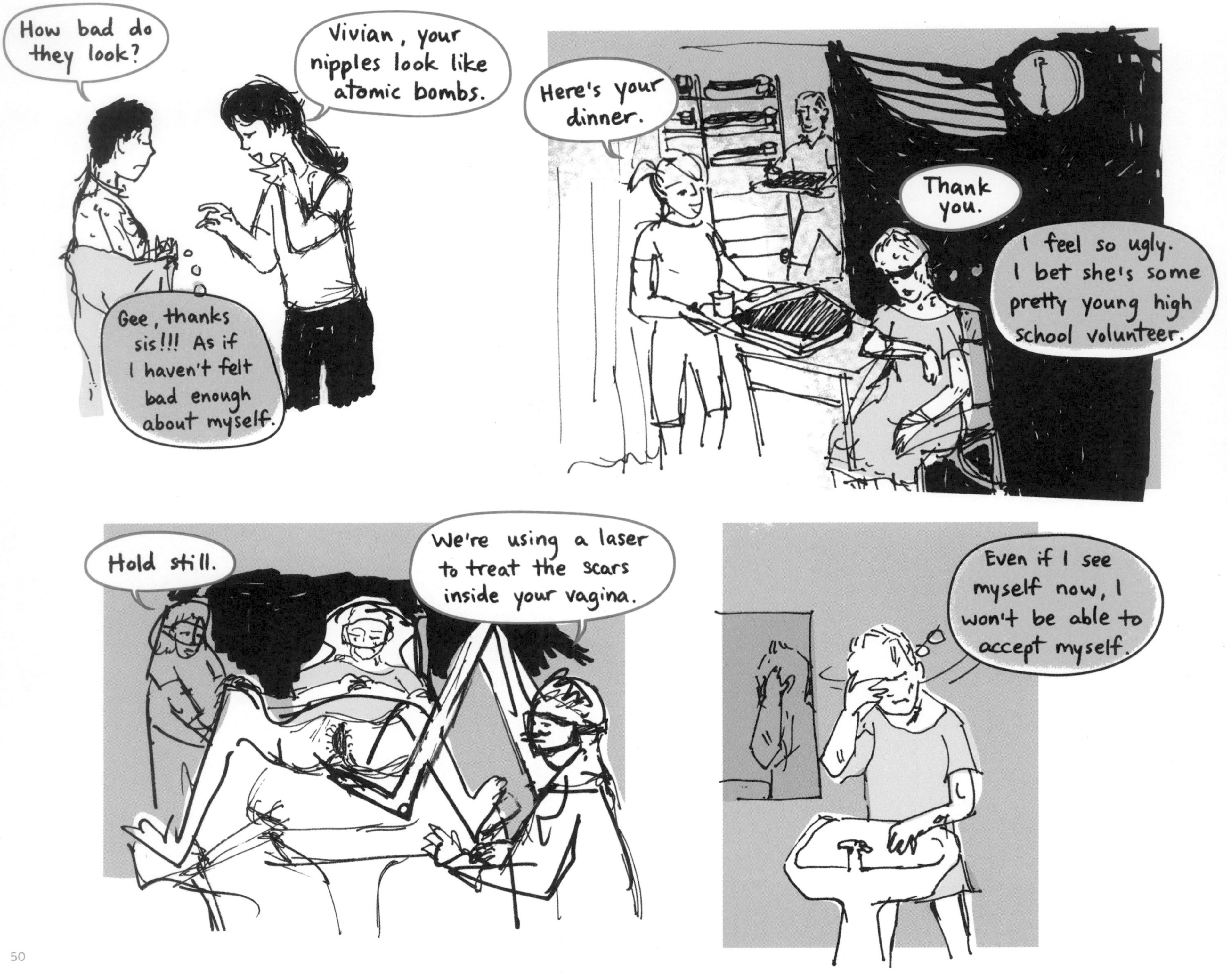
How bad do they look?
Vivian, your nipples look like atomic bombs.
Gee, thanks sis!!! As if I haven't felt bad enough about myself.
Here's your dinner.
Thank you.
I feel so ugly. I bet she's some pretty young high school volunteer.
Hold still.
We're using a laser to treat the scars inside your vagina.
Even if I see myself now, I won't be able to accept myself.

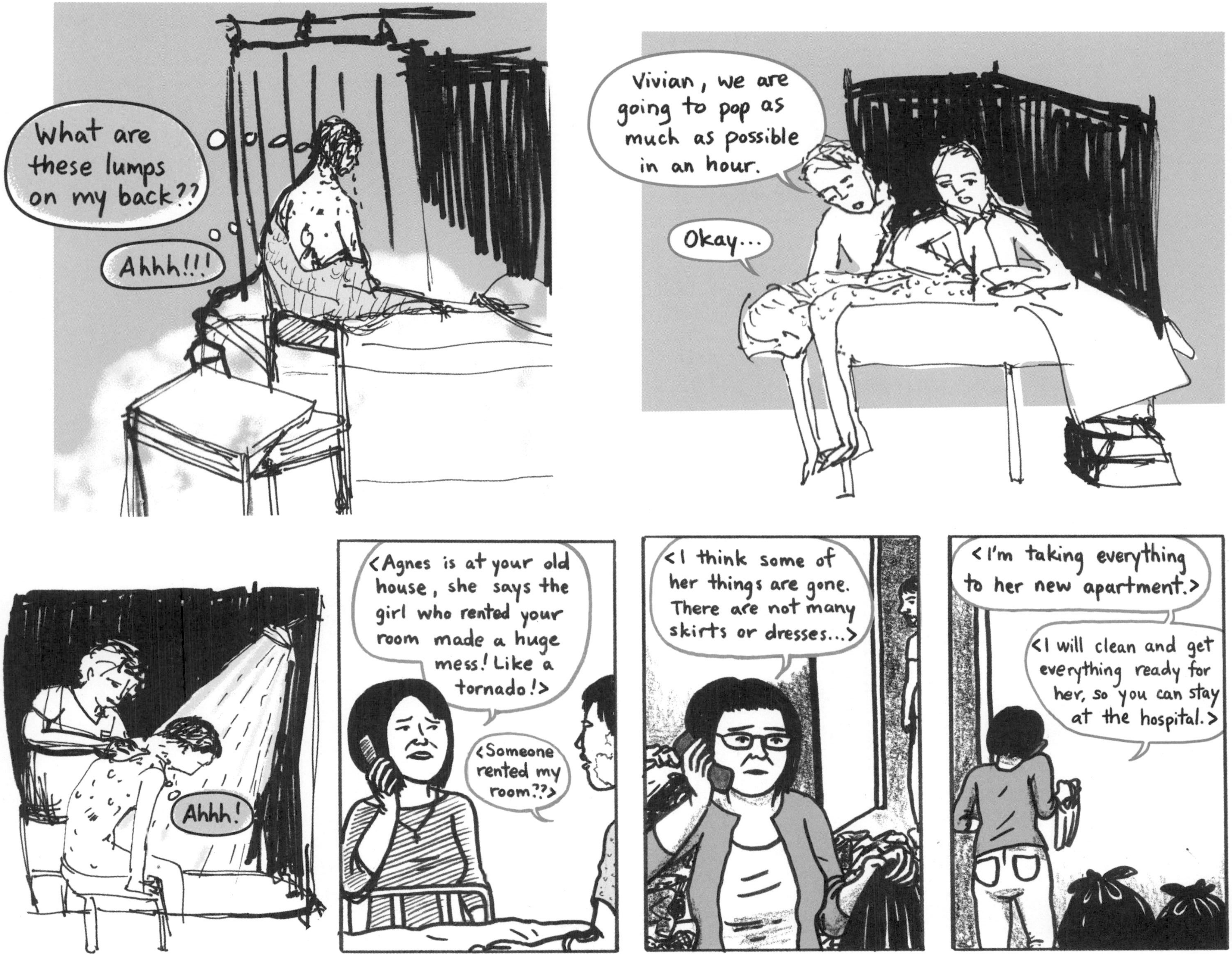
What are these lumps on my back??
Ahhh!!!
Vivian, we are going to pop as much as possible in an hour.
Okay...
Ahhh!
<Agnes is at your old house, she says the girl who rented your room made a huge mess! Like a tornado!>
<Someone rented my room??>
<I think some of her things are gone. There are not many skirts or dresses...>
<I'm taking everything to her new apartment.>
<I will clean and get everything ready for her, so you can stay at the hospital.>

Vivian, you have a phone call!

Who is calling me here?

This is so crazy, are you okay now?

There's so much to tell you, and I want to hear all about...

Will you get out of the hospital someday soon?

Hello?

Vivian, oh my god I finally found you!

Marguerite?

YES! Vivian how ARE you? I had to hunt you down, I've called your house about fifty times since January! Seth said you were still on vacation!

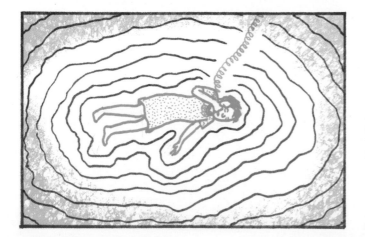

At first I was like, "Hell yeah, have fun!" But then it seemed way too long, and Seth wouldn't tell me anything. Finally I wore him down, and he told me where you were.

I can't believe him!

!!!

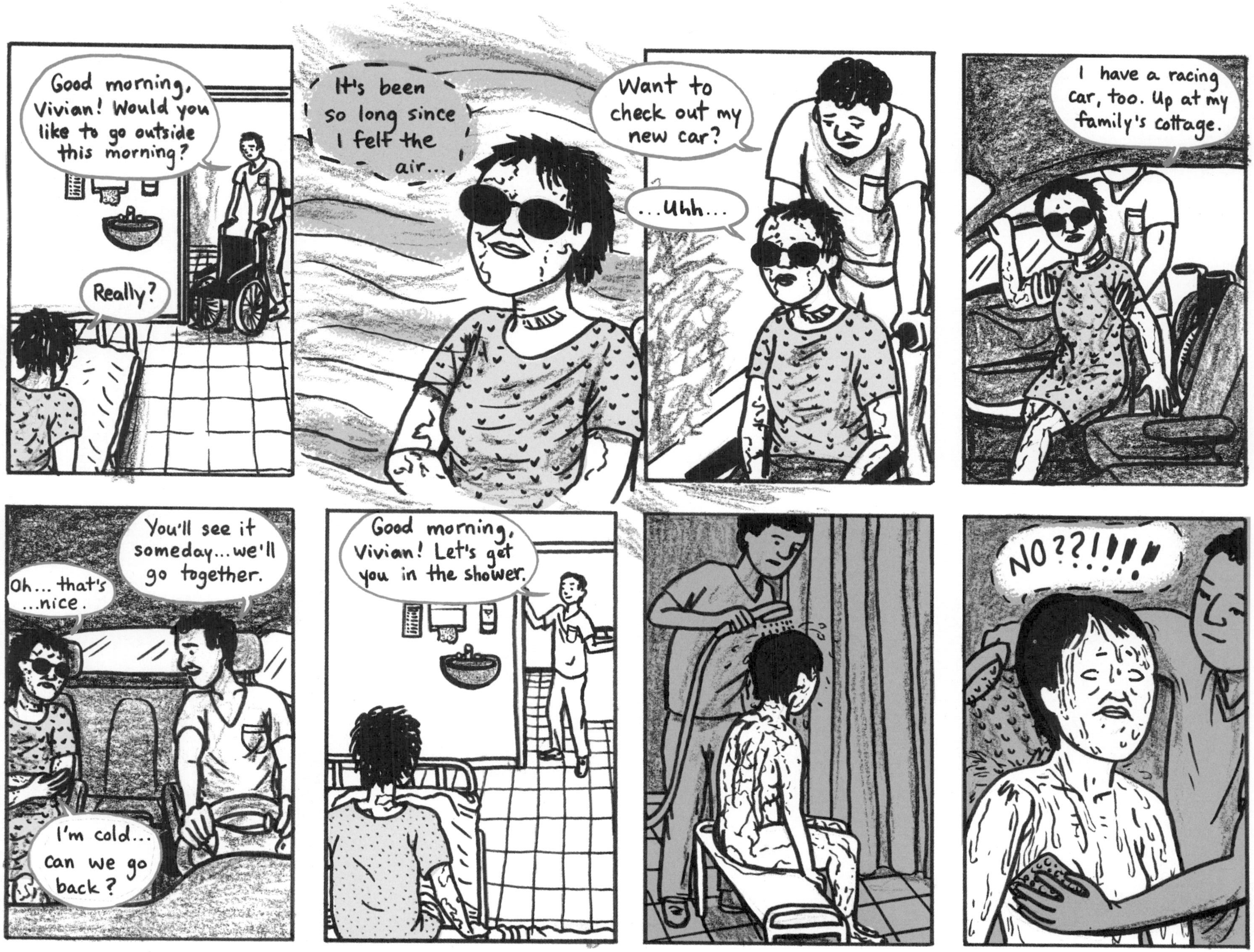
Good morning, Vivian! Would you like to go outside this morning?
Really?
It's been so long since I felt the air...
Want to check out my new car?
...Uhh...
I have a racing car, too. Up at my family's cottage.
You'll see it someday... we'll go together.
Oh... that's ...nice.
I'm cold... can we go back?
Good morning, Vivian! Let's get you in the shower.
NO??!!!!!

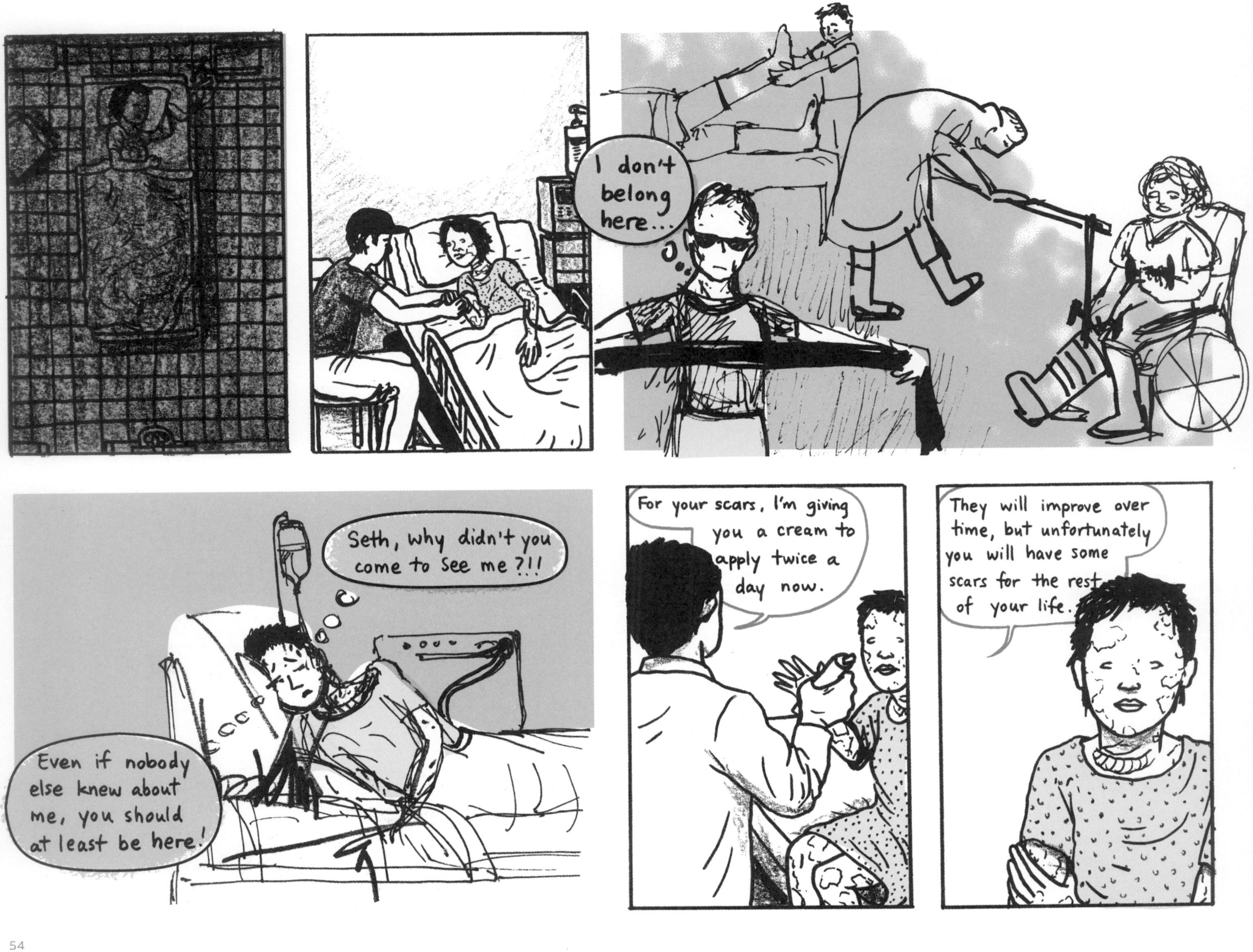

I don't belong here...
Seth, why didn't you come to see me?!!
Even if nobody else knew about me, you should at least be here!
For your scars, I'm giving you a cream to apply twice a day now.
They will improve over time, but unfortunately you will have some scars for the rest of your life.

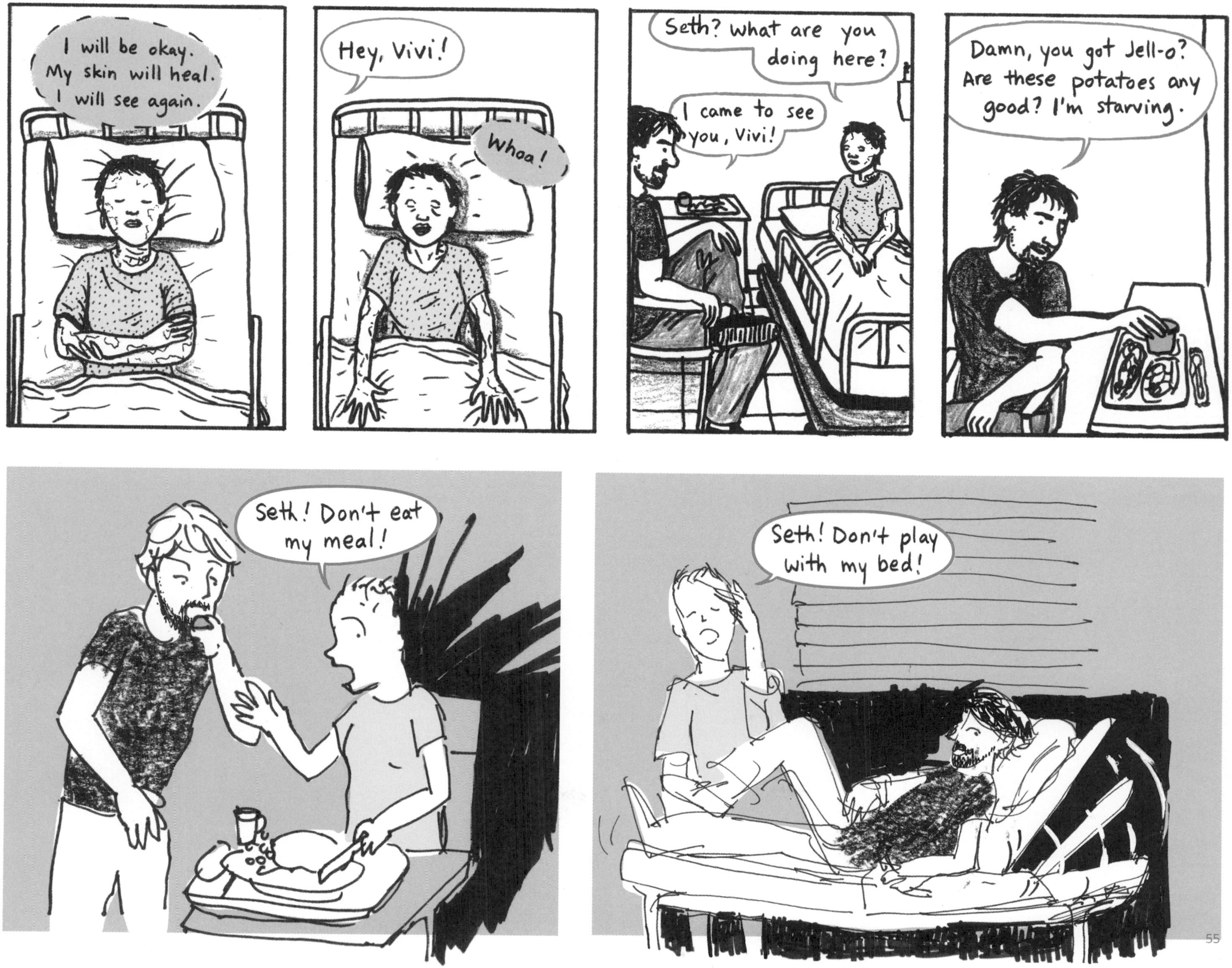
I will be okay. My skin will heal. I will see again.
Hey, Vivi!
Whoa!
Seth? What are you doing here?
I came to see you, Vivi!
Damn, you got Jell-o? Are these potatoes any good? I'm starving.
Seth! Don't eat my meal!
Seth! Don't play with my bed!

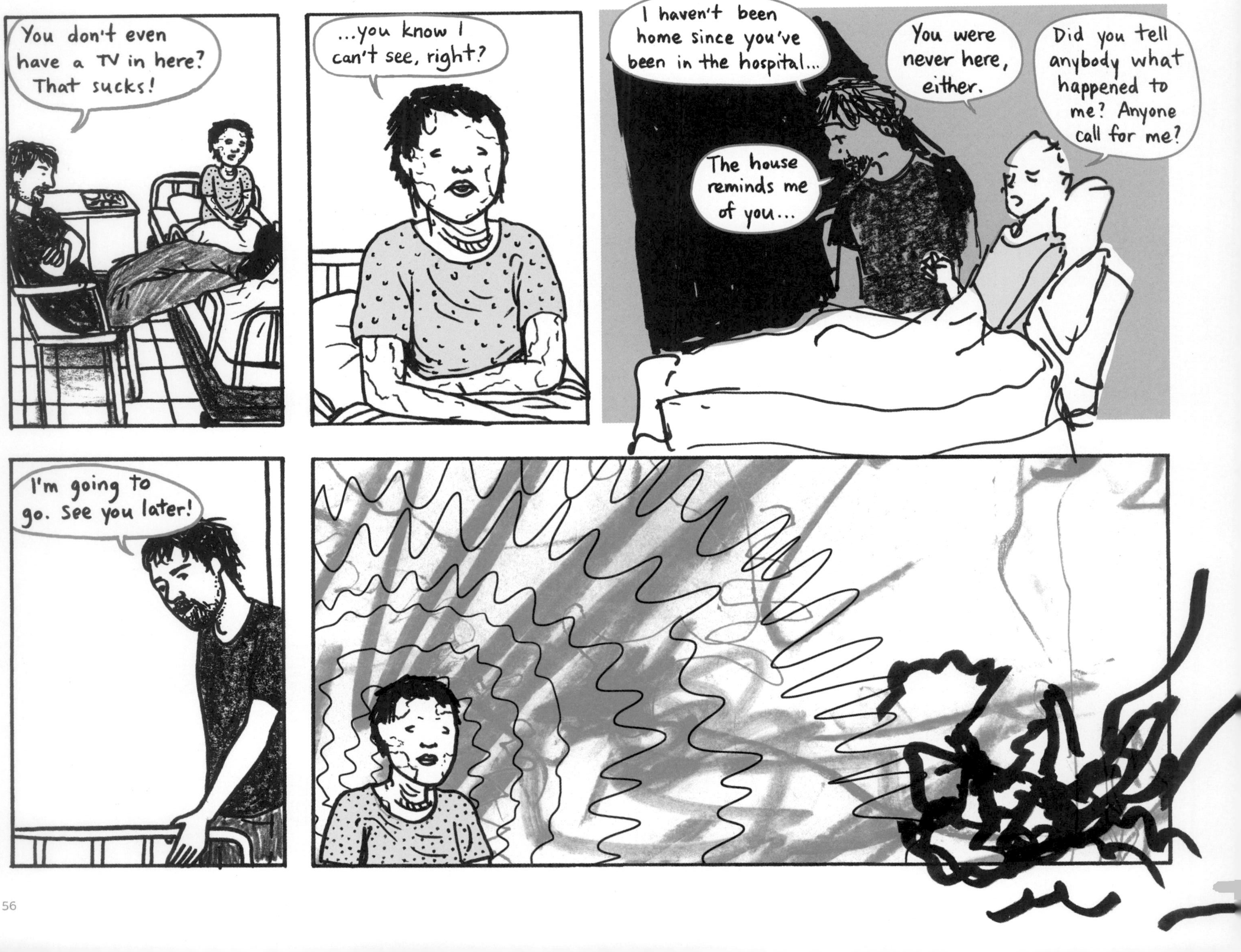
You don't even have a TV in here? That sucks!
...you know I can't see, right?
I haven't been home since you've been in the hospital...
The house reminds me of you...
You were never here, either.
Did you tell anybody what happened to me? Anyone call for me?
I'm going to go. See you later!

<It's okay, Mom. Michael will be here. Thank you for helping me.>

<The caretaker is all lined up. I have to go back to work.>

<It'll be okay. Remember to smile.>

<I'm about to get on my flight home to Hong Kong... Aunt Agnes said the apartment will be ready a day early.>

Five

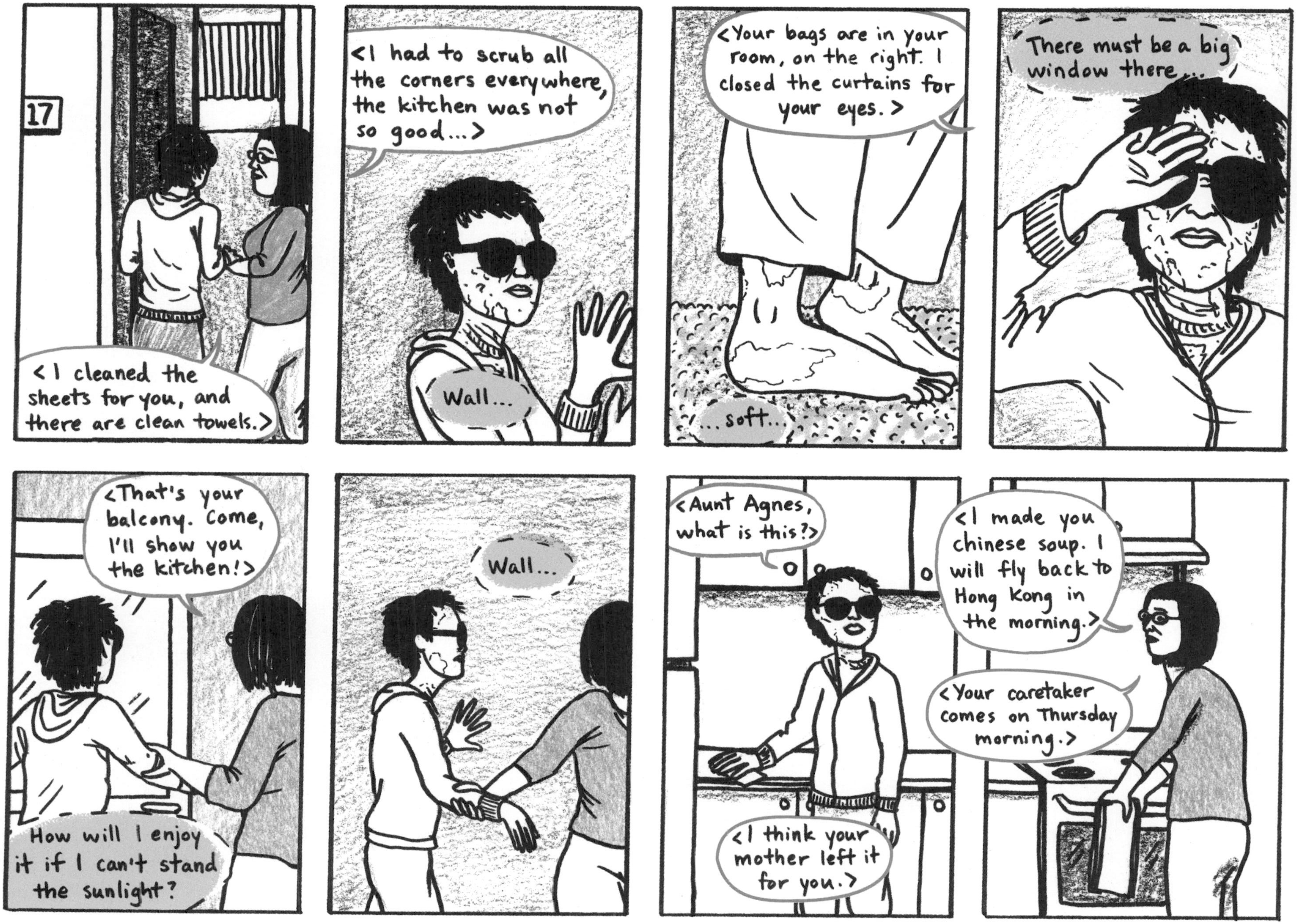
17
<I cleaned the sheets for you, and there are clean towels.>
<I had to scrub all the corners everywhere, the kitchen was not so good...>
Wall...
<Your bags are in your room, on the right. I closed the curtains for your eyes.>
...soft...
There must be a big window there...
<That's your balcony. Come, I'll show you the kitchen!>
How will I enjoy it if I can't stand the sunlight?
Wall...
<Aunt Agnes, what is this?>
<I think your mother left it for you.>
<I made you chinese soup. I will fly back to Hong Kong in the morning.>
<Your caretaker comes on Thursday morning.>

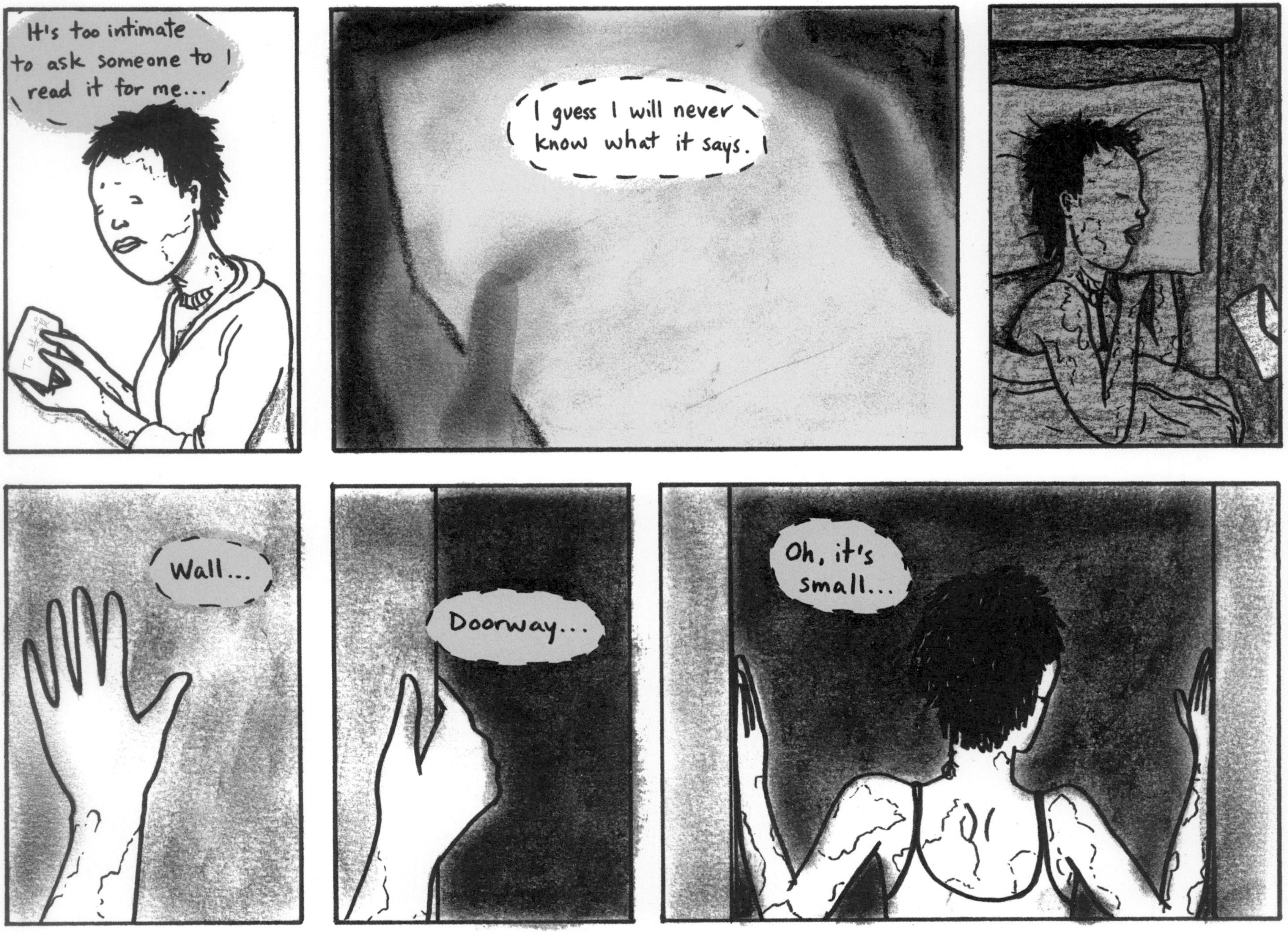
It's too intimate to ask someone to read it for me...
I guess I will never know what it says.
Wall...
Doorway...
Oh, it's small...

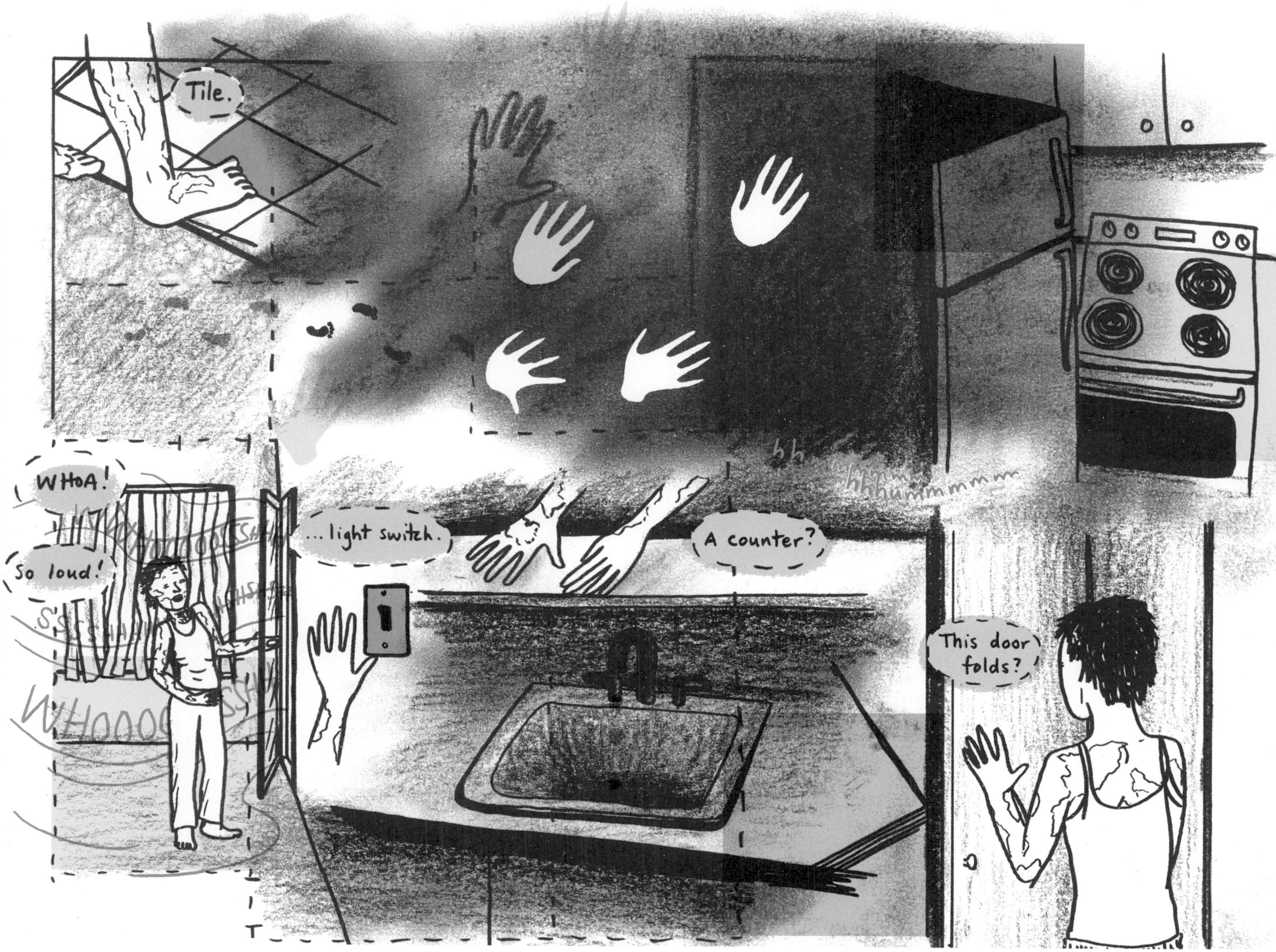
Tile.
WHOA!
So loud!
WHOOOOSSSH
...light switch.
A counter?
hhhummmmm
This door folds?

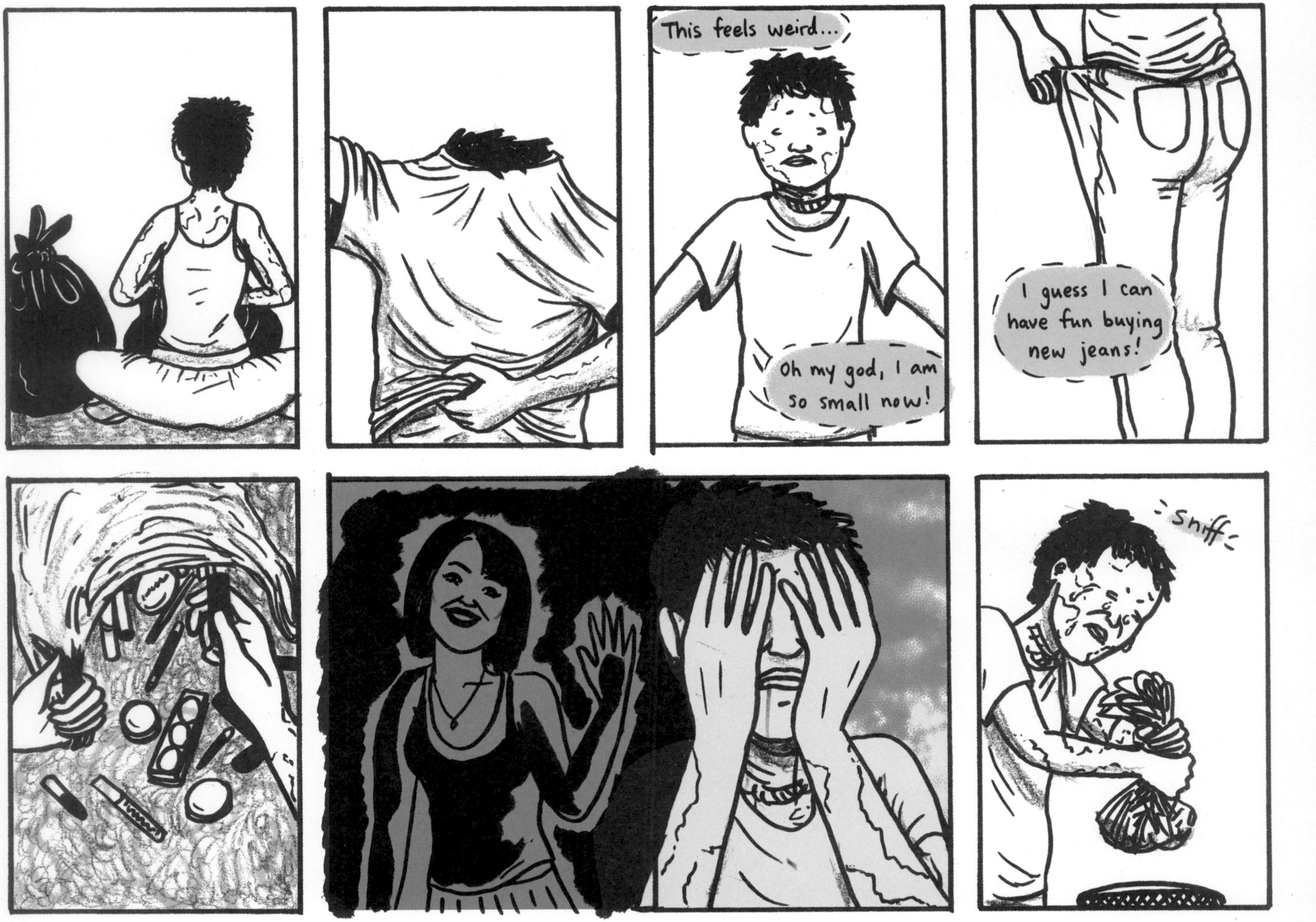
This feels weird...
Oh my god, I am so small now!
I guess I can have fun buying new jeans!
Sniff

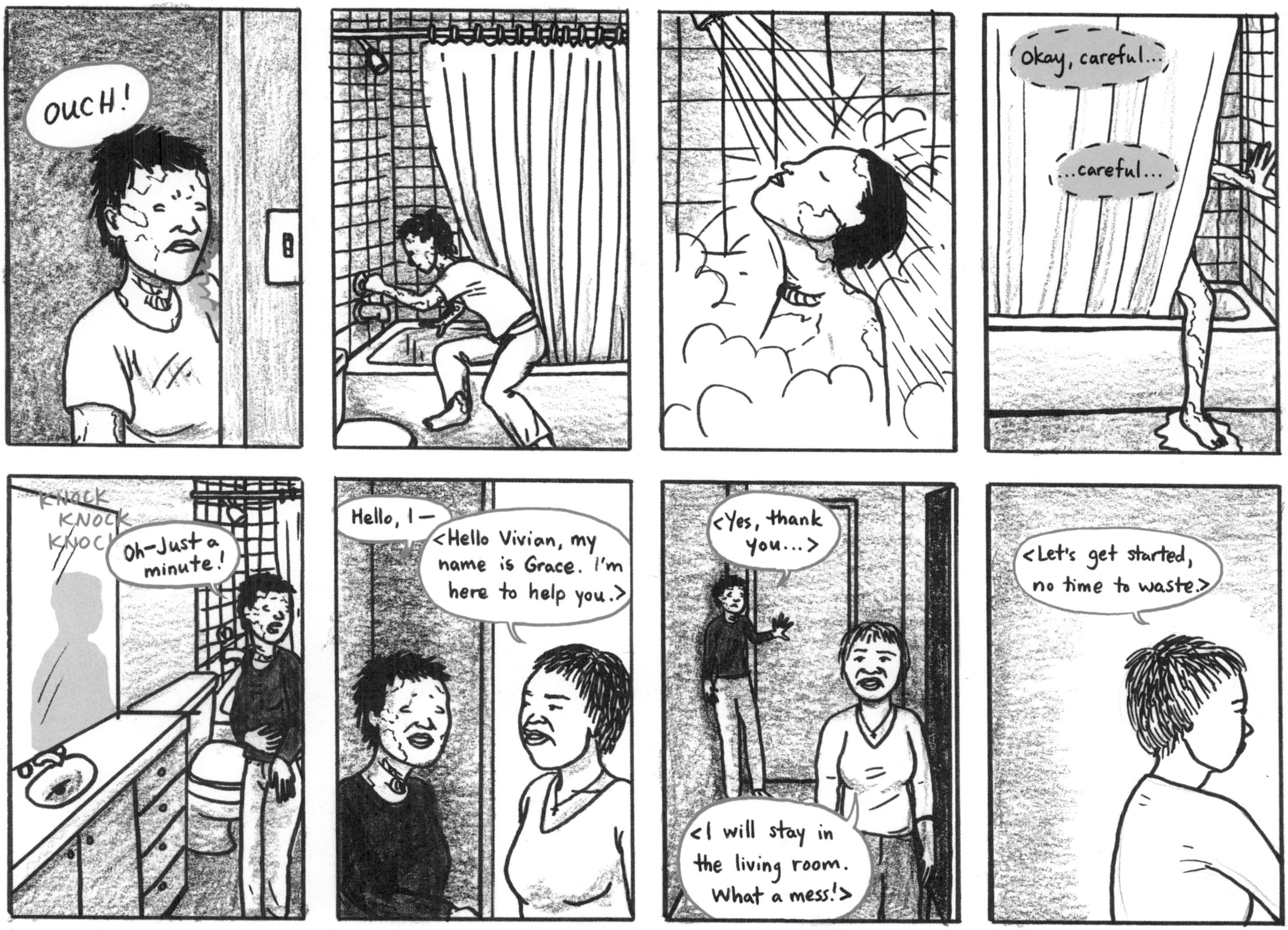
OUCH!
Okay, careful...
...careful...
KNOCK KNOCK KNOCK
Oh—Just a minute!
Hello, I—
<Hello Vivian, my name is Grace. I'm here to help you.>
<Yes, thank you...>
<I will stay in the living room. What a mess!>
<Let's get started, no time to waste.>

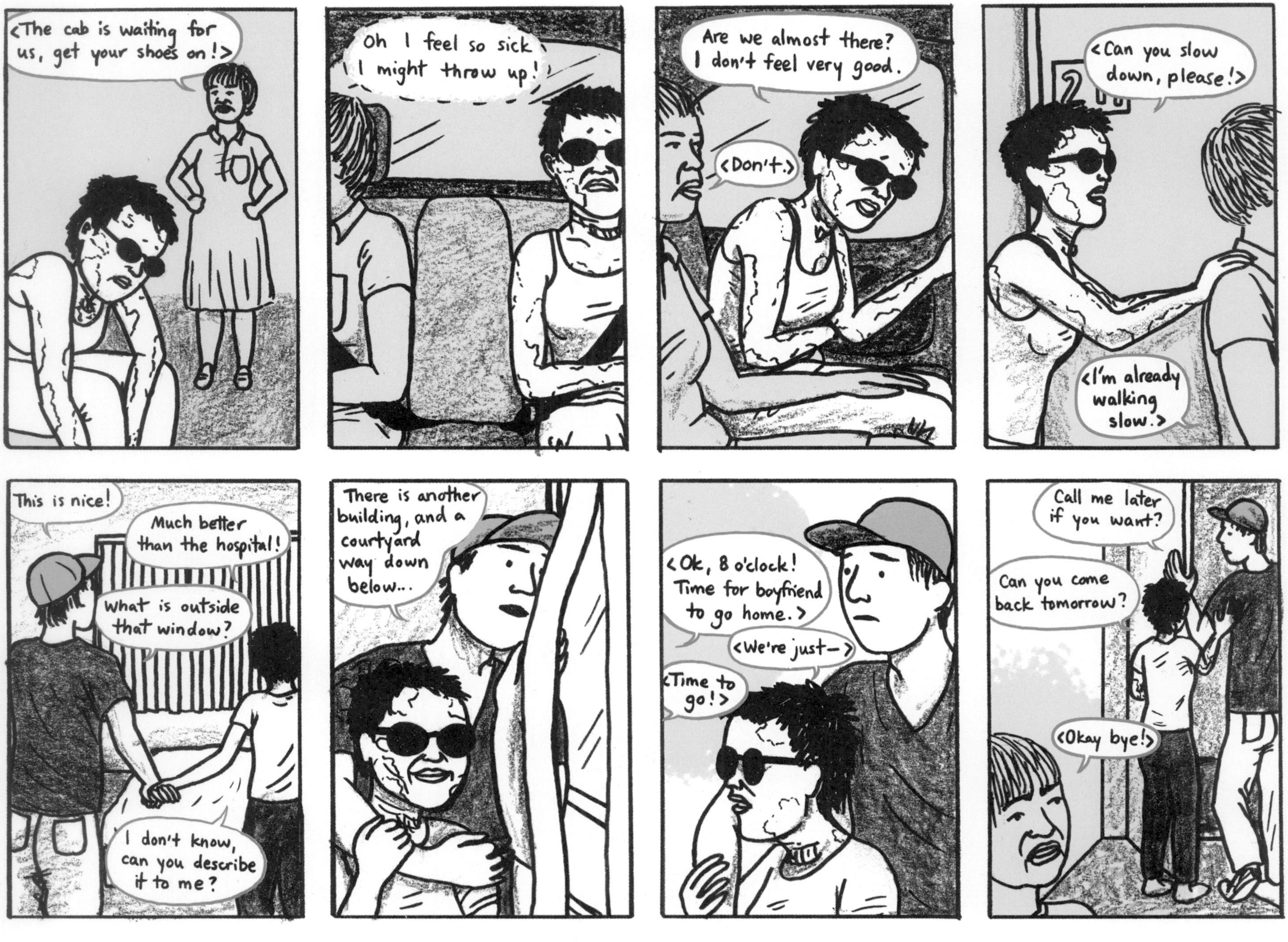
<The cab is waiting for us, get your shoes on!>
Oh I feel so sick I might throw up!
Are we almost there? I don't feel very good.
<Don't.>
<Can you slow down, please!>
<I'm already walking slow.>
This is nice!
Much better than the hospital!
What is outside that window?
I don't know, can you describe it to me?
There is another building, and a courtyard way down below...
<Ok, 8 o'clock! Time for boyfriend to go home.>
<We're just—>
<Time to go!>
Call me later if you want?
Can you come back tomorrow?
<Okay bye!>

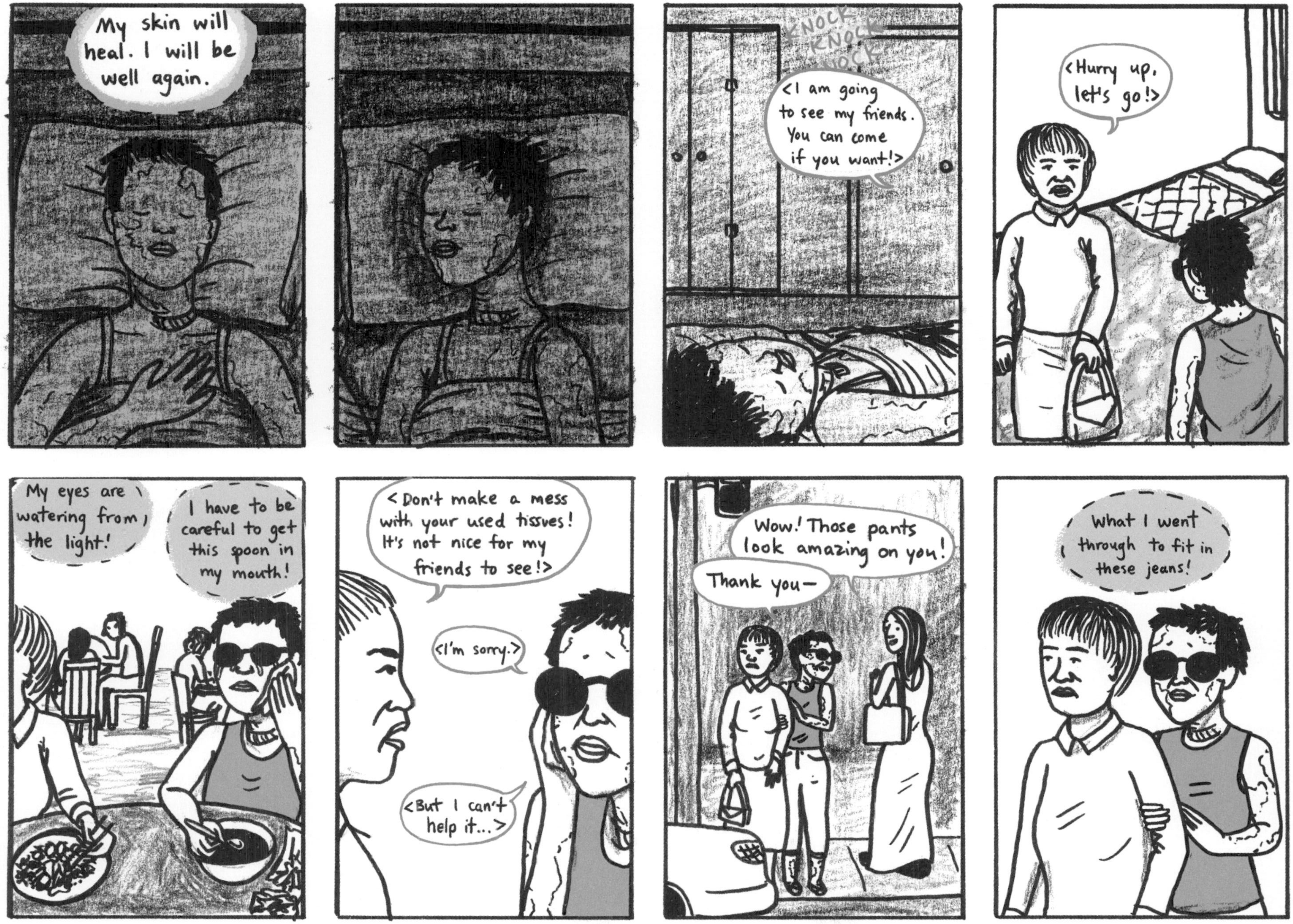
My skin will heal. I will be well again.
KNOCK KNOCK KNOCK
<I am going to see my friends. You can come if you want!>
<Hurry up, let's go!>
My eyes are watering from the light!
I have to be careful to get this spoon in my mouth!
<Don't make a mess with your used tissues! It's not nice for my friends to see!>
<I'm sorry.>
<But I can't help it...>
Wow! Those pants look amazing on you!
Thank you—
What I went through to fit in these jeans!

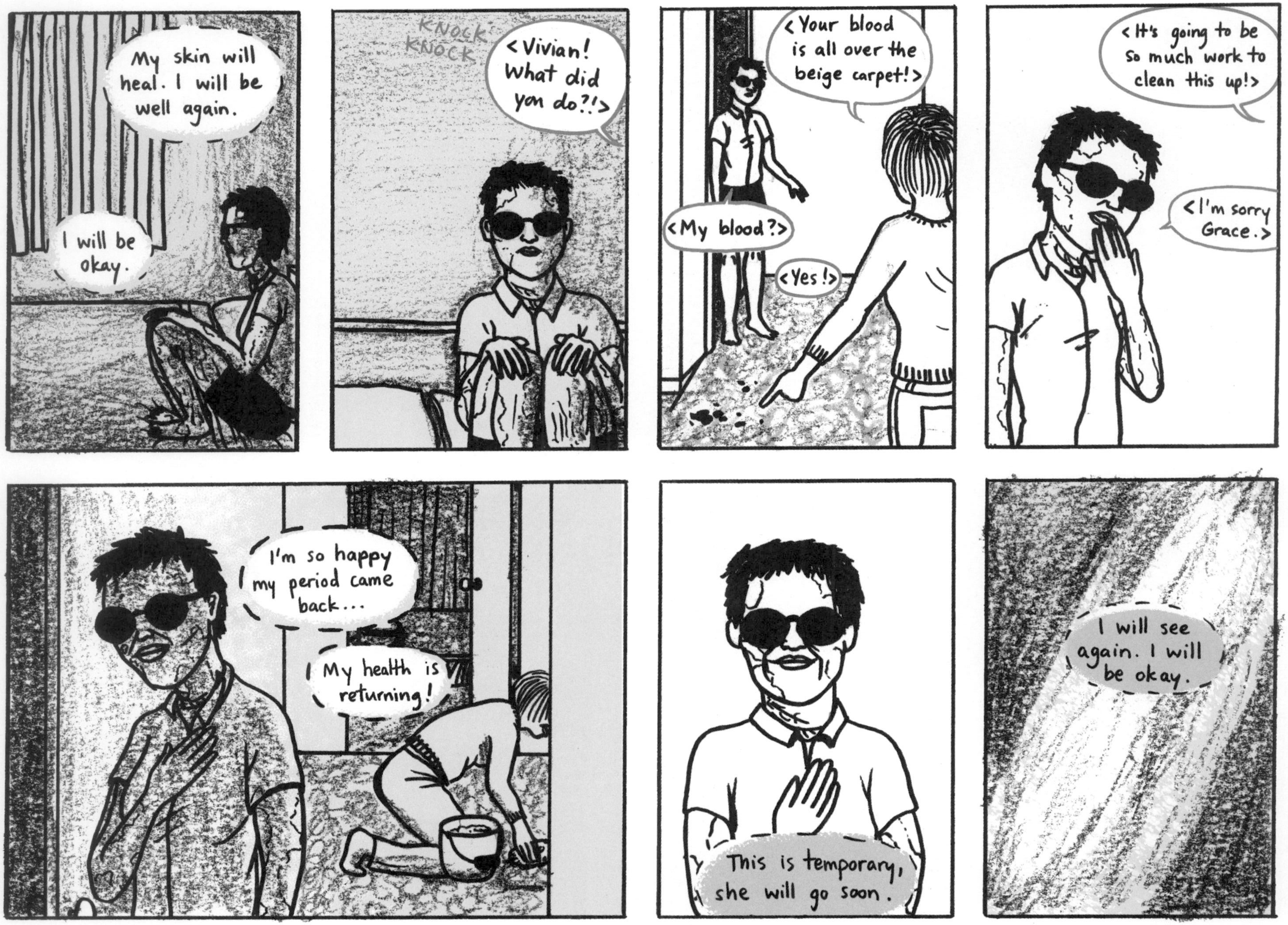
My skin will heal. I will be well again.
I will be okay.
KNOCK KNOCK
<Vivian! What did you do?!>
<Your blood is all over the beige carpet!>
<My blood?>
<Yes!>
<It's going to be so much work to clean this up!>
<I'm sorry Grace.>
I'm so happy my period came back...
My health is returning!
This is temporary, she will go soon.
I will see again. I will be okay.

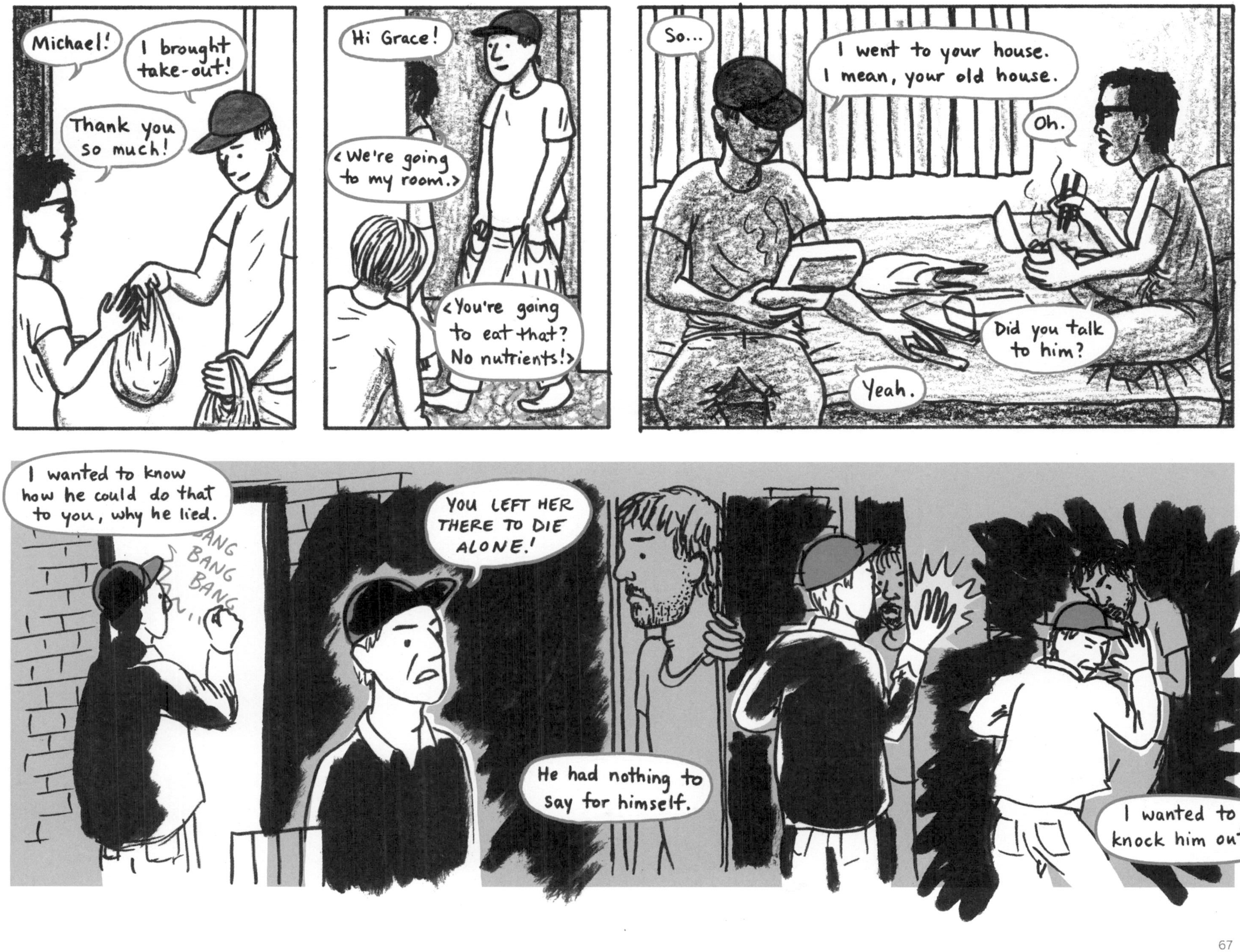
Michael!
I brought take-out!
Thank you so much!
Hi Grace!
<We're going to my room.>
<You're going to eat that? No nutrients!>
So...
I went to your house. I mean, your old house.
Oh.
Did you talk to him?
Yeah.
I wanted to know how he could do that to you, why he lied.
BANG BANG BANG
YOU LEFT HER THERE TO DIE ALONE!
He had nothing to say for himself.
I wanted to knock him out...

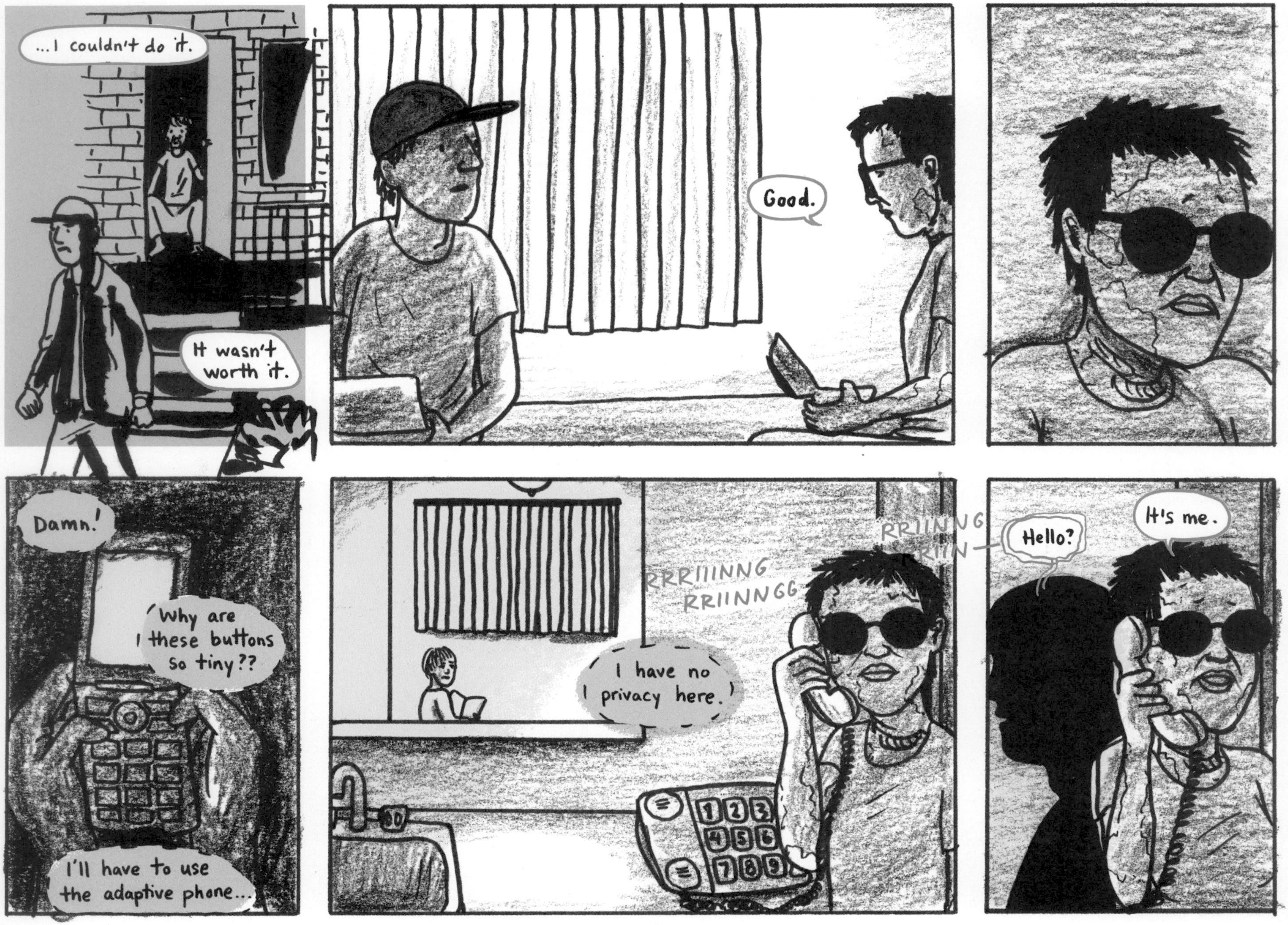
...I couldn't do it.
It wasn't worth it.
Good.
Damn!
Why are these buttons so tiny??
I'll have to use the adaptive phone...
I have no privacy here.
RRRIIINNG
RRIINNGG
RRIINNG
RRIIN—
Hello?
It's me.

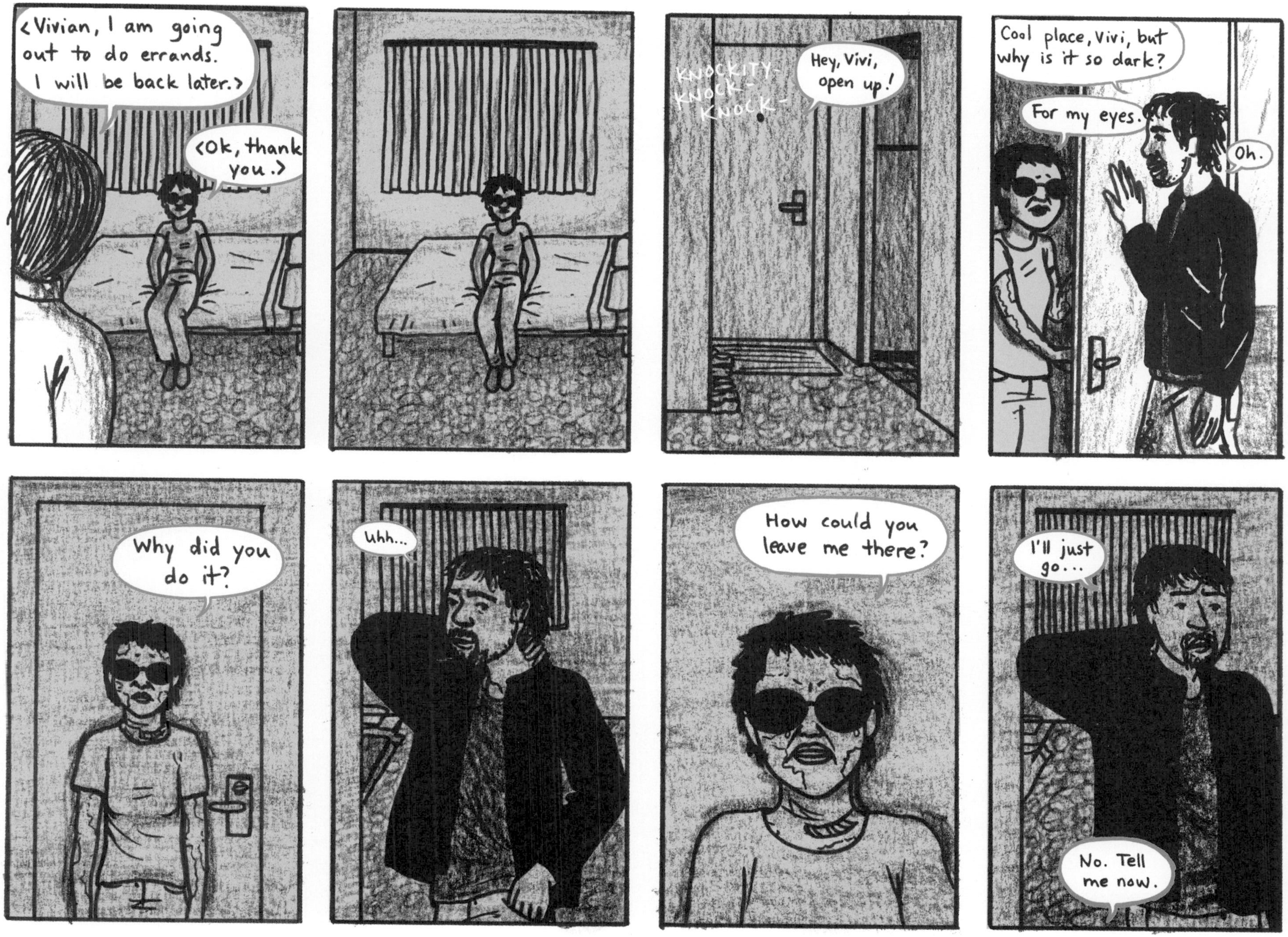

<Vivian, I am going out to do errands. I will be back later.>
<Ok, thank you.>
KNOCKITY-KNOCK-KNOCK-
Hey, Vivi, open up!
Cool place, Vivi, but why is it so dark?
For my eyes.
Oh.
Why did you do it?
Uhh...
How could you leave me there?
I'll just go...
No. Tell me now.

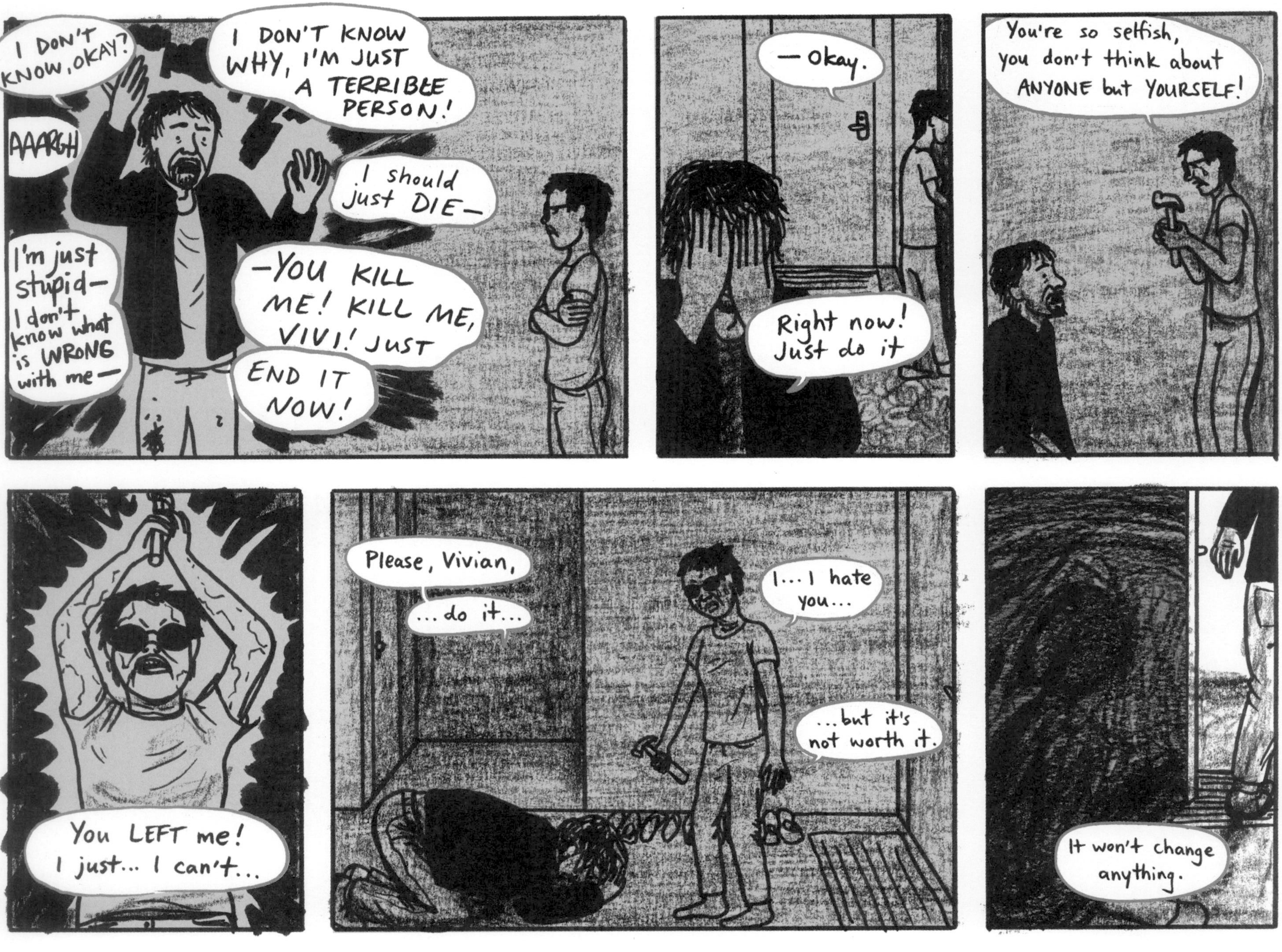
I DON'T KNOW, OKAY?
AAARGH
I'm just stupid—
I don't know what is WRONG with me—
I DON'T KNOW WHY, I'M JUST A TERRIBLEE PERSON!
I should just DIE—
—YOU KILL ME! KILL ME, VIVI! JUST
END IT NOW!
—Okay.
Right now! Just do it
You're so selfish, you don't think about ANYONE but YOURSELF!
You LEFT me! I just... I can't...
Please, Vivian,
... do it...
I... I hate you...
...but it's not worth it.
It won't change anything.

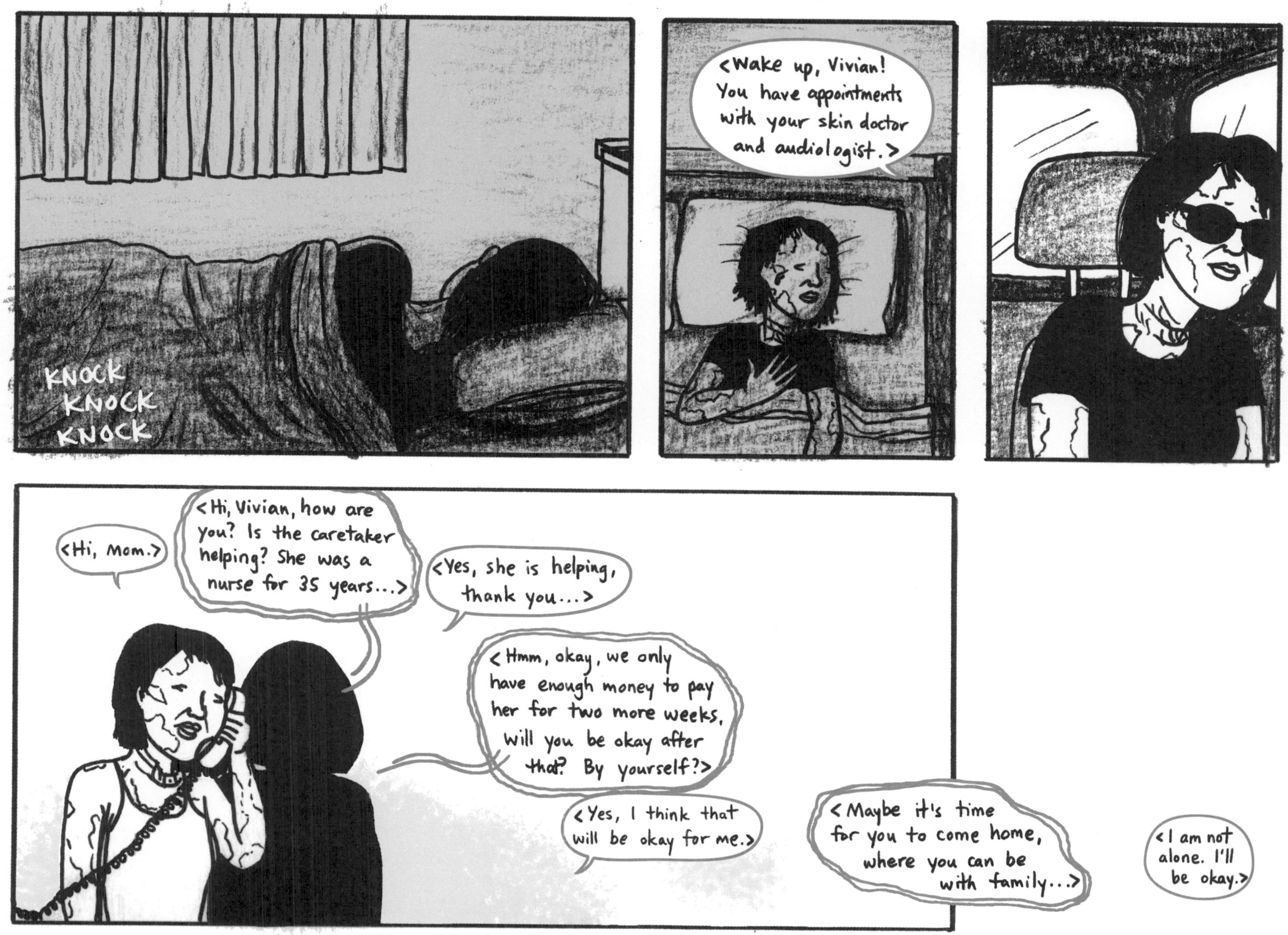
KNOCK KNOCK KNOCK
<Wake up, Vivian! You have appointments with your skin doctor and audiologist.>
<Hi, Mom.>
<Hi, Vivian, how are you? Is the caretaker helping? She was a nurse for 35 years...>
<Yes, she is helping, thank you...>
<Hmm, okay, we only have enough money to pay her for two more weeks, will you be okay after that? By yourself?>
<Yes, I think that will be okay for me.>
<Maybe it's time for you to come home, where you can be with family...>
<I am not alone. I'll be okay.>

Six

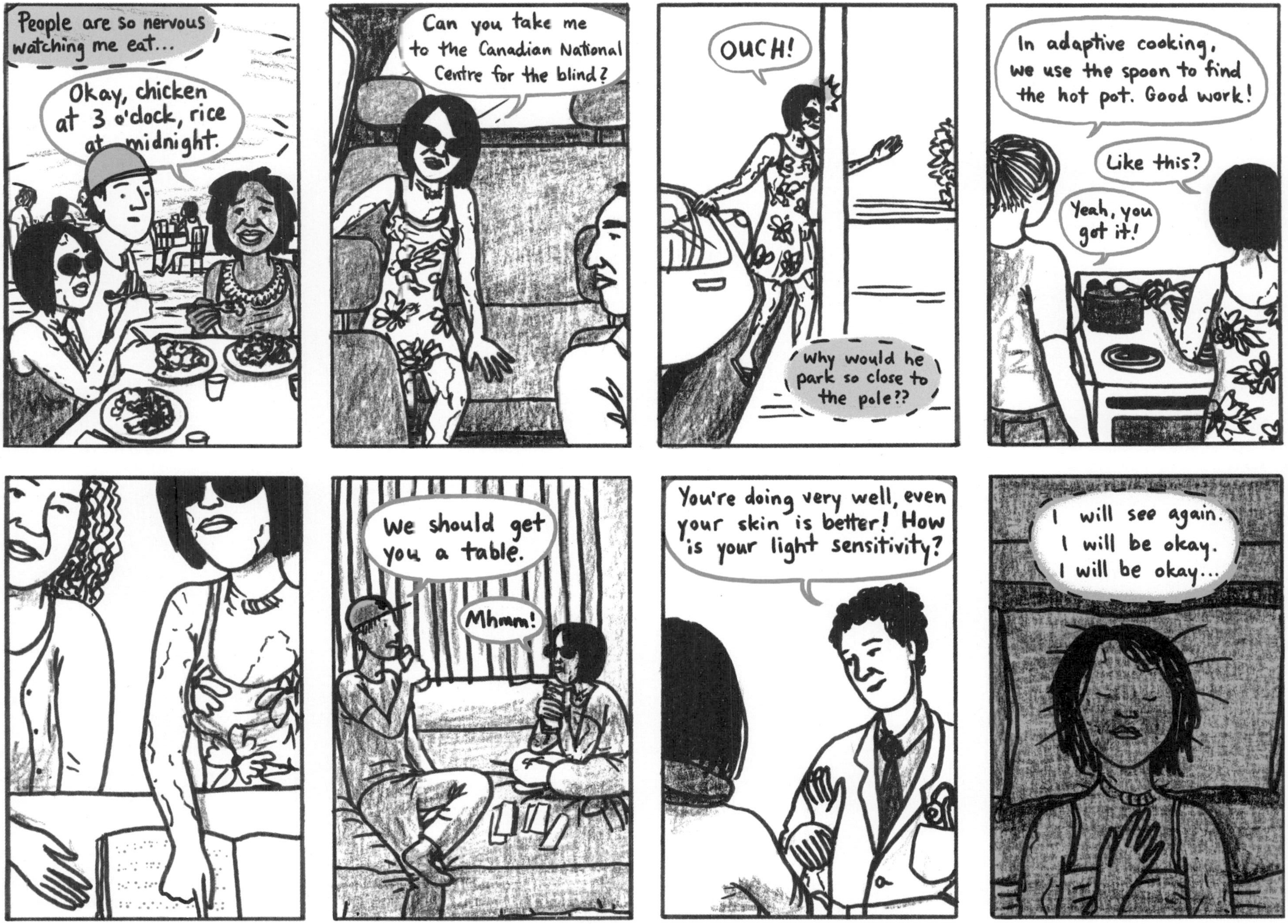
People are so nervous watching me eat...
Okay, chicken at 3 o'clock, rice at midnight.
Can you take me to the Canadian National Centre for the blind?
OUCH!
Why would he park so close to the pole??
In adaptive cooking, we use the spoon to find the hot pot. Good work!
Like this?
Yeah, you got it!
We should get you a table.
Mhmm!
You're doing very well, even your skin is better! How is your light sensitivity?
I will see again.
I will be okay.
I will be okay...

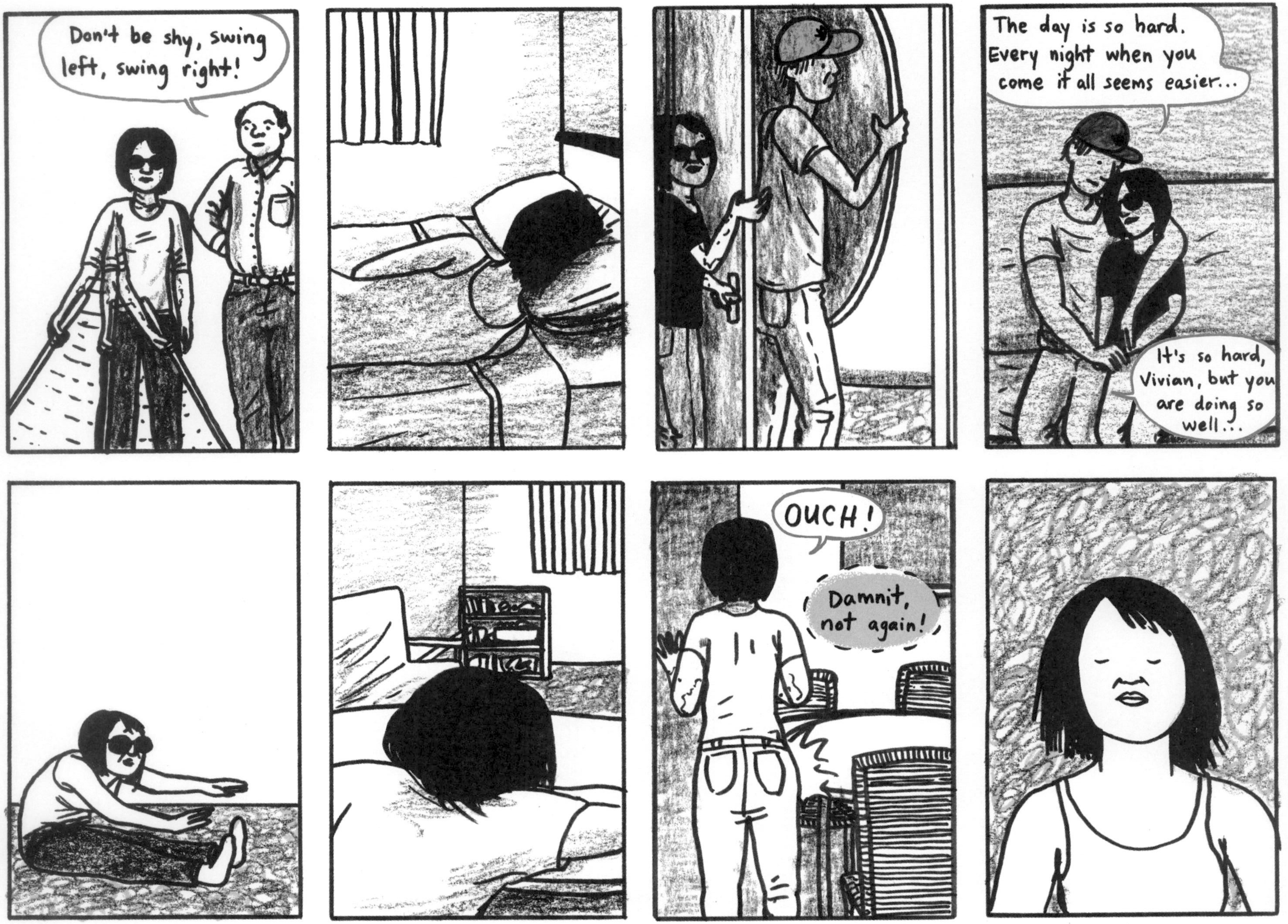
Don't be shy, swing left, swing right!
The day is so hard. Every night when you come it all seems easier...
It's so hard, Vivian, but you are doing so well...
OUCH!
Damnit, not again!

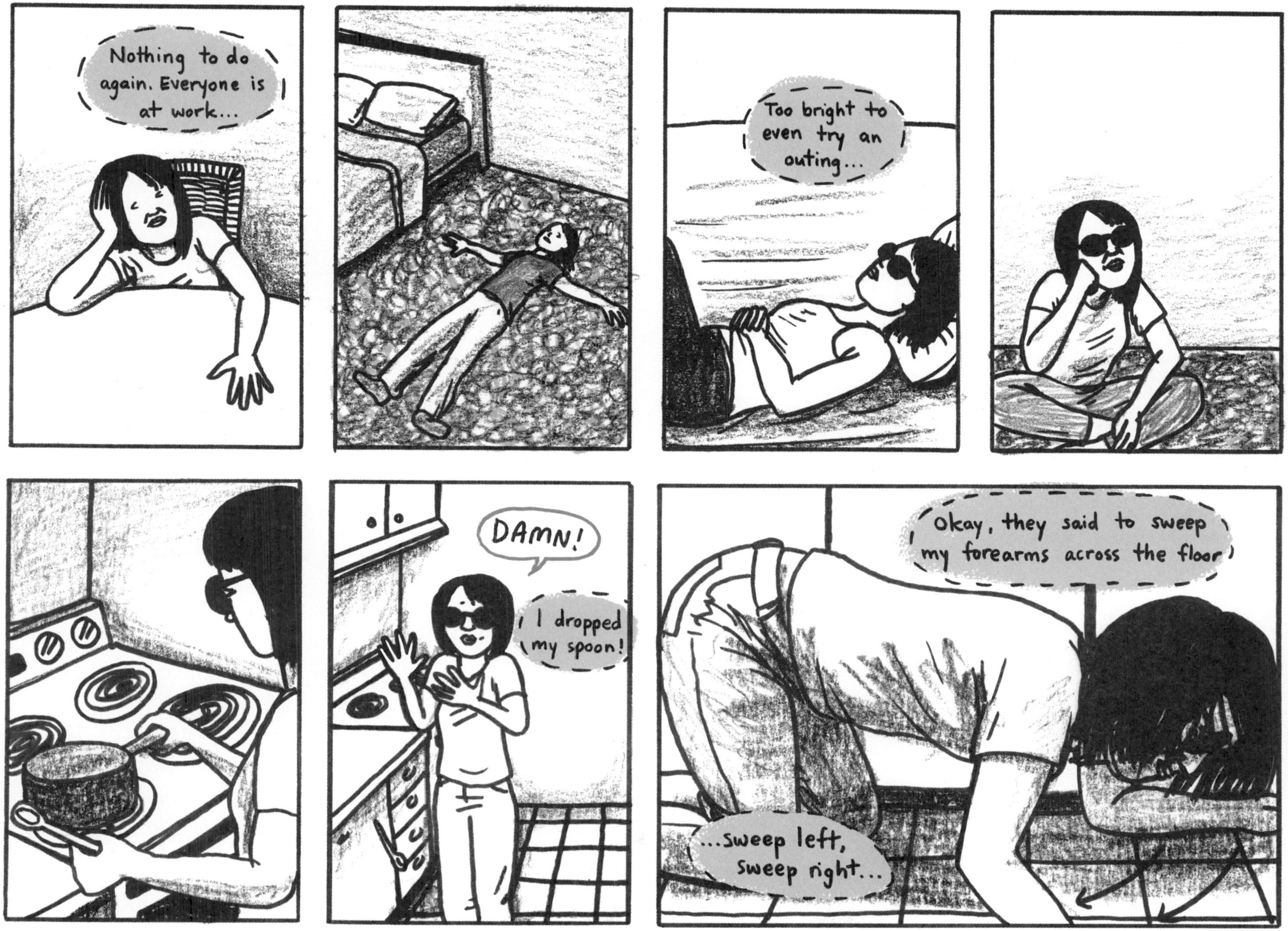

Nothing to do again. Everyone is at work...
Too bright to even try an outing...
DAMN!
I dropped my spoon!
Okay, they said to sweep my forearms across the floor
...sweep left, sweep right...

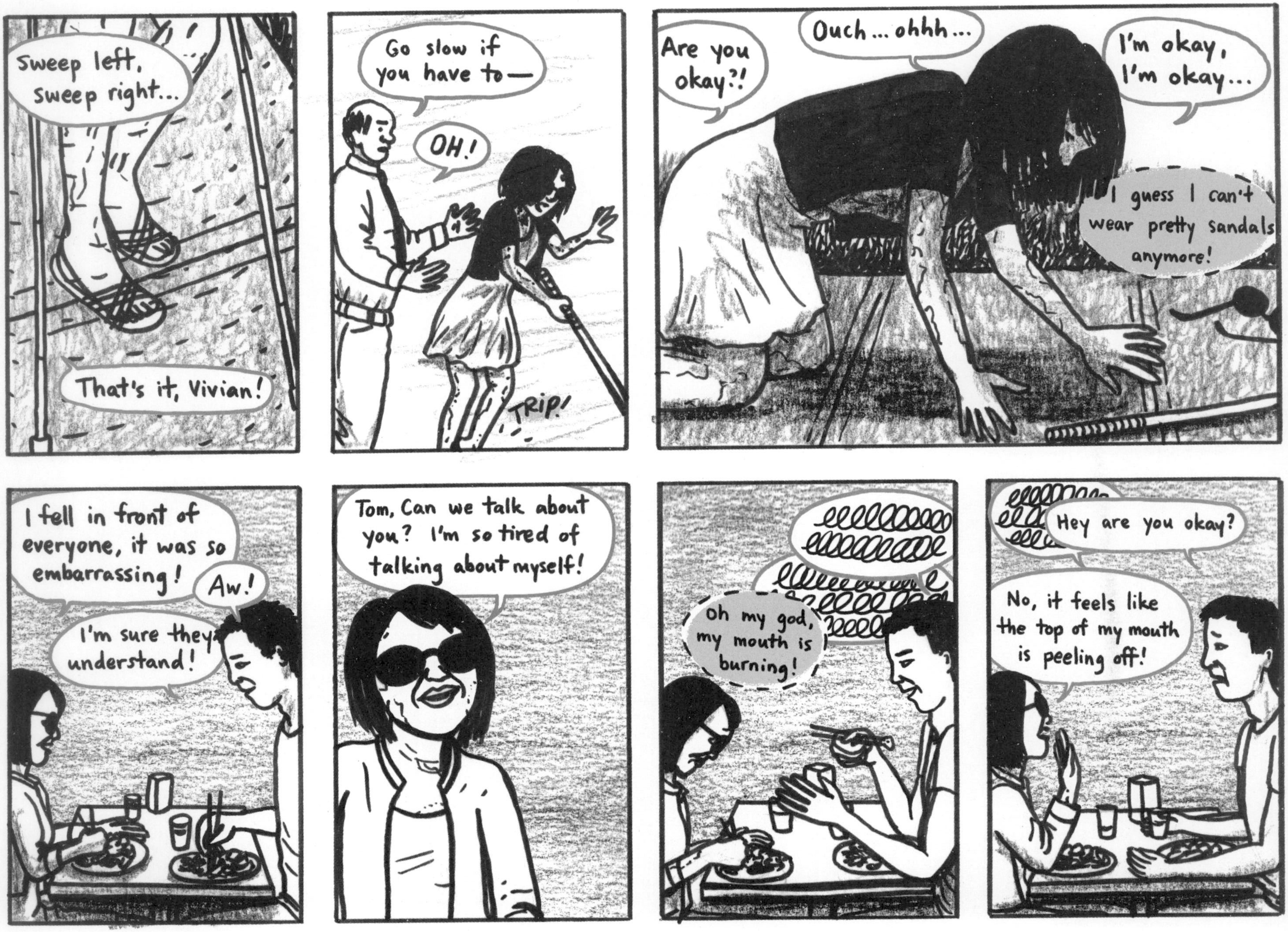
Sweep left, sweep right...
That's it, Vivian!
Go slow if you have to—
OH!
TRIP!
Are you okay?!
Ouch... ohhh...
I'm okay, I'm okay...
I guess I can't wear pretty sandals anymore!
I fell in front of everyone, it was so embarrassing!
Aw!
I'm sure they understand!
Tom, Can we talk about you? I'm so tired of talking about myself!
Oh my god, my mouth is burning!
Hey are you okay?
No, it feels like the top of my mouth is peeling off!

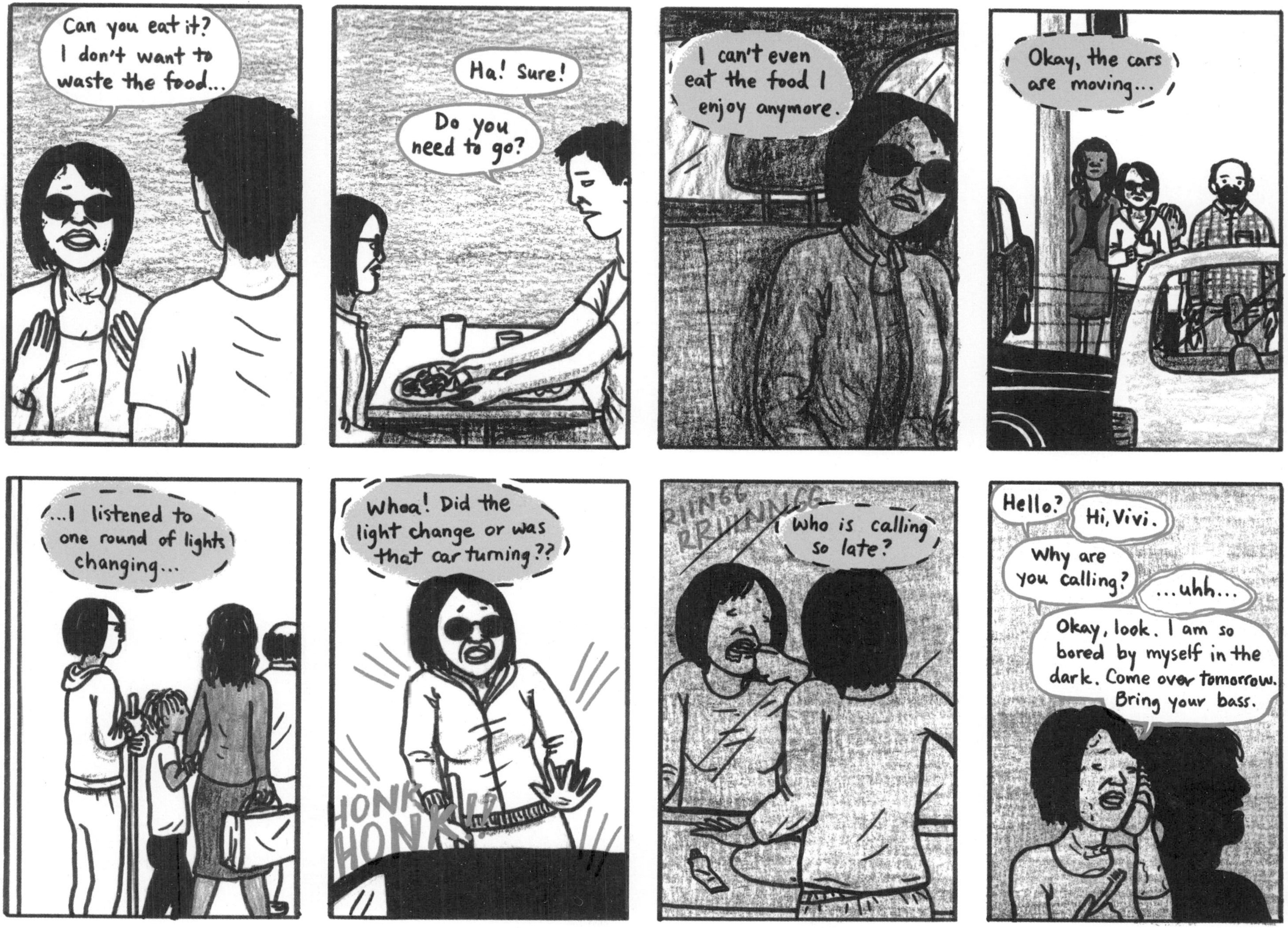
Can you eat it? I don't want to waste the food...
Ha! Sure!
Do you need to go?
I can't even eat the food I enjoy anymore.
Okay, the cars are moving...
...I listened to one round of lights changing...
Whoa! Did the light change or was that car turning??
HONK! HONK!!
RRIIING RRIIINNGG
Who is calling so late?
Hello?
Hi, Vivi.
Why are you calling?
...uhh...
Okay, look. I am so bored by myself in the dark. Come over tomorrow. Bring your bass.

Vivian, I'm here!
KNOCK KNOCK KNOCK
Hellooo! I brought food...
Vivian! It's Michael.!

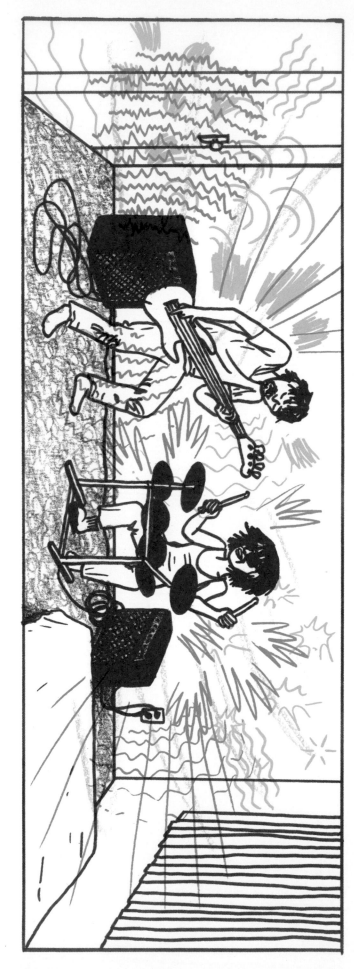

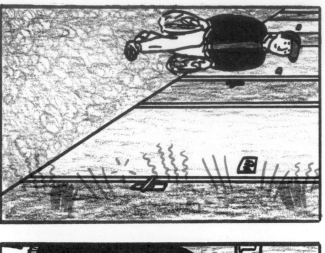

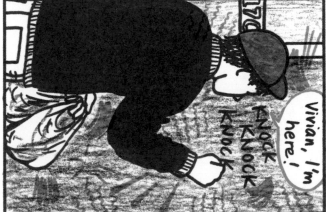

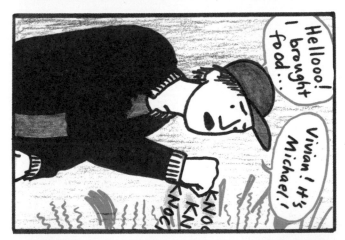

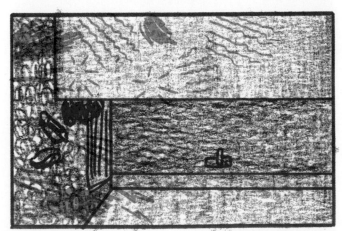

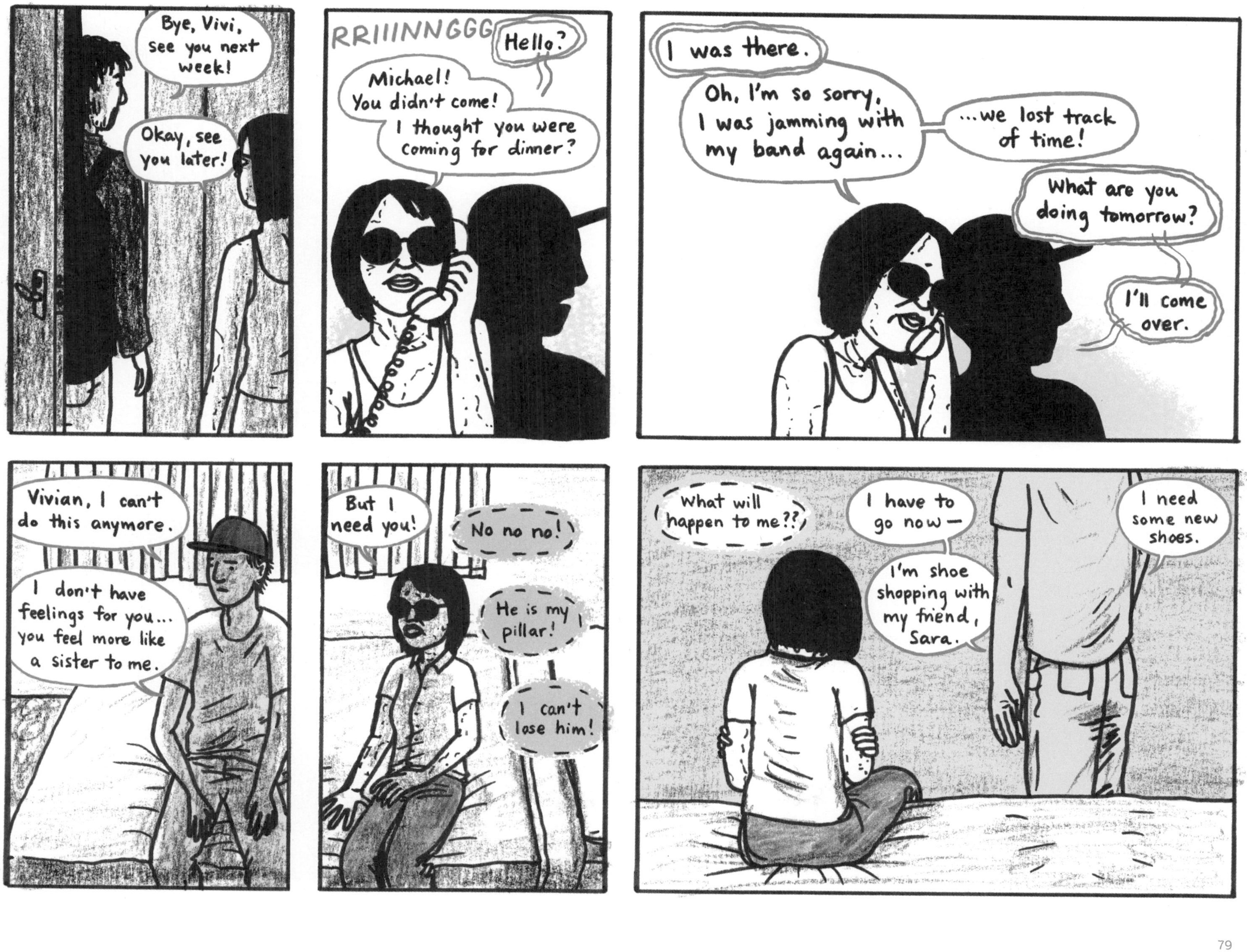
Bye, Vivi, see you next week!
Okay, see you later!
RRIIINNGGG
Hello?
Michael! You didn't come!
I thought you were coming for dinner?
I was there.
Oh, I'm so sorry, I was jamming with my band again...
...we lost track of time!
What are you doing tomorrow?
I'll come over.
Vivian, I can't do this anymore.
I don't have feelings for you... you feel more like a sister to me.
But I need you!
No no no!
He is my pillar!
I can't lose him!
What will happen to me??
I have to go now—
I'm shoe shopping with my friend, Sara.
I need some new shoes.

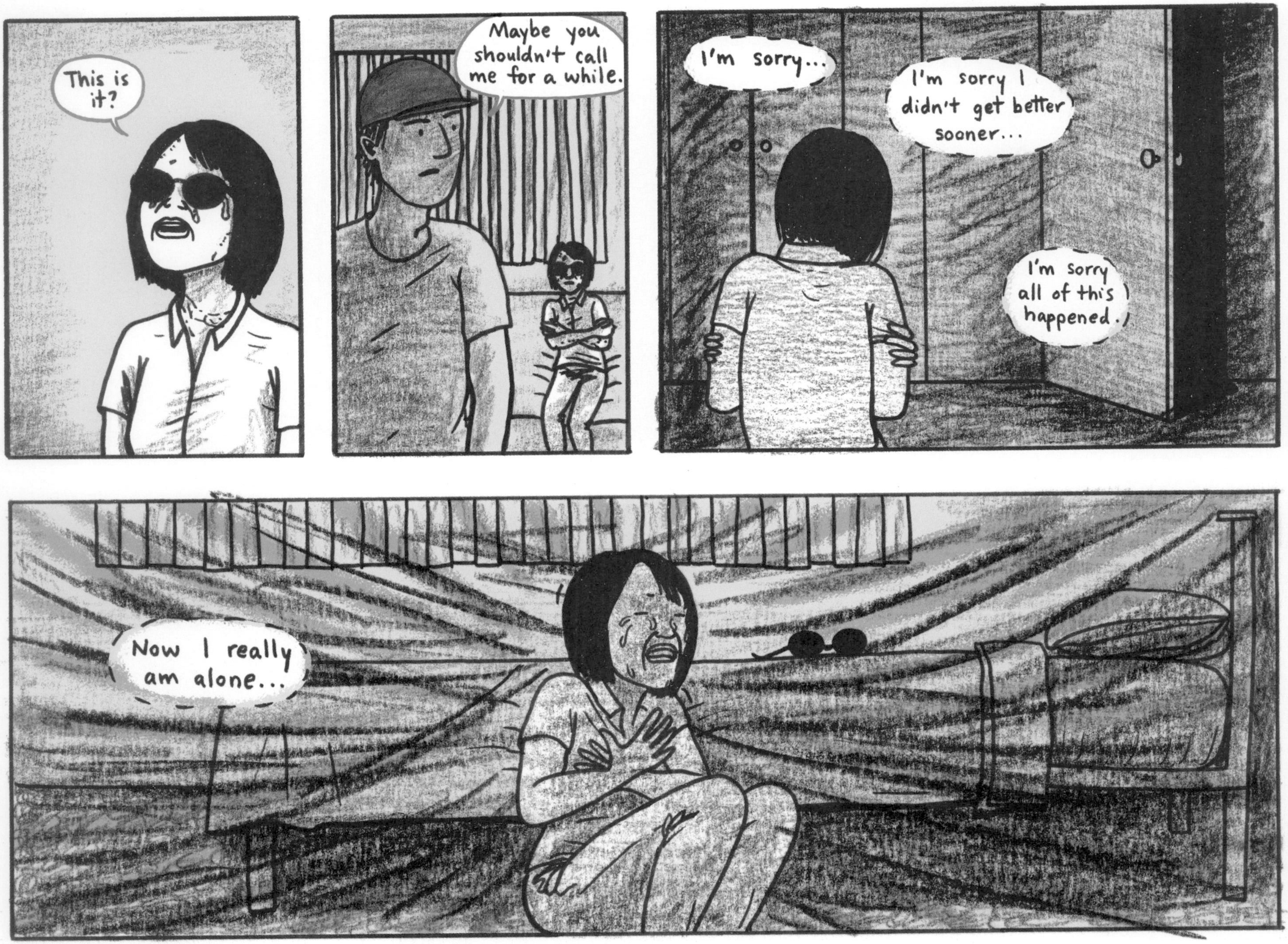
This is it?
Maybe you shouldn't call me for a while.
I'm sorry...
I'm sorry I didn't get better sooner...
I'm sorry all of this happened.
Now I really am alone...

Seven

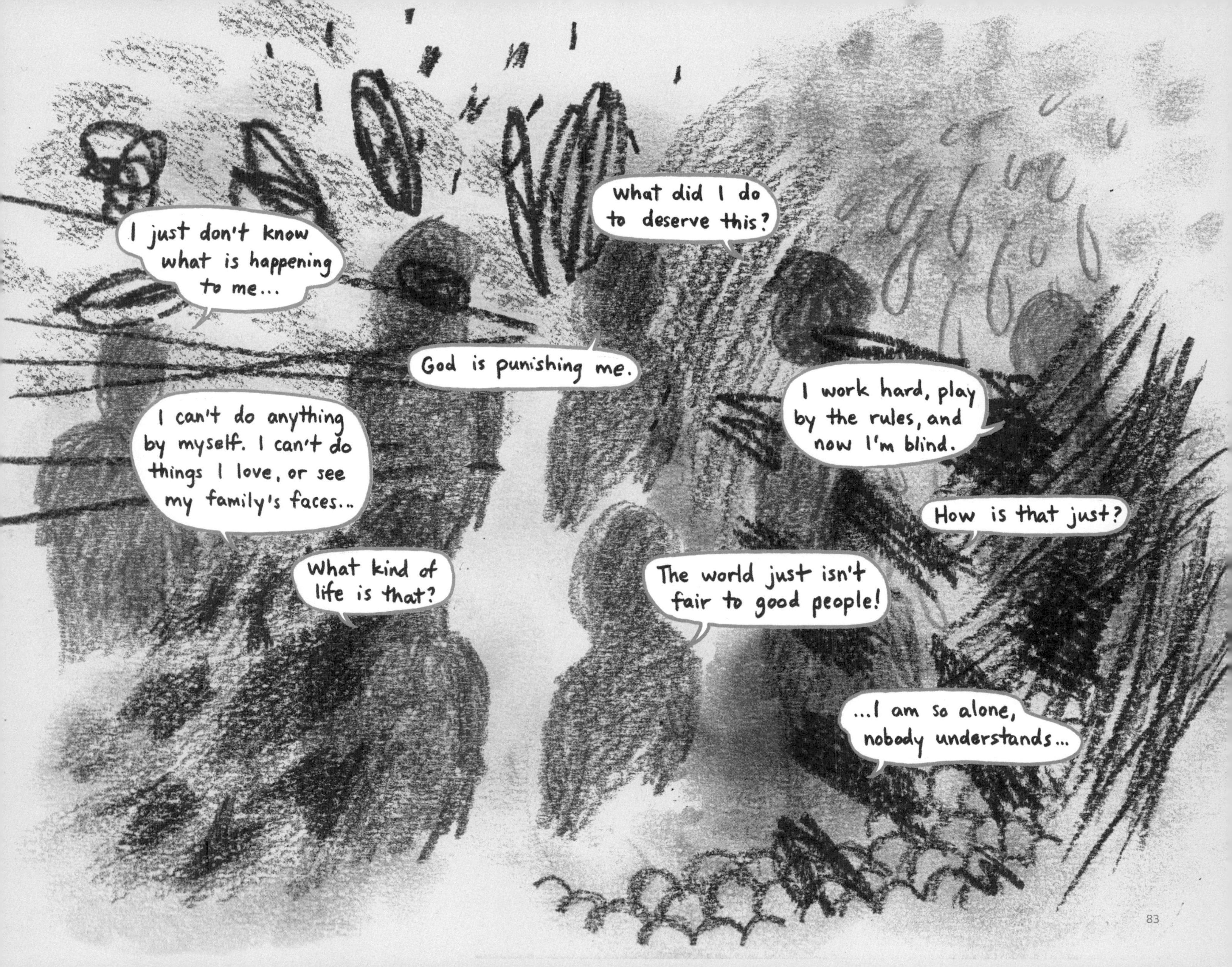
I just don't know what is happening to me...
I can't do anything by myself. I can't do things I love, or see my family's faces...
What kind of life is that?
God is punishing me.
What did I do to deserve this?
The world just isn't fair to good people!
I work hard, play by the rules, and now I'm blind.
How is that just?
...I am so alone, nobody understands...

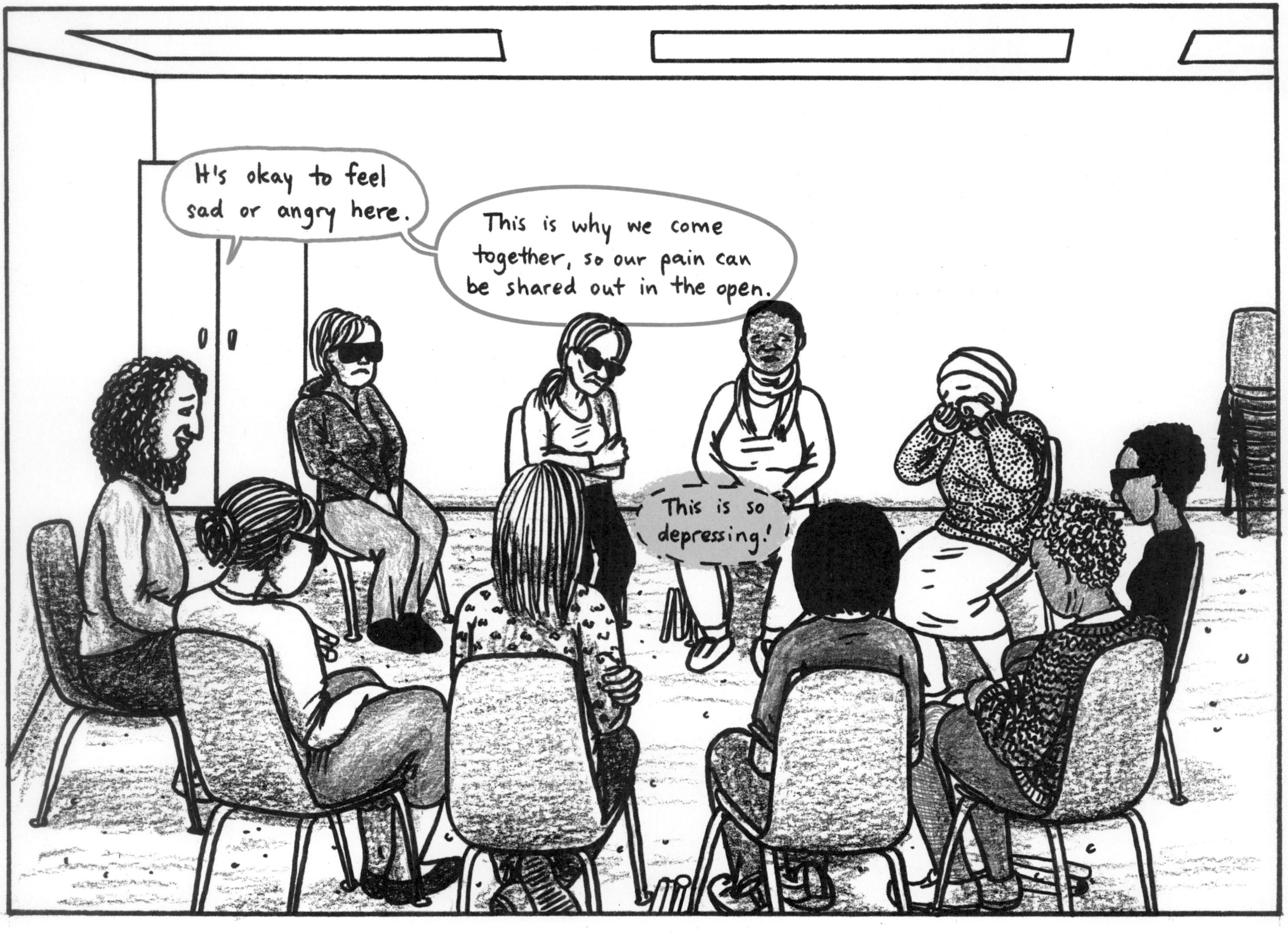
It's okay to feel sad or angry here.
This is why we come together, so our pain can be shared out in the open.
This is so depressing!

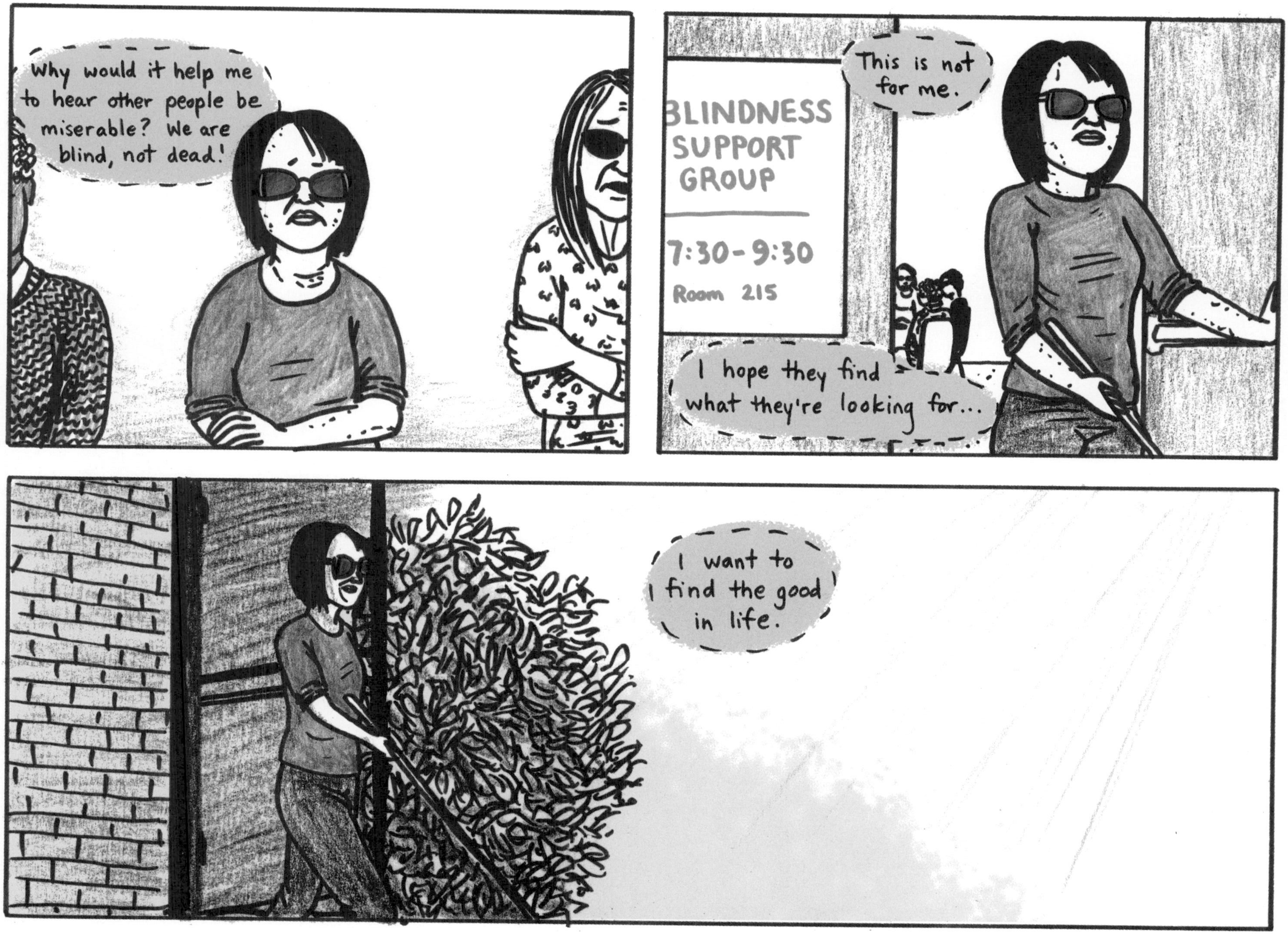
Why would it help me to hear other people be miserable? We are blind, not dead!
BLINDNESS SUPPORT GROUP
7:30-9:30
Room 215
This is not for me.
I hope they find what they're looking for...
I want to find the good in life.

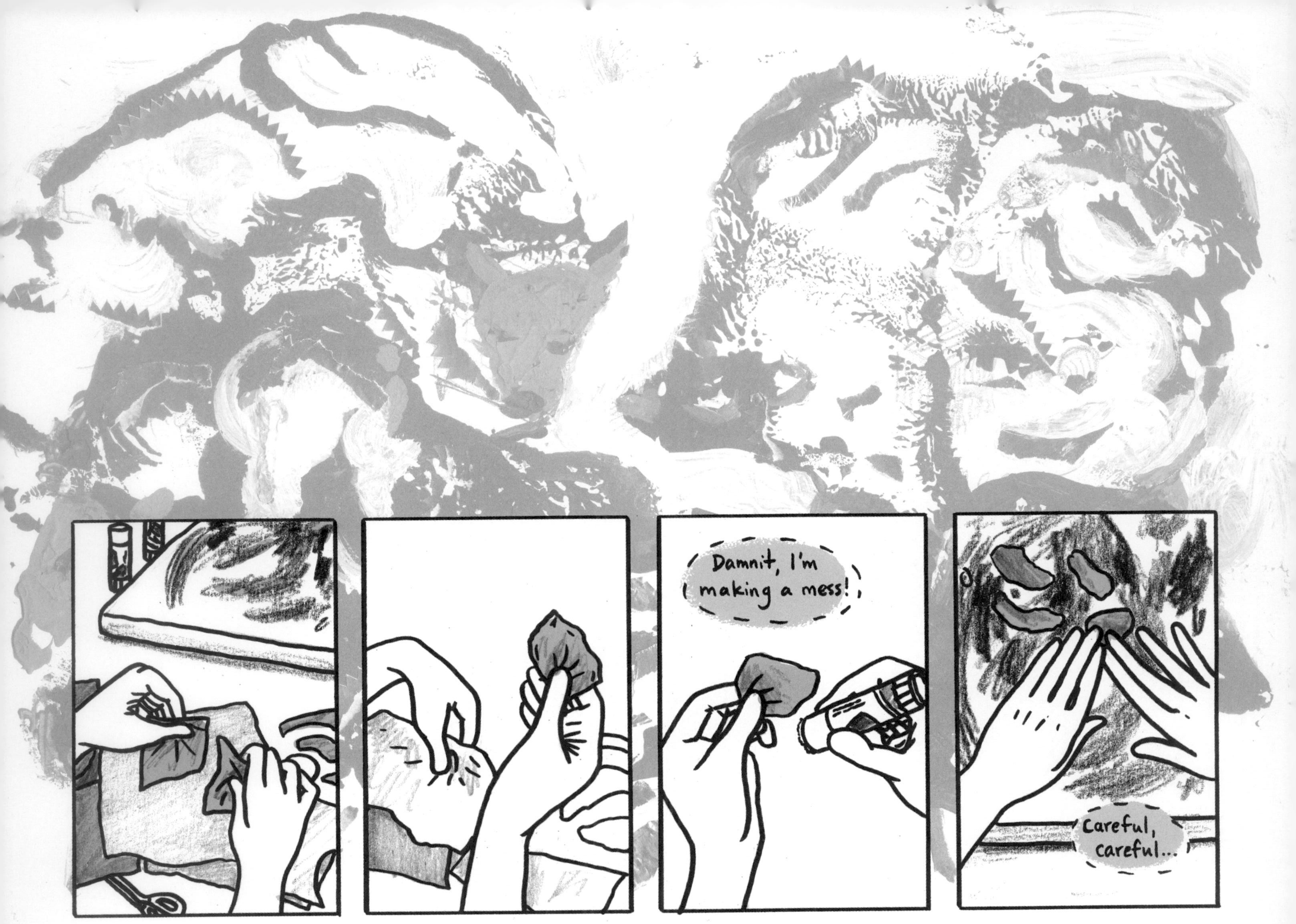
Damnit, I'm making a mess!
Careful, careful...

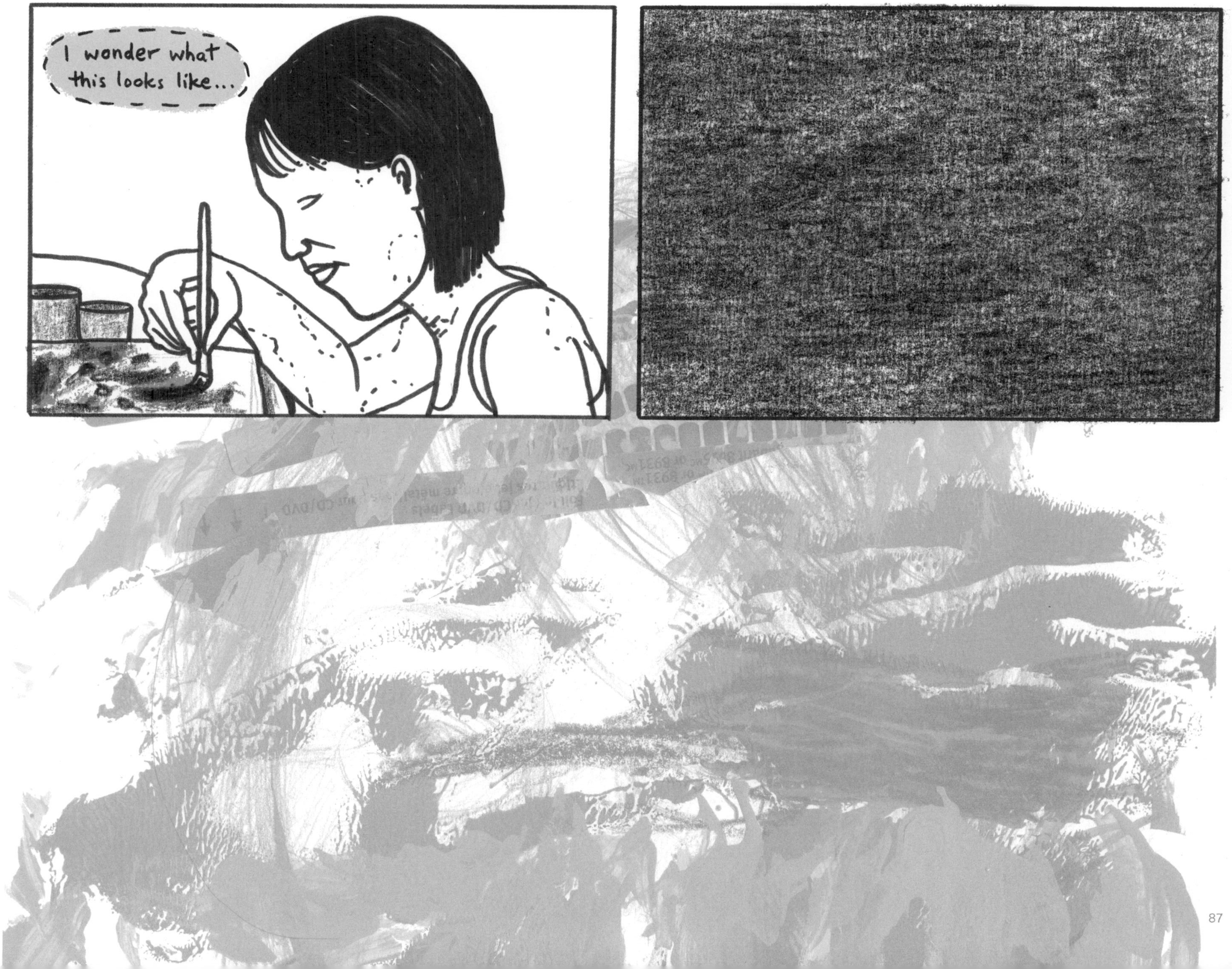
I wonder what this looks like...

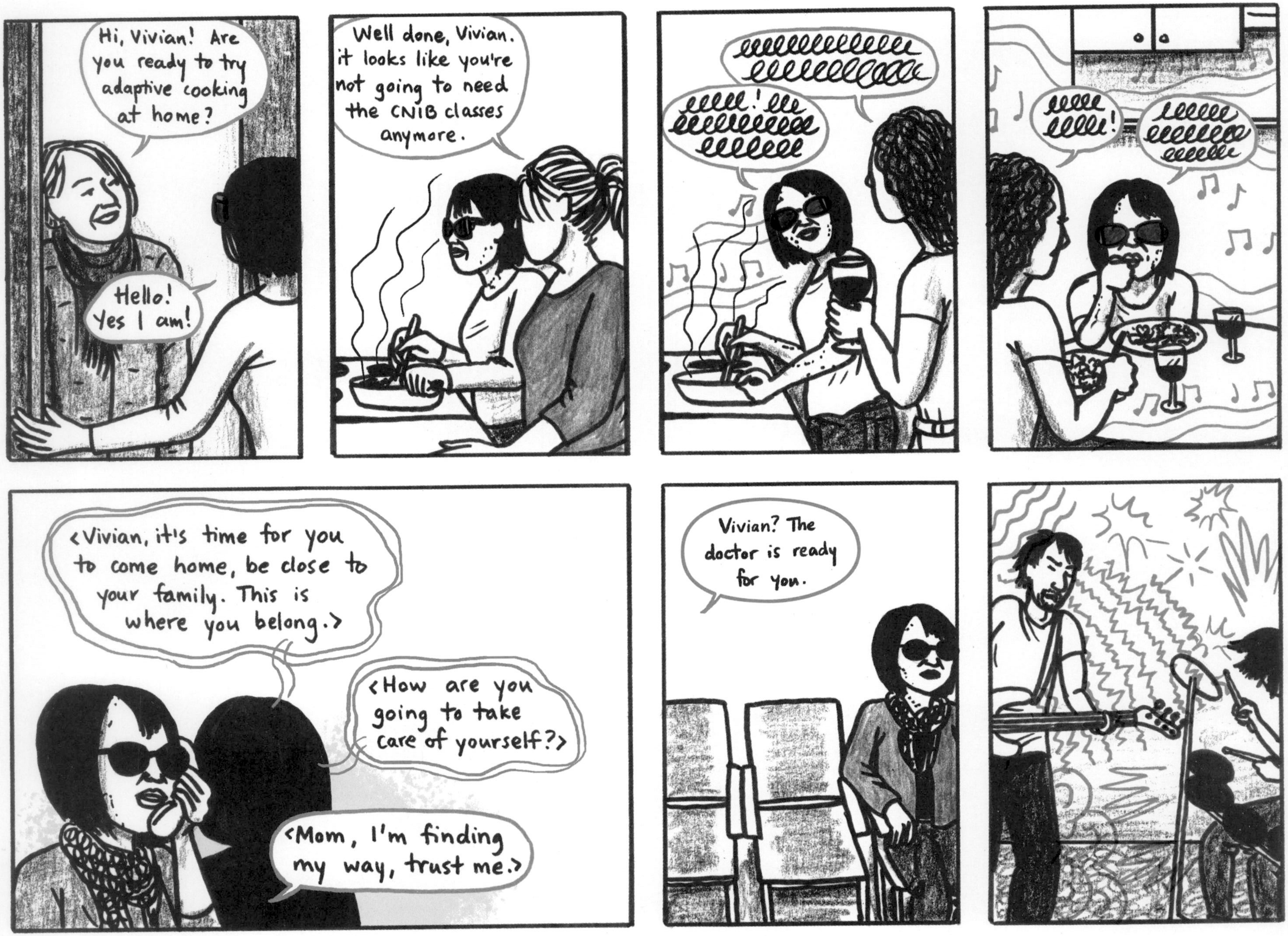
Hi, Vivian! Are you ready to try adaptive cooking at home?
Hello! Yes I am!
Well done, Vivian. it looks like you're not going to need the CNIB classes anymore.
<Vivian, it's time for you to come home, be close to your family. This is where you belong.>
<How are you going to take care of yourself?>
<Mom, I'm finding my way, trust me.>
Vivian? The doctor is ready for you.

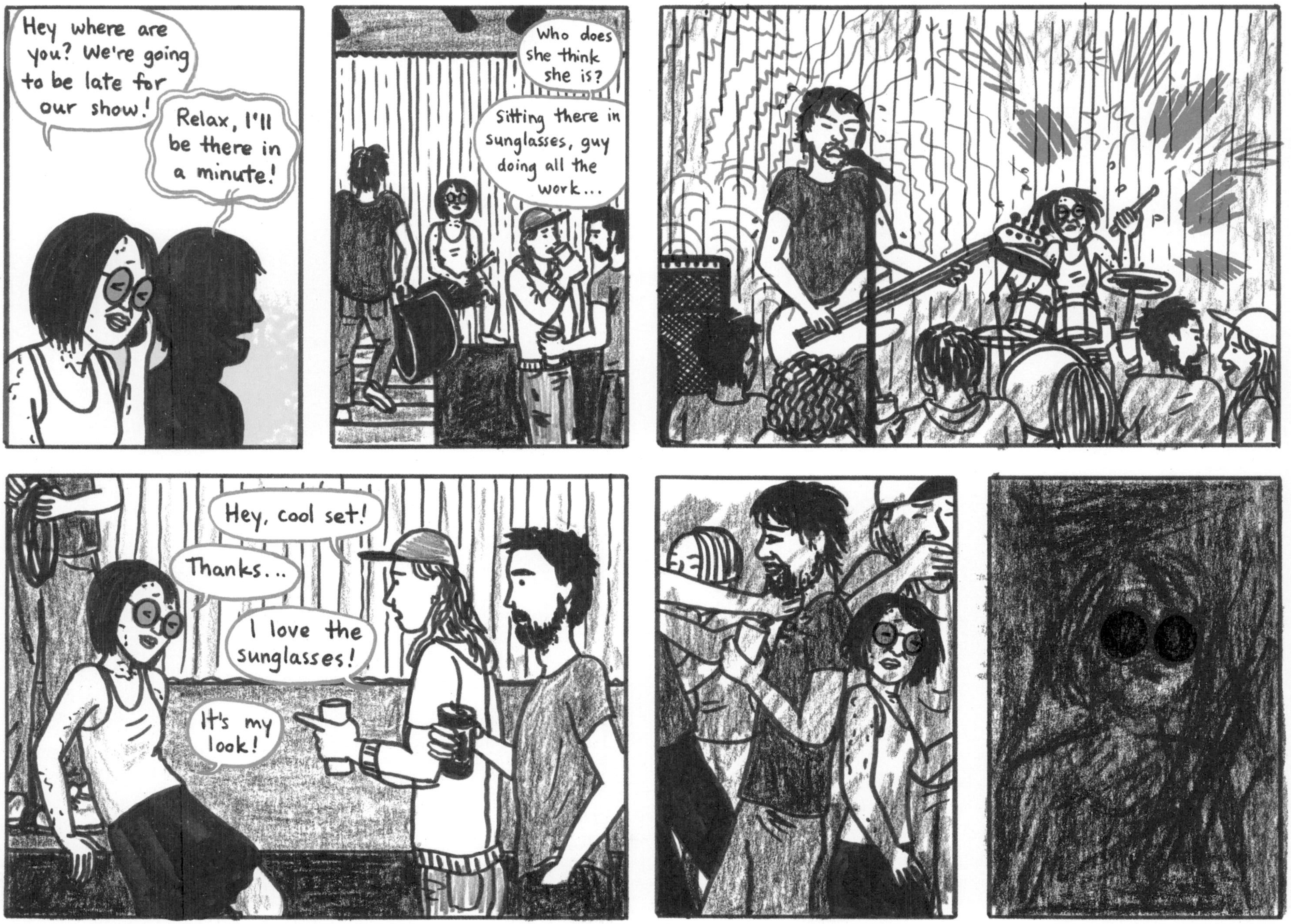
Hey where are you? We're going to be late for our show!
Relax, I'll be there in a minute!
Who does she think she is?
Sitting there in sunglasses, guy doing all the work...
Hey, cool set!
Thanks...
I love the sunglasses!
It's my look!

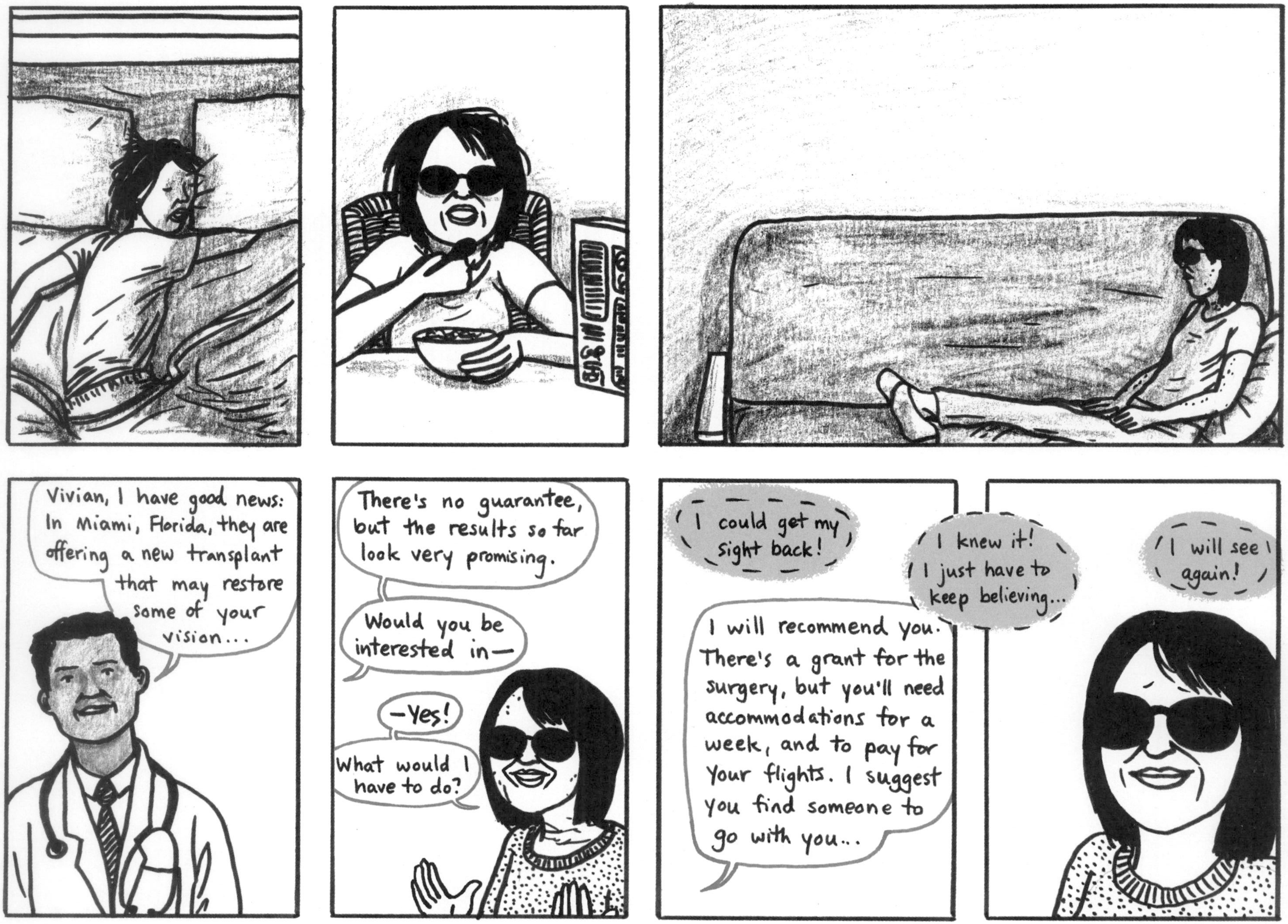
Vivian, I have good news: In Miami, Florida, they are offering a new transplant that may restore some of your vision...
There's no guarantee, but the results so far look very promising.
Would you be interested in—
—Yes!
What would I have to do?
I could get my sight back!
I will recommend you. There's a grant for the surgery, but you'll need accommodations for a week, and to pay for your flights. I suggest you find someone to go with you...
I knew it! I just have to keep believing...
I will see again!

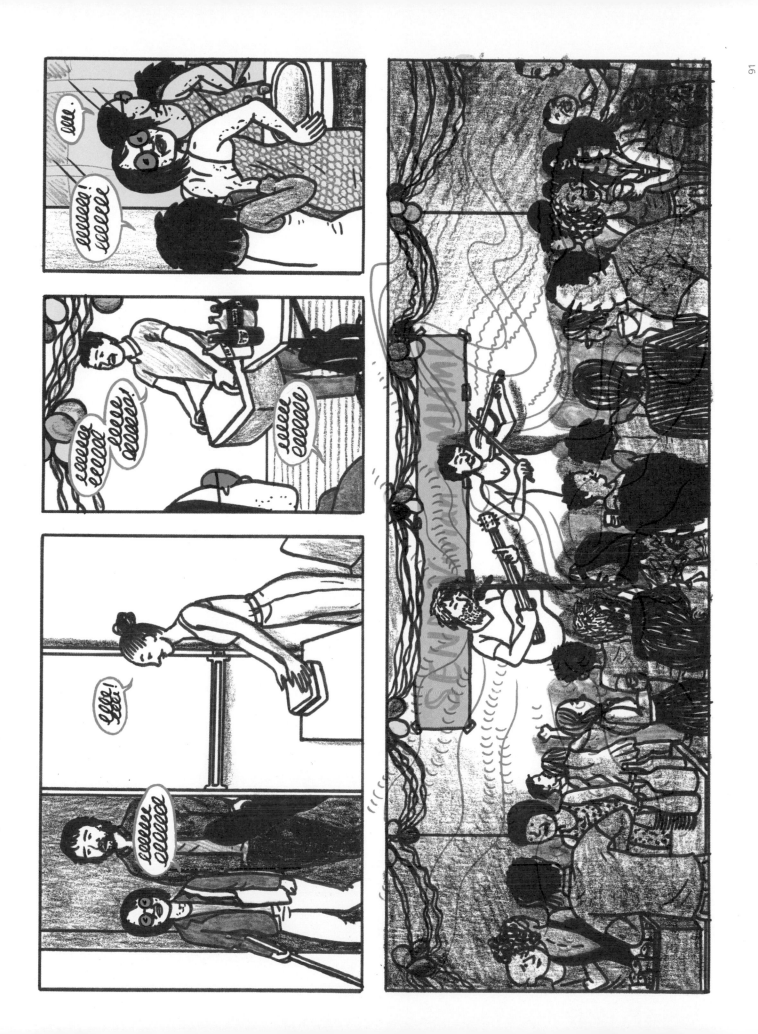

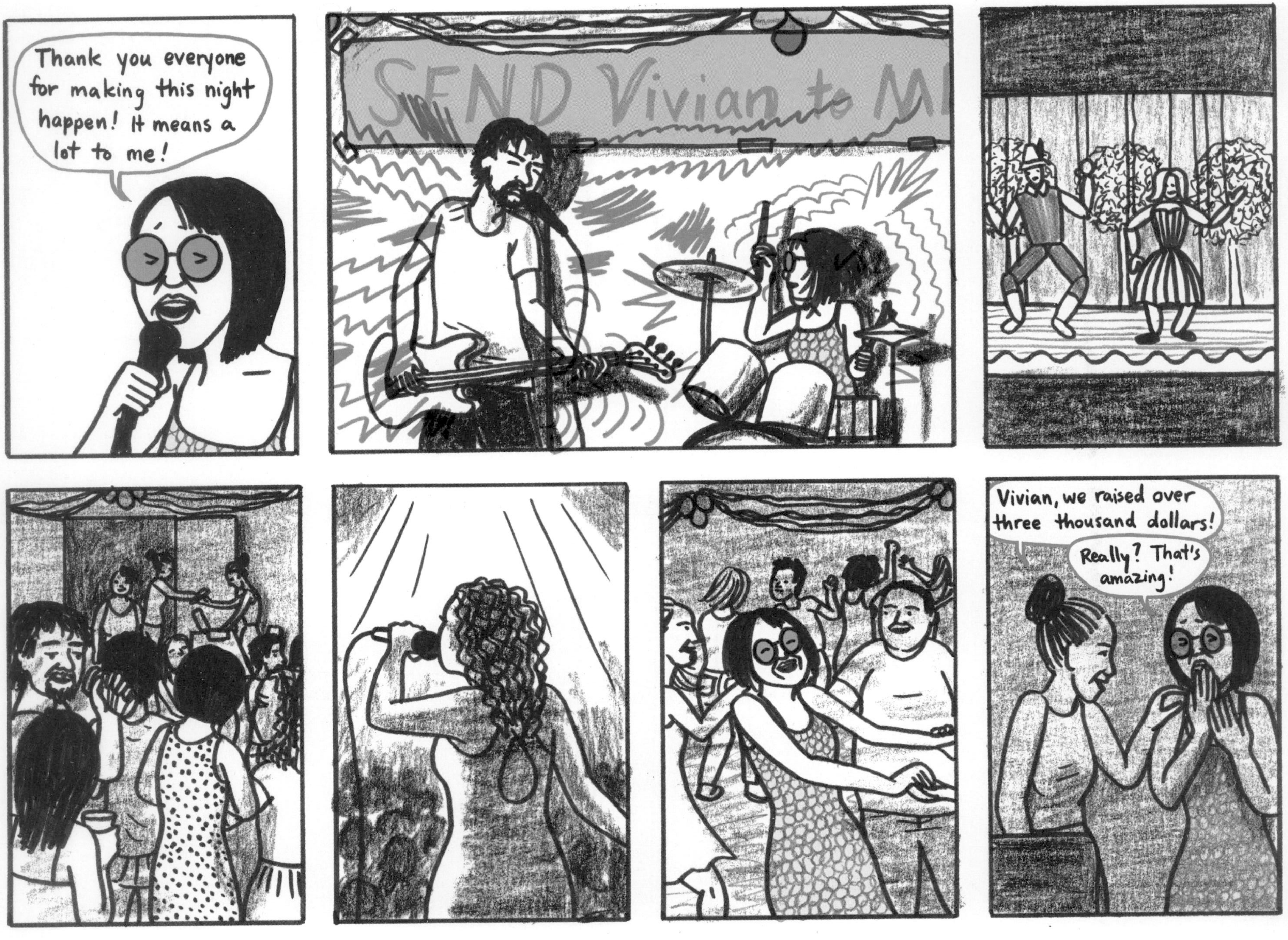
Thank you everyone for making this night happen! It means a lot to me!
SEND Vivian to M
Vivian, we raised over three thousand dollars!
Really? That's amazing!

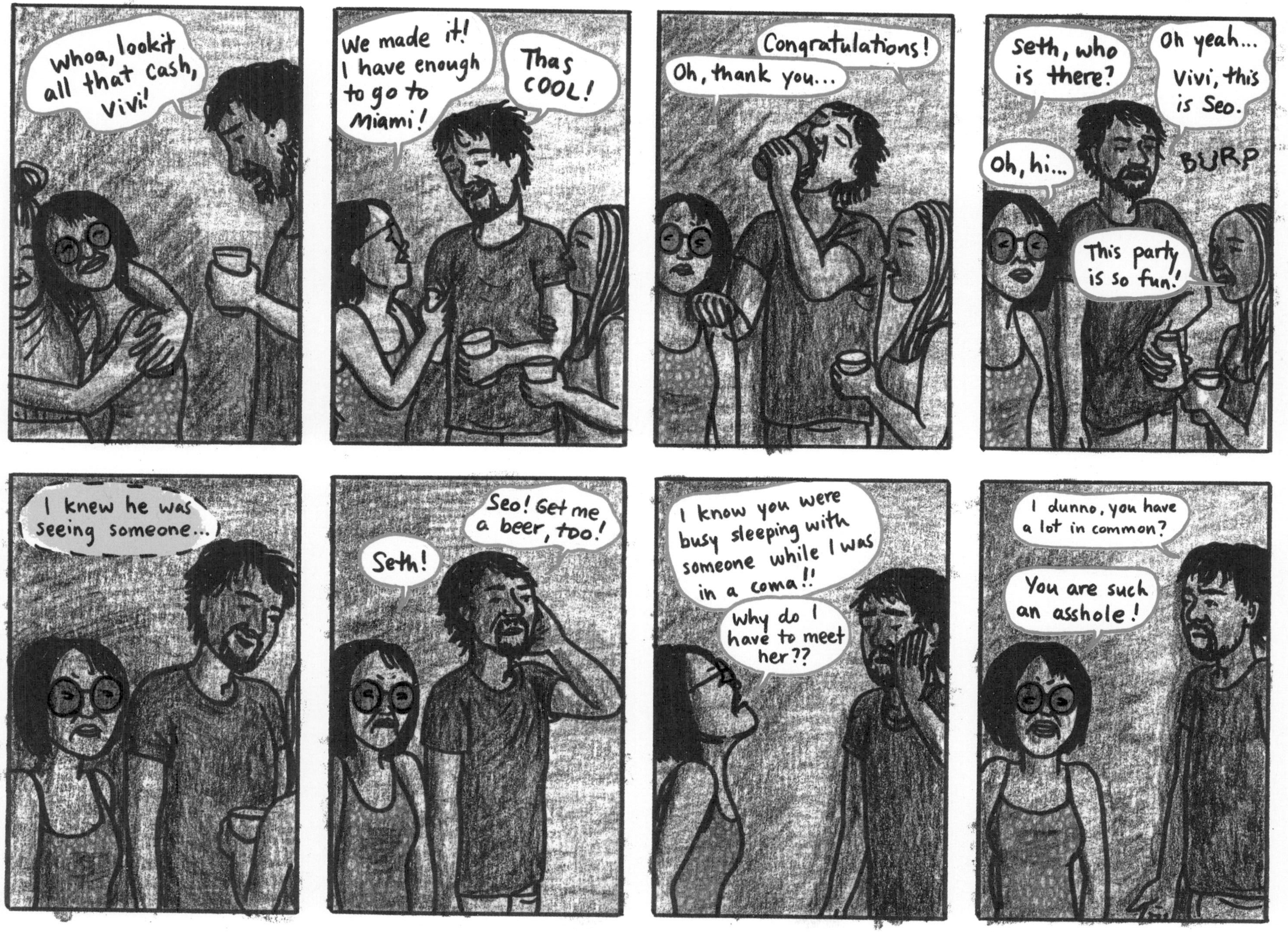
Whoa, lookit all that cash, Vivi!
We made it! I have enough to go to Miami!
Thas COOL!
Oh, thank you...
Congratulations!
Seth, who is there?
Oh yeah... Vivi, this is Seo.
BURP
Oh, hi...
This party is so fun!
I knew he was seeing someone...
Seth!
Seo! Get me a beer, too!
I know you were busy sleeping with someone while I was in a coma!!
Why do I have to meet her??
I dunno, you have a lot in common?
You are such an asshole!

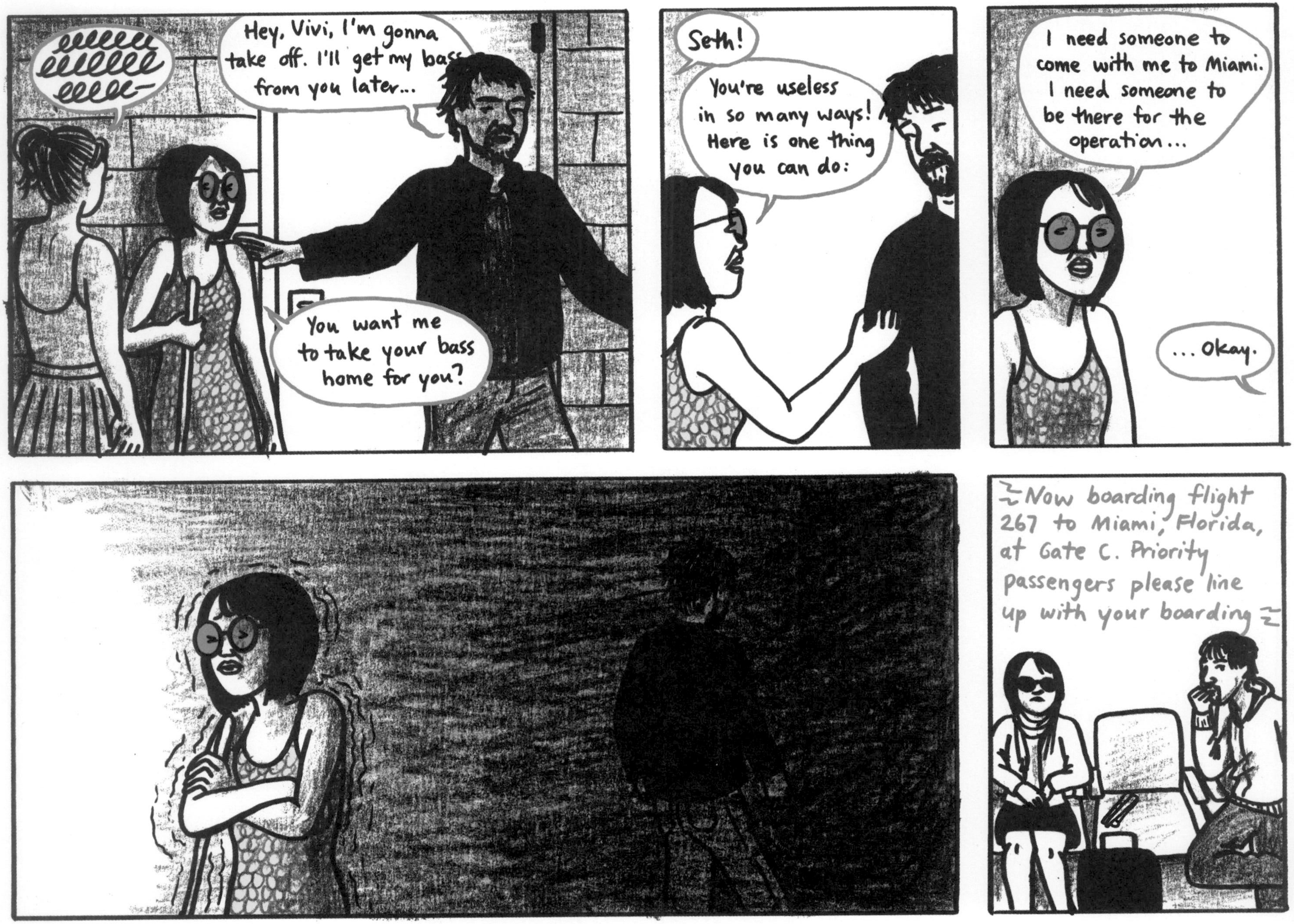
eeeeee eeeeeee eeeee—
Hey, Vivi, I'm gonna take off. I'll get my bass from you later...
You want me to take your bass home for you?
Seth!
You're useless in so many ways! Here is one thing you can do:
I need someone to come with me to Miami. I need someone to be there for the operation...
...Okay.
Now boarding flight 267 to Miami, Florida, at Gate C. Priority passengers please line up with your boarding

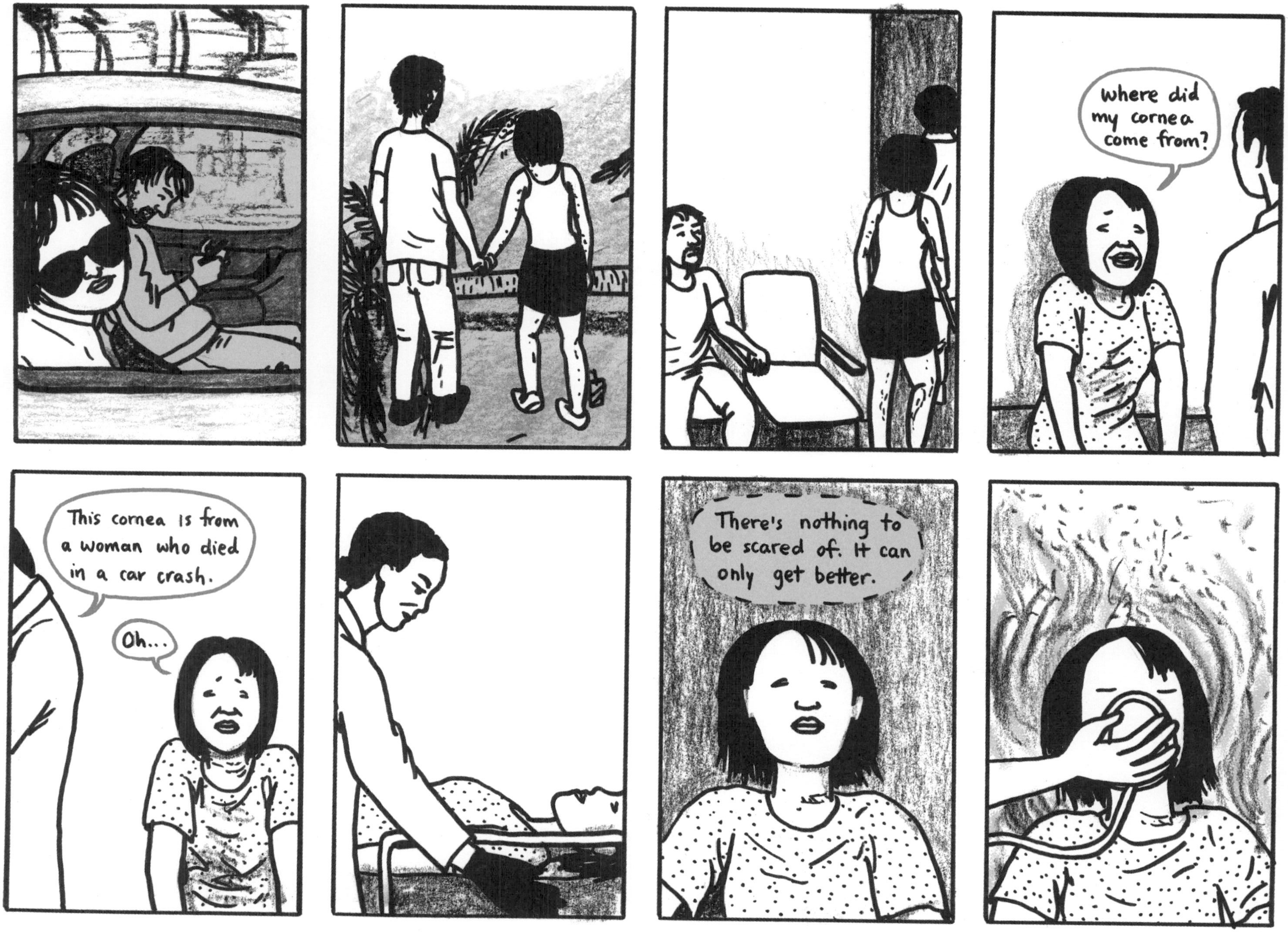
Where did my cornea come from?
This cornea is from a woman who died in a car crash.
Oh...
There's nothing to be scared of. It can only get better.

Eight

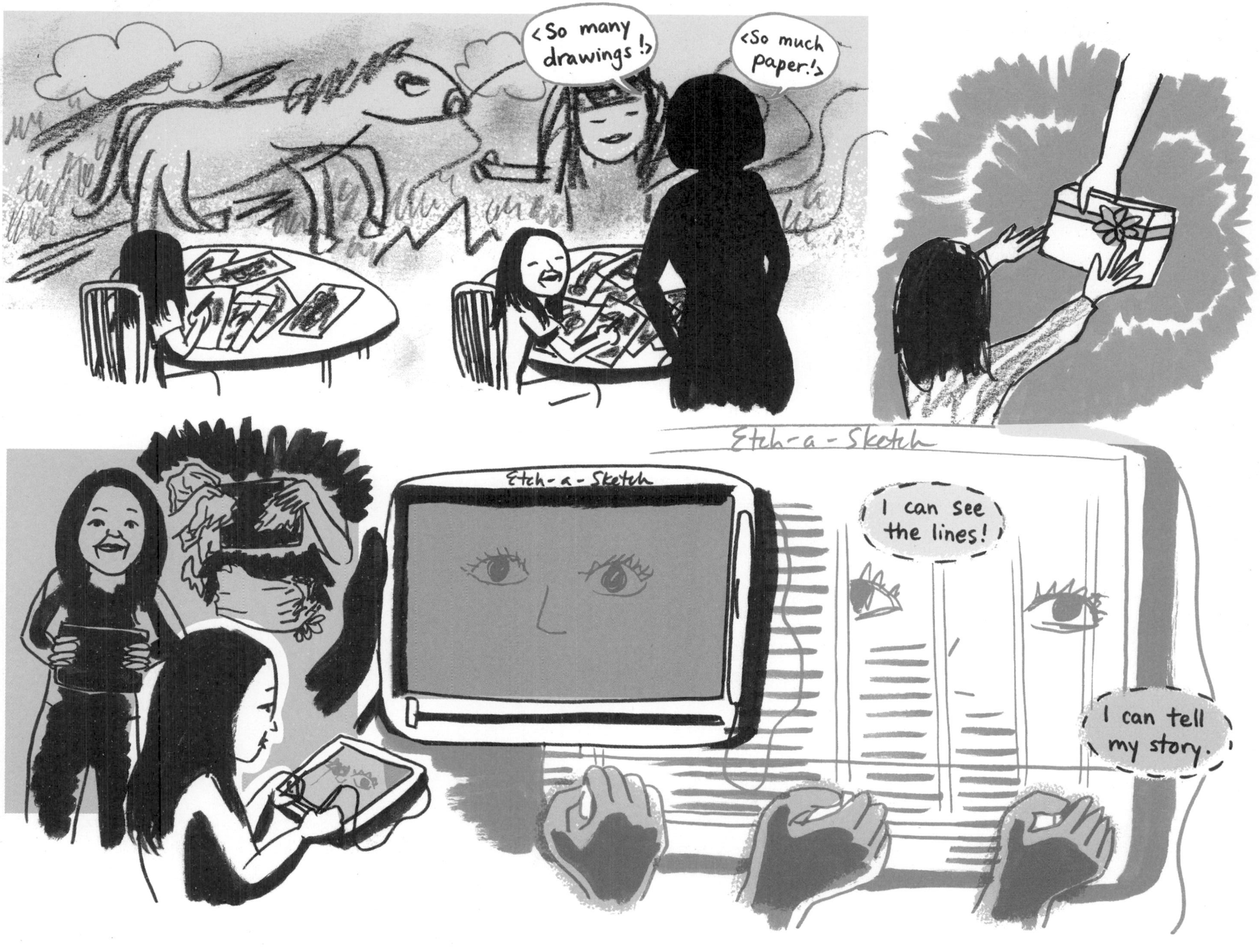
<So many drawings!>
<So much paper!>
Etch-a-Sketch
Etch-a-Sketch
I can see the lines!
I can tell my story.

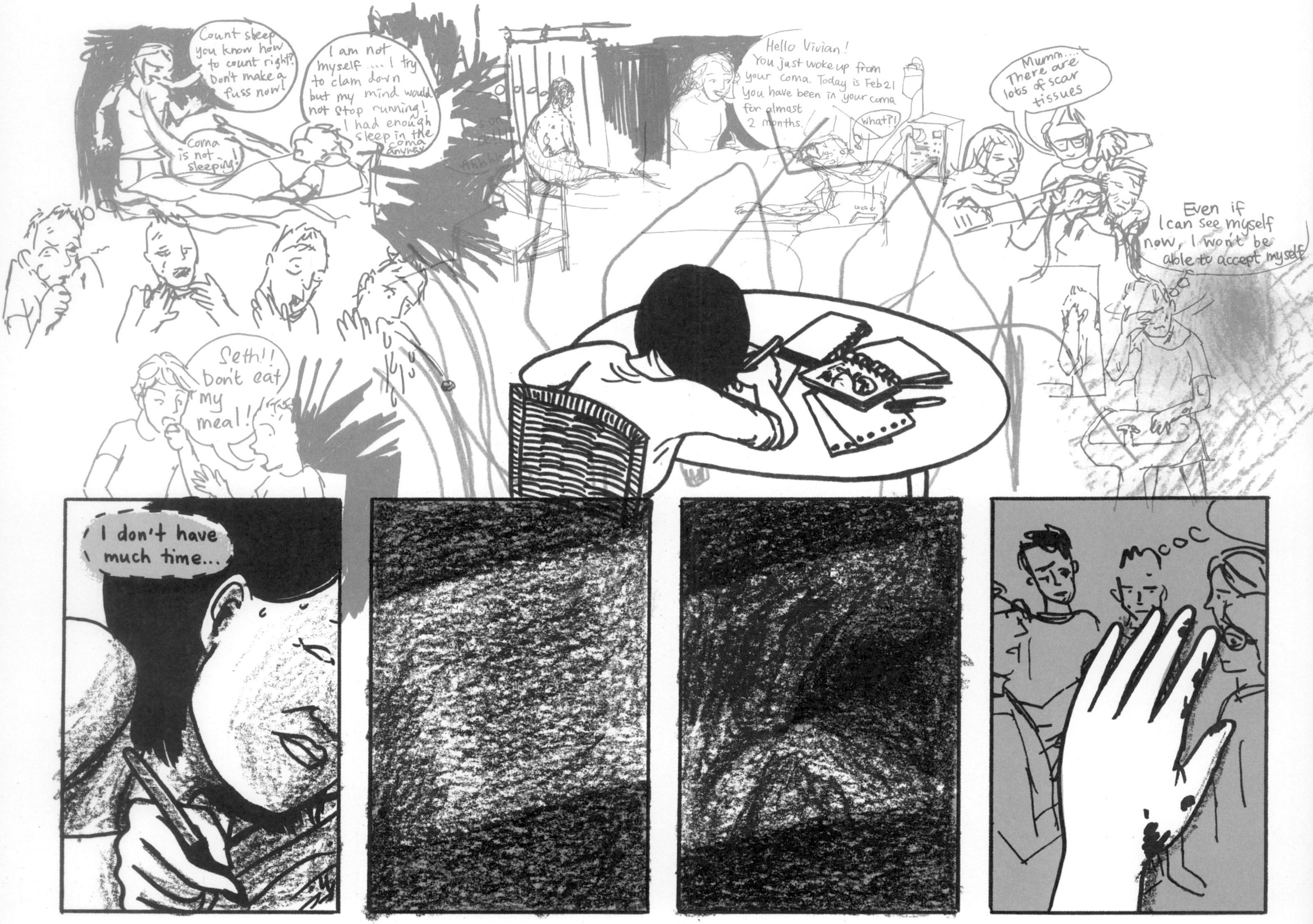
Count sleep you know how to count right? Don't make a fuss now!
Coma is not sleeping.
I am not myself .... I try to clam down but my mind would not stop running! I had enough sleep in the coma anyway
Hello Vivian! You just woke up from your coma. Today is Feb 21 You have been in your coma for almost 2 months.
What?!
Mumm.... There are lots of scar tissues
Even if I can see myself now, I won't be able to accept myself
Seth!! Don't eat my meal!!
I don't have much time...

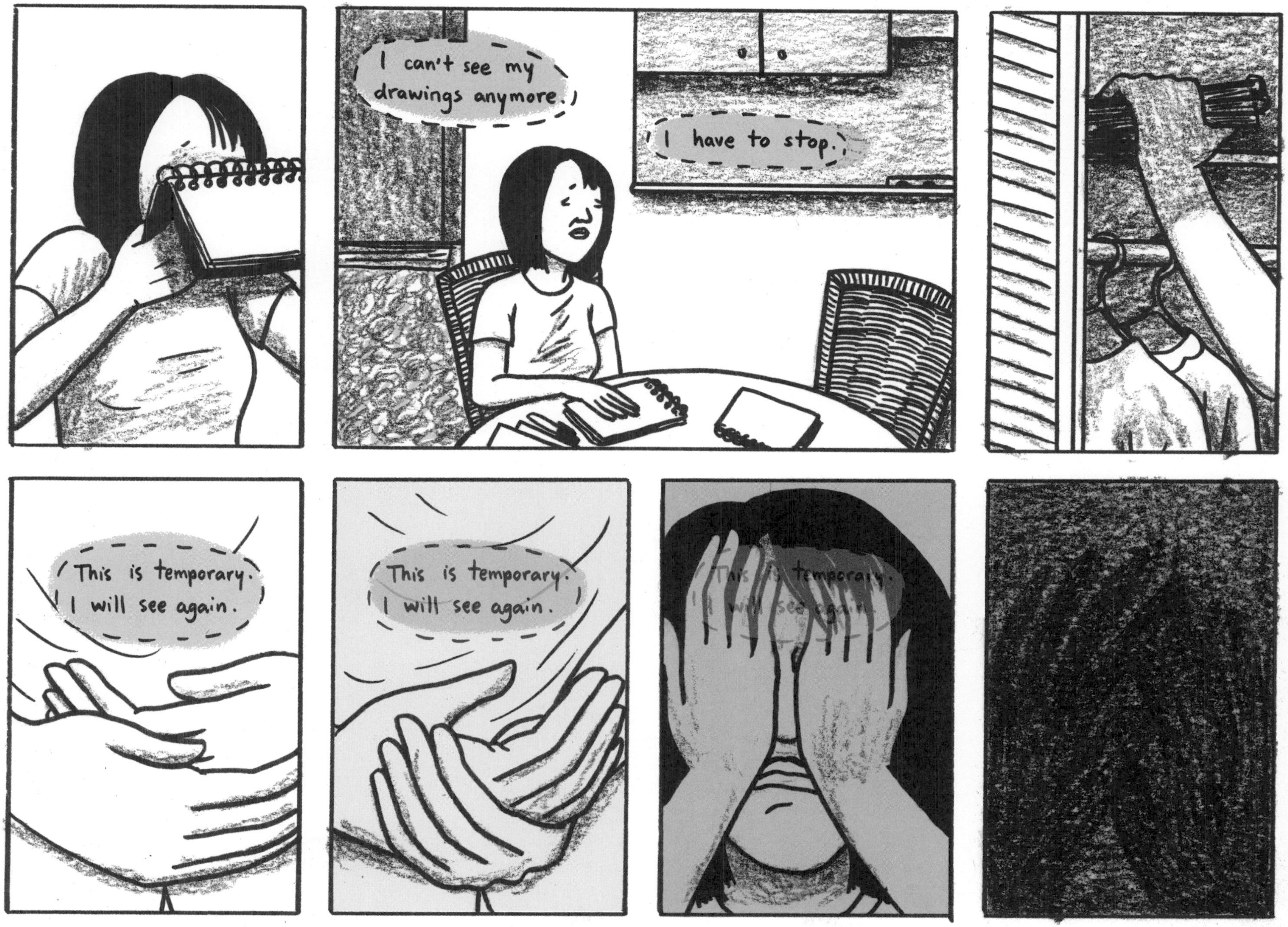
I can't see my drawings anymore.
I have to stop.
This is temporary. I will see again.
This is temporary. I will see again.
This is temporary. I will see again.

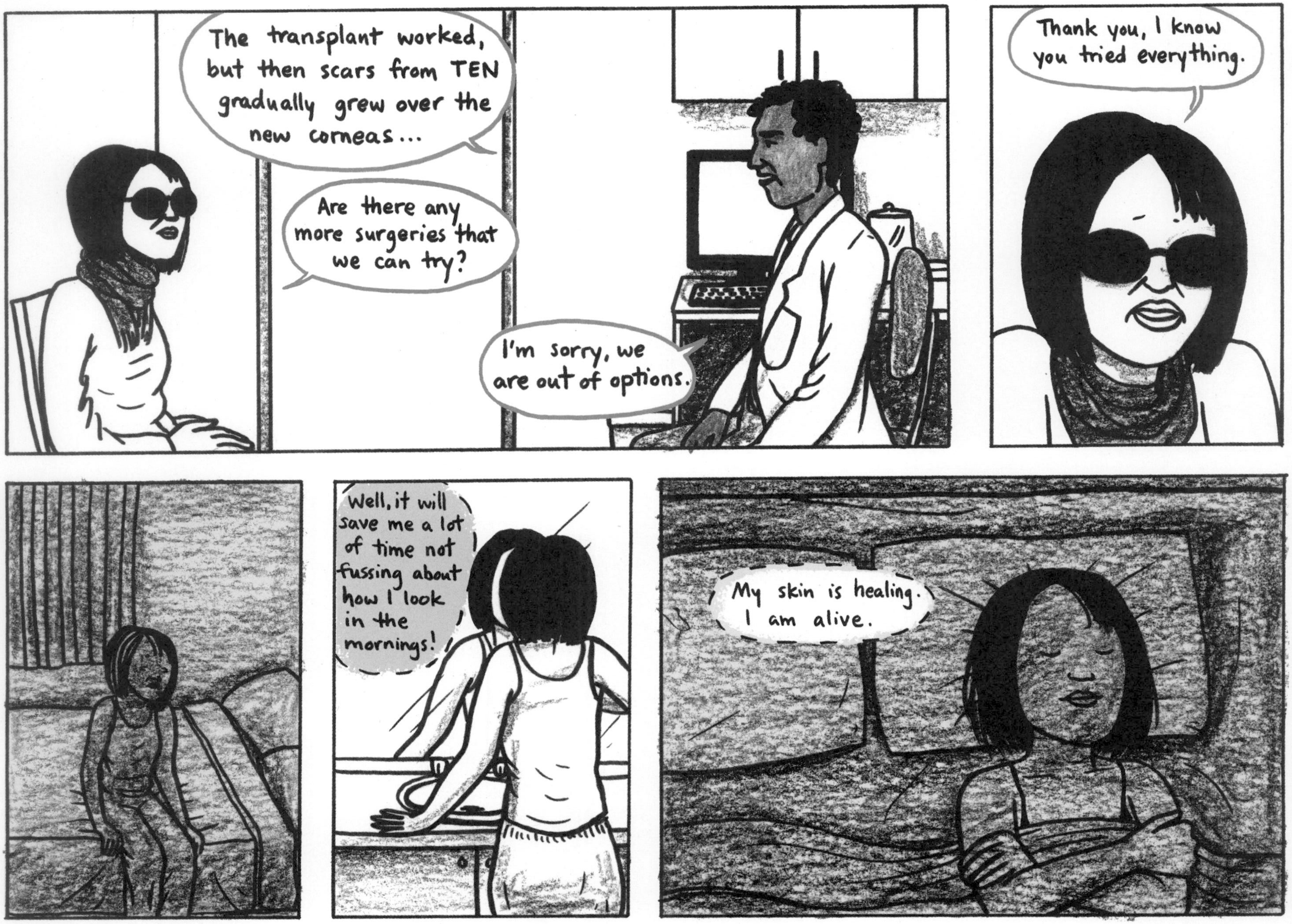
The transplant worked, but then scars from TEN gradually grew over the new corneas...
Are there any more surgeries that we can try?
I'm sorry, we are out of options.
Thank you, I know you tried everything.
Well, it will save me a lot of time not fussing about how I look in the mornings!
My skin is healing. I am alive.

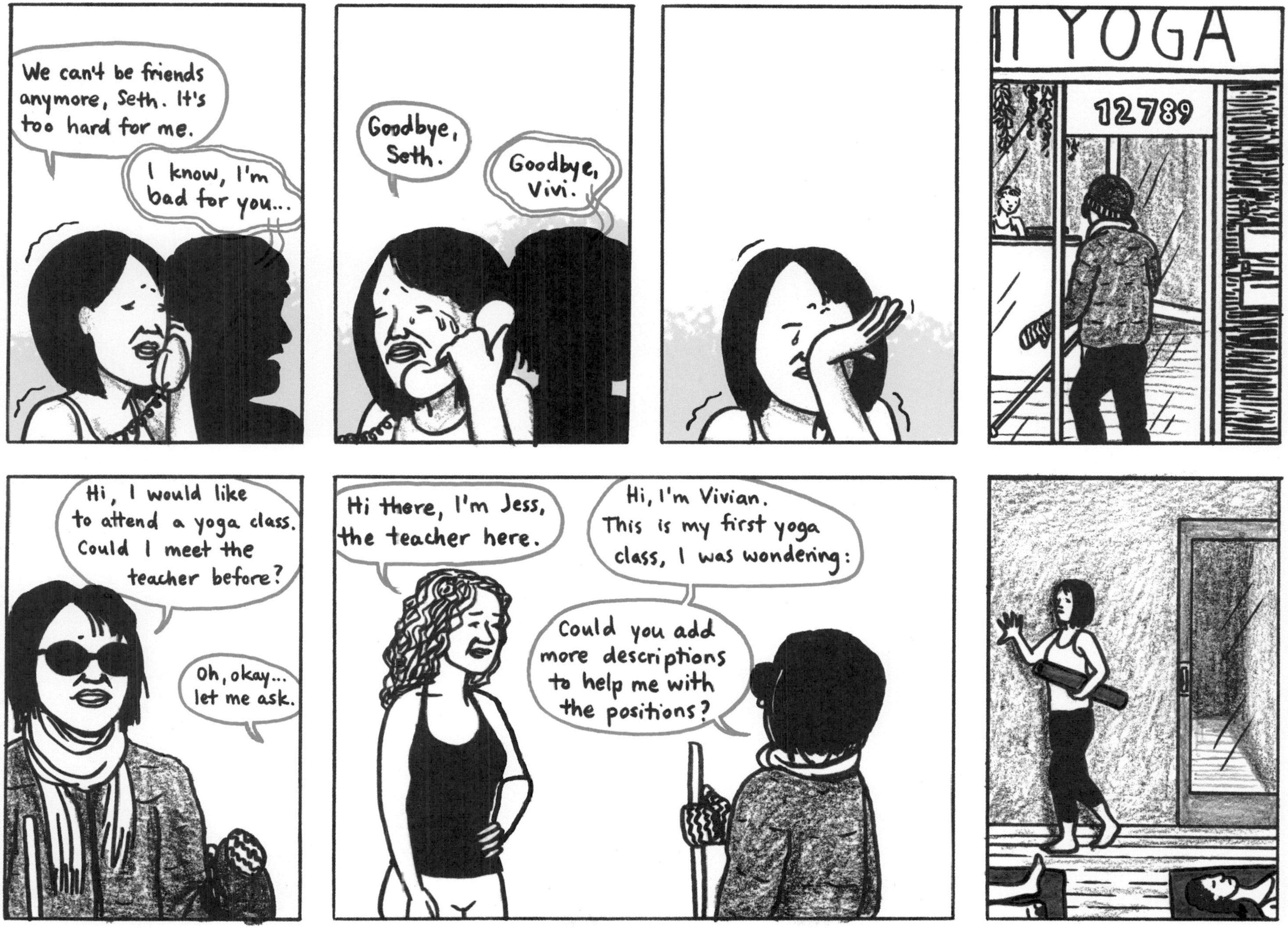
We can't be friends anymore, Seth. It's too hard for me.
I know, I'm bad for you...
Goodbye, Seth.
Goodbye, Vivi.
YOGA
12789
Hi, I would like to attend a yoga class. Could I meet the teacher before?
Oh, okay... let me ask.
Hi there, I'm Jess, the teacher here.
Hi, I'm Vivian. This is my first yoga class, I was wondering:
Could you add more descriptions to help me with the positions?

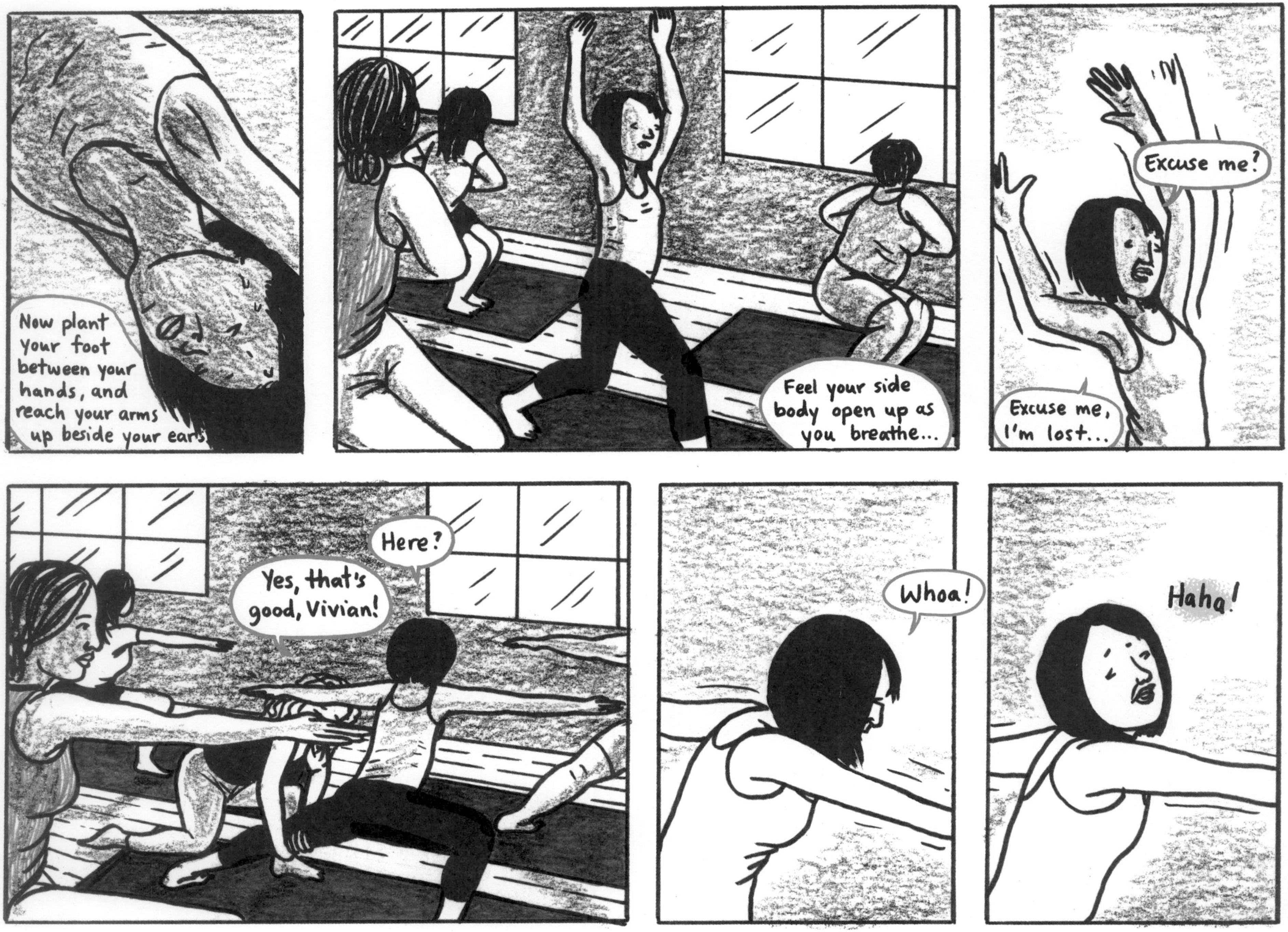

Now plant your foot between your hands, and reach your arms up beside your ears
Feel your side body open up as you breathe...
Excuse me?
Excuse me, I'm lost...
Here?
Yes, that's good, Vivian!
Whoa!
Haha!

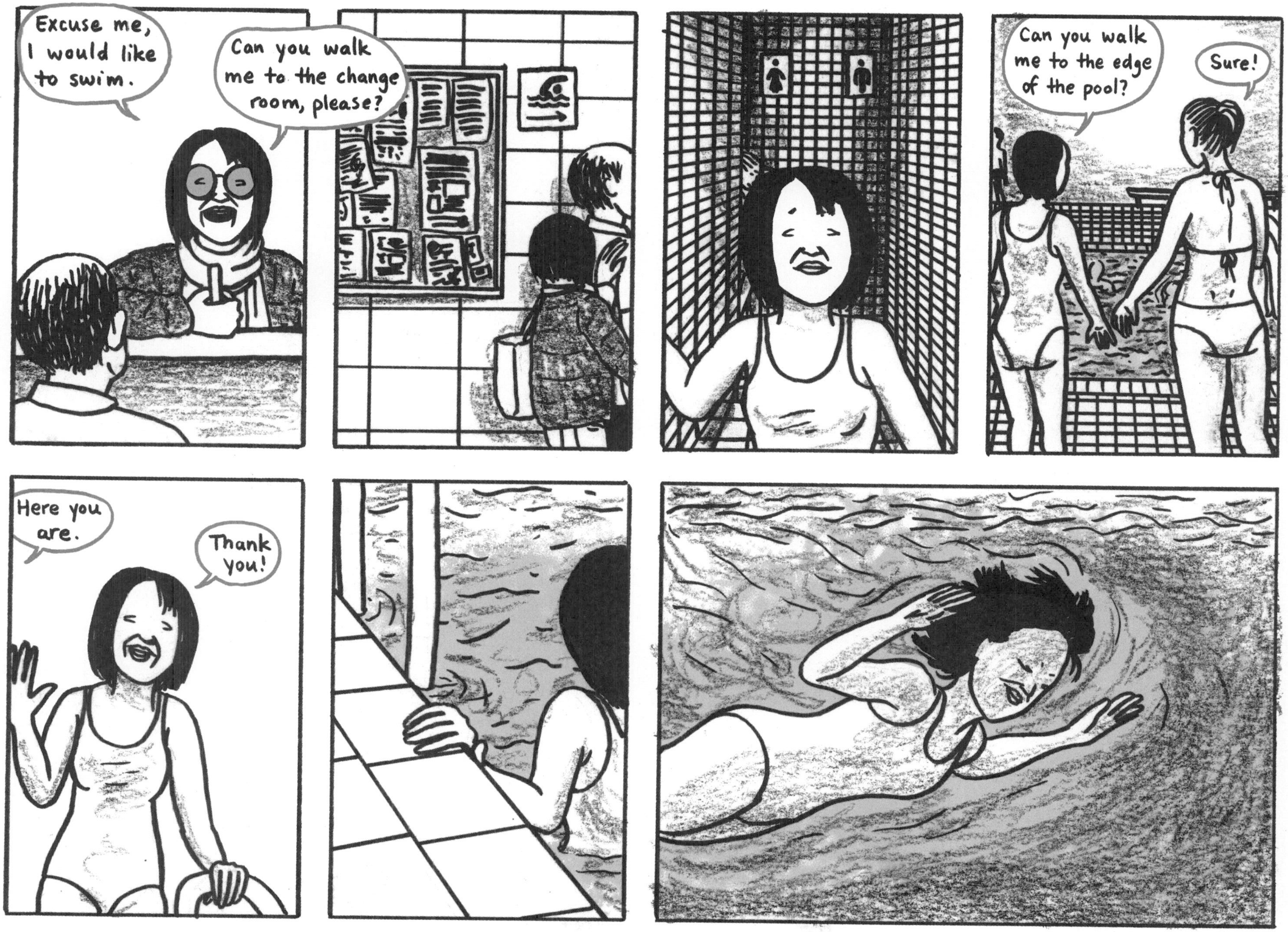
Excuse me, I would like to swim.
Can you walk me to the change room, please?
Can you walk me to the edge of the pool?
Sure!
Here you are.
Thank you!

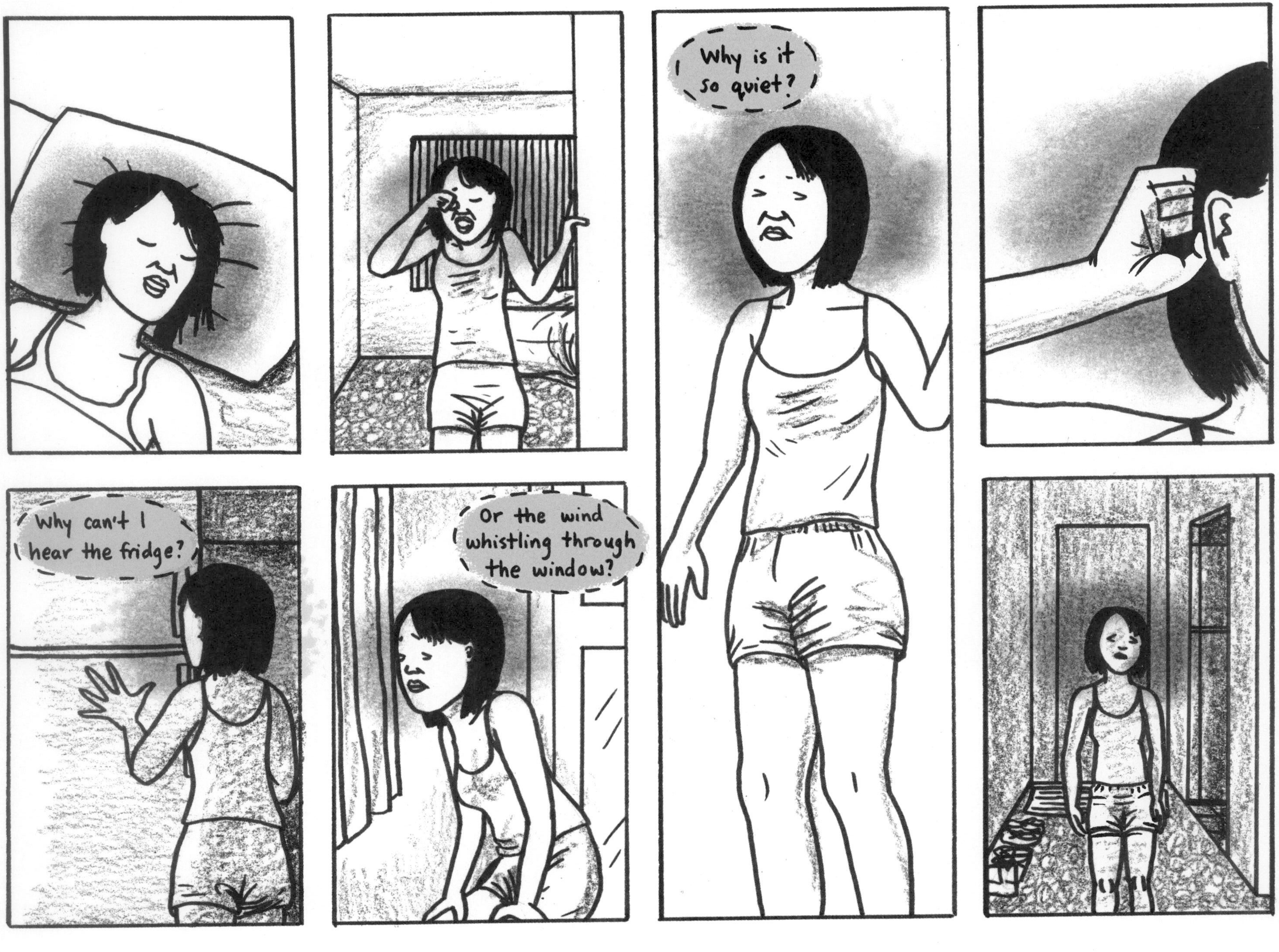
Why can't I hear the fridge?
Or the wind whistling through the window?
Why is it so quiet?

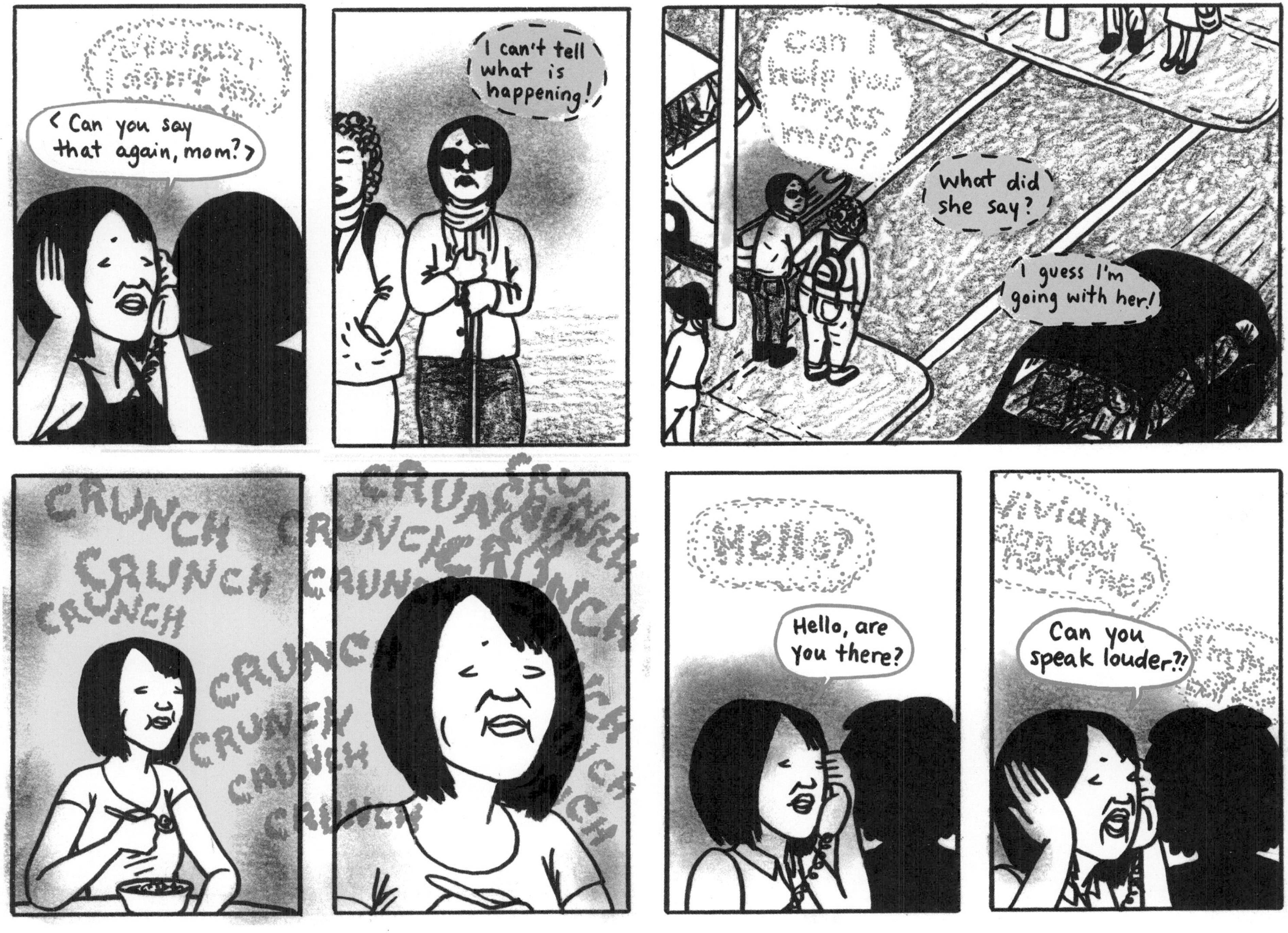
‹Can you say that again, mom?›
I can't tell what is happening!
Can I help you cross, miss?
What did she say?
I guess I'm going with her!
CRUNCH
CRUNCH
Hello?
Hello, are you there?
Can you speak louder-?!

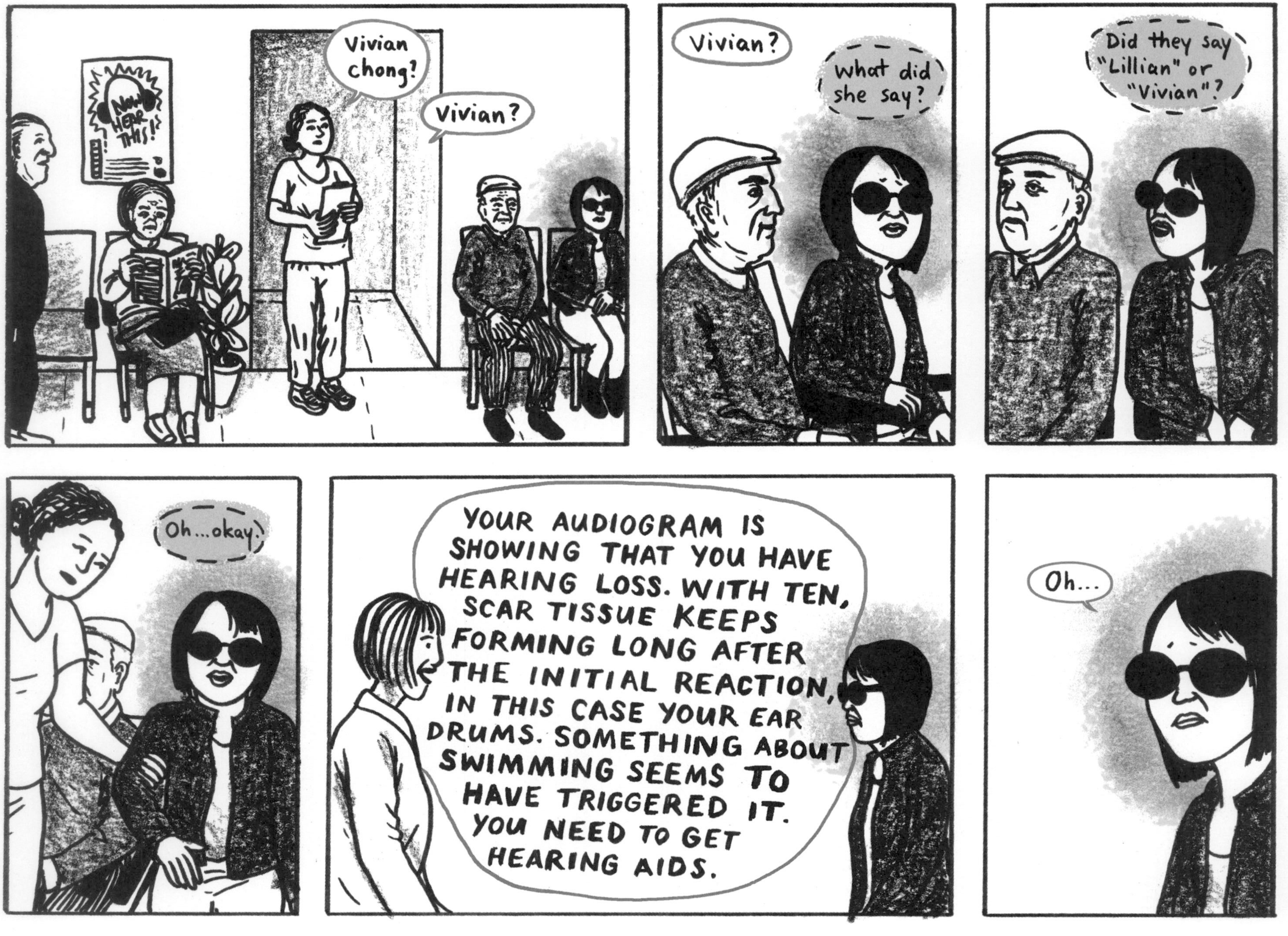
NOW HEAR THIS!
Vivian chong?
Vivian?
Vivian?
What did she say?
Did they say "Lillian" or "Vivian"?
Oh...okay.
YOUR AUDIOGRAM IS SHOWING THAT YOU HAVE HEARING LOSS. WITH TEN, SCAR TISSUE KEEPS FORMING LONG AFTER THE INITIAL REACTION, IN THIS CASE YOUR EAR DRUMS. SOMETHING ABOUT SWIMMING SEEMS TO HAVE TRIGGERED IT. YOU NEED TO GET HEARING AIDS.
Oh...

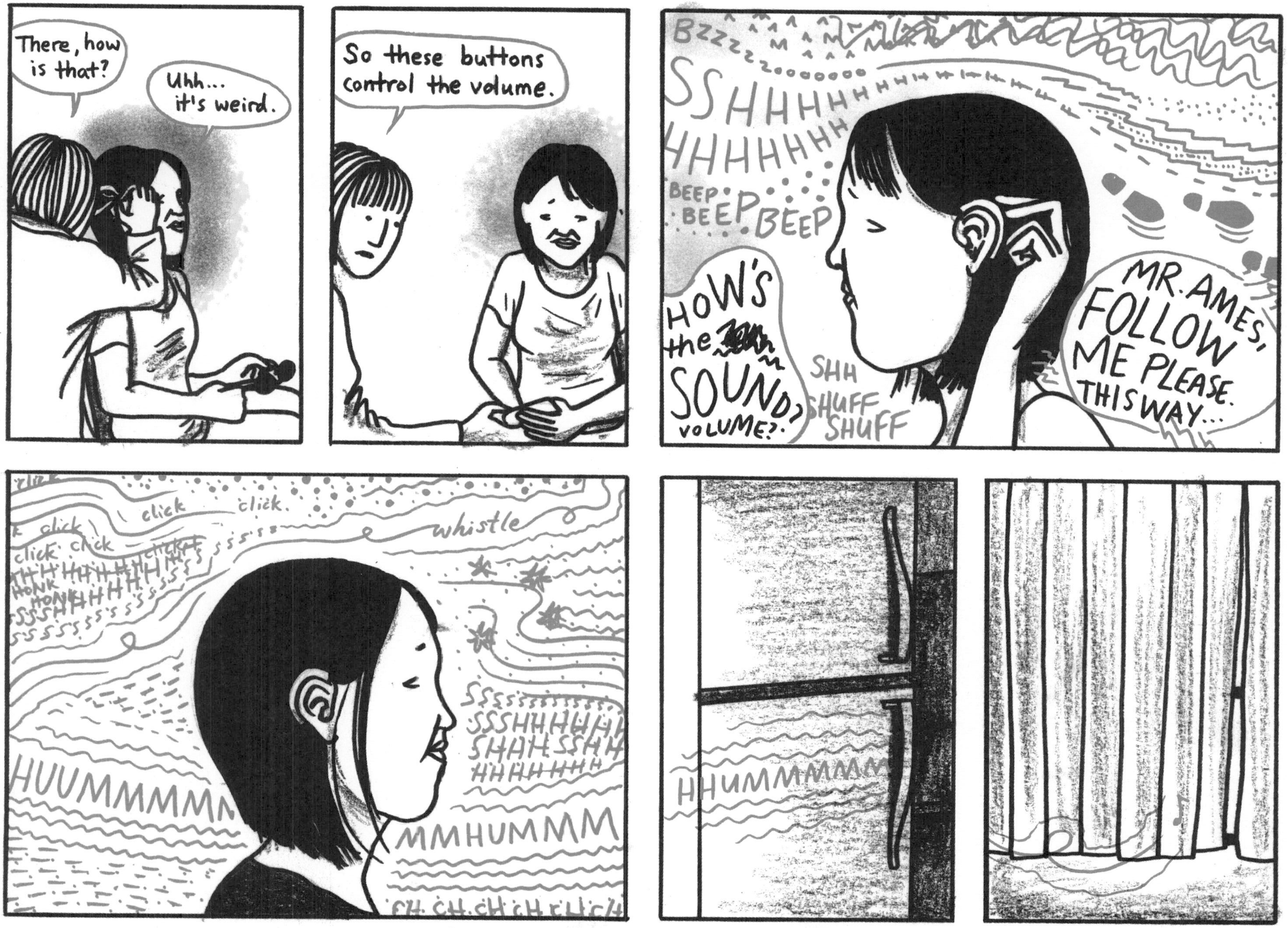
There, how is that?
Uhh... it's weird.
So these buttons control the volume.
BZZZZ
SSHHHH HHHHHHH
BEEP BEEP BEEP
HOW'S the SOUND? VOLUME?
SHH
SHUFF SHUFF
MR. AMES, FOLLOW ME PLEASE. THIS WAY...
click click click click
whistle
HONK HONK
HUUMMMMM
MMHUMMM
HHUMMMMM

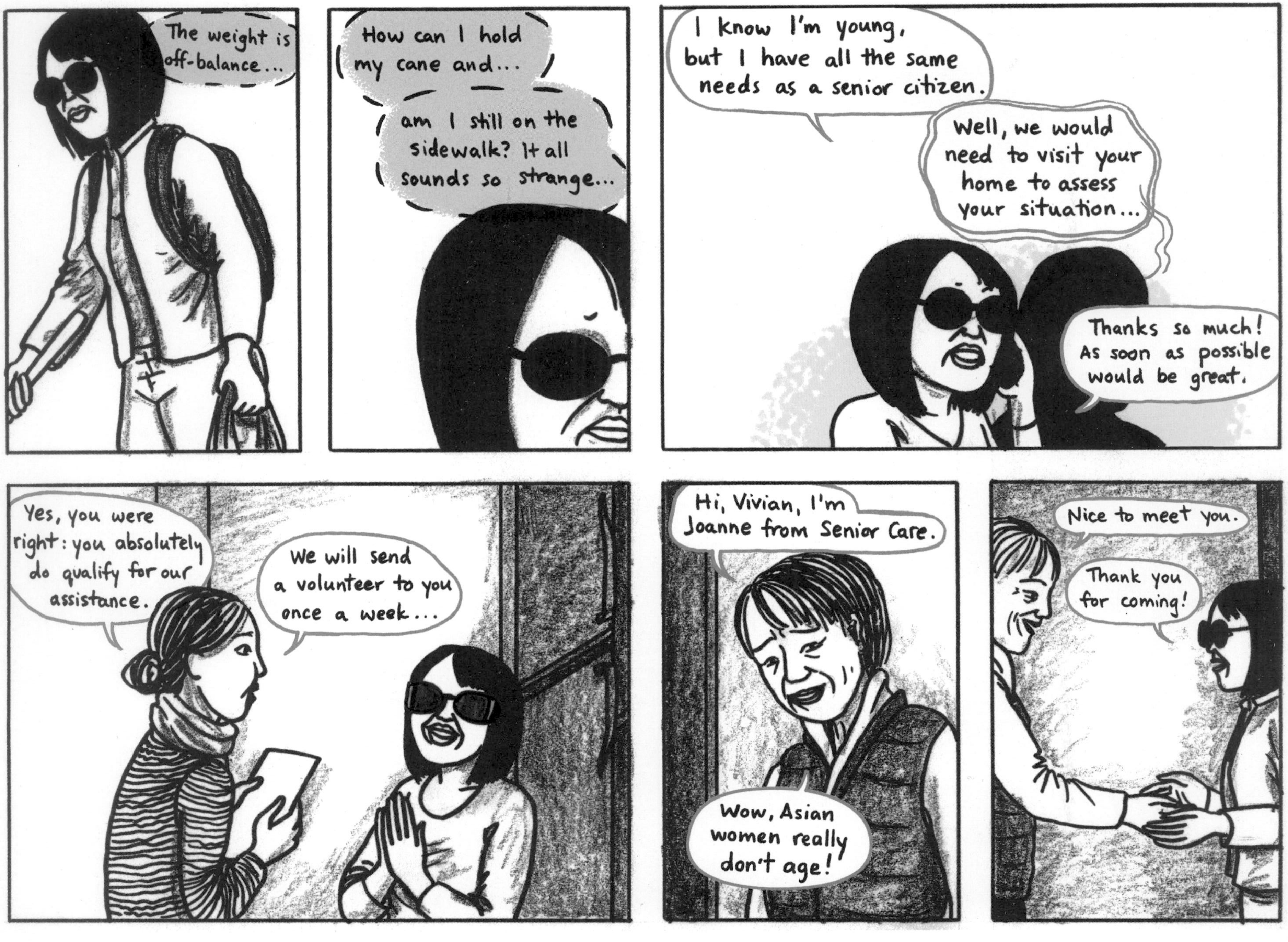
The weight is off-balance...
How can I hold my cane and...
am I still on the sidewalk? It all sounds so strange...
I know I'm young, but I have all the same needs as a senior citizen.
Well, we would need to visit your home to assess your situation...
Thanks so much! As soon as possible would be great.
Yes, you were right: you absolutely do qualify for our assistance.
We will send a volunteer to you once a week...
Hi, Vivian, I'm Joanne from Senior Care.
Wow, Asian women really don't age!
Nice to meet you.
Thank you for coming!

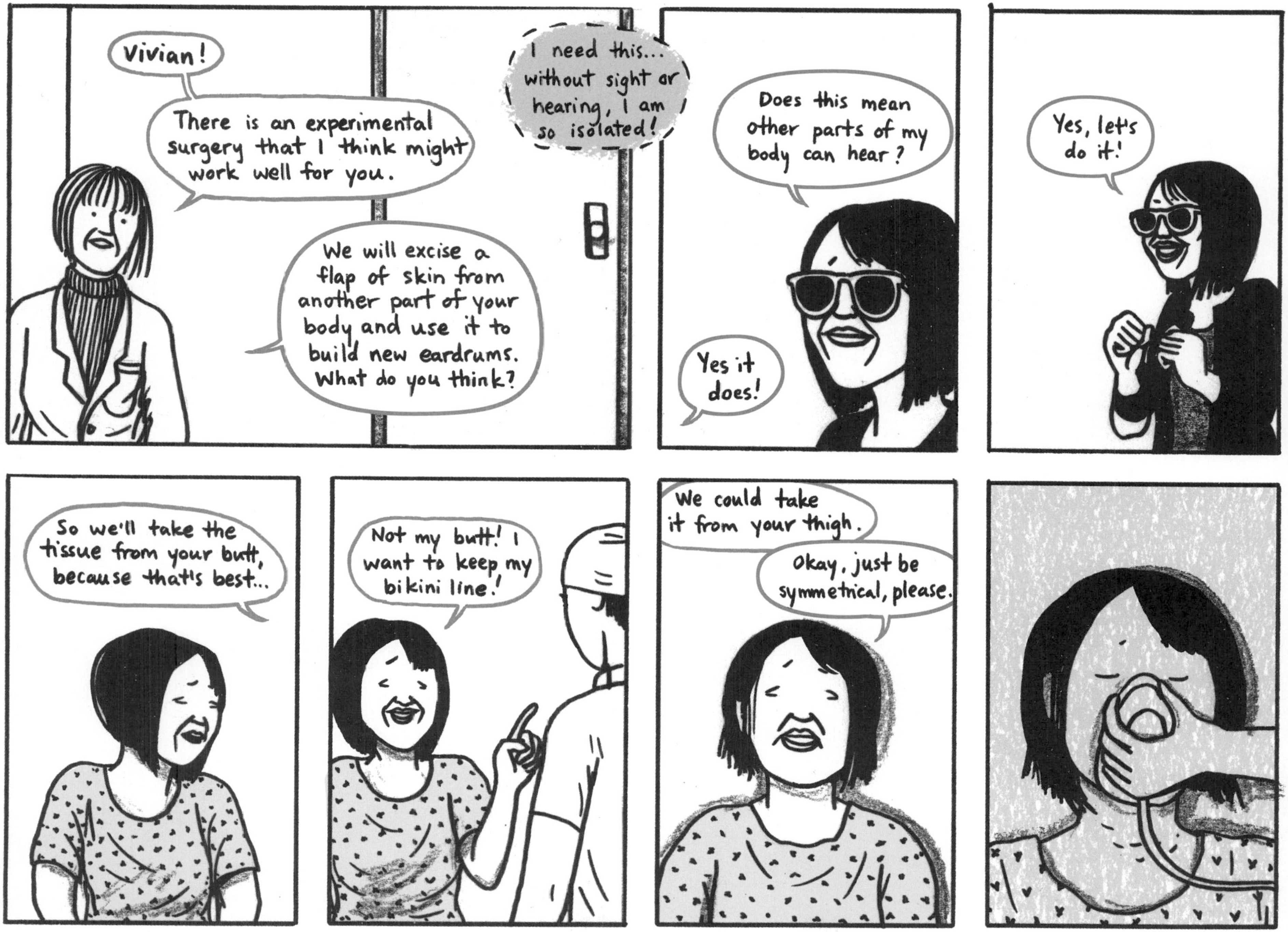
Vivian!
There is an experimental surgery that I think might work well for you.
We will excise a flap of skin from another part of your body and use it to build new eardrums. What do you think?
I need this... without sight or hearing, I am so isolated!
Does this mean other parts of my body can hear?
Yes it does!
Yes, let's do it!
So we'll take the tissue from your butt, because that's best...
Not my butt! I want to keep my bikini line!
We could take it from your thigh.
Okay, just be symmetrical, please.

Nine

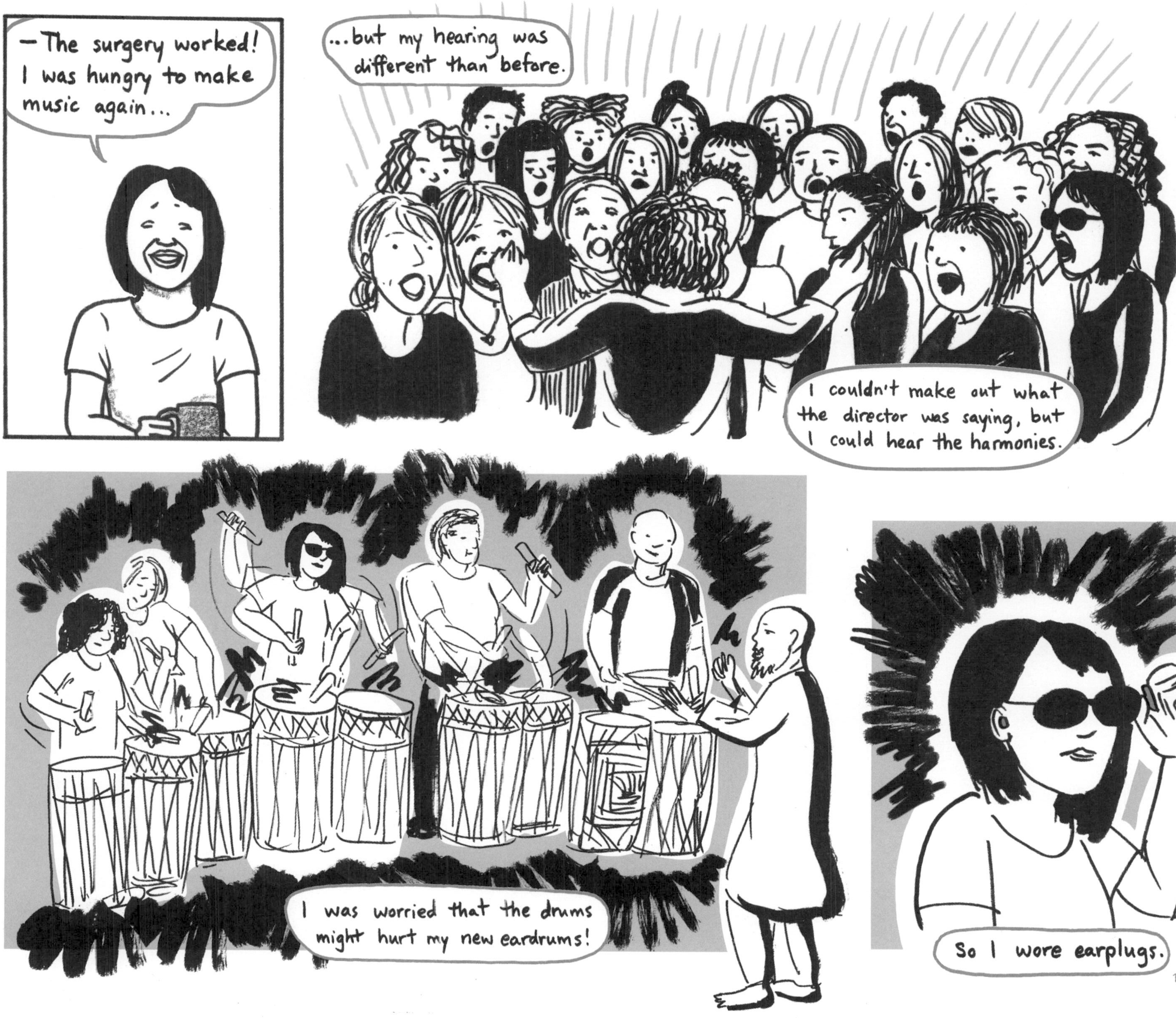
—The surgery worked! I was hungry to make music again...
...but my hearing was different than before.
I couldn't make out what the director was saying, but I could hear the harmonies.
I was worried that the drums might hurt my new eardrums!
So I wore earplugs.

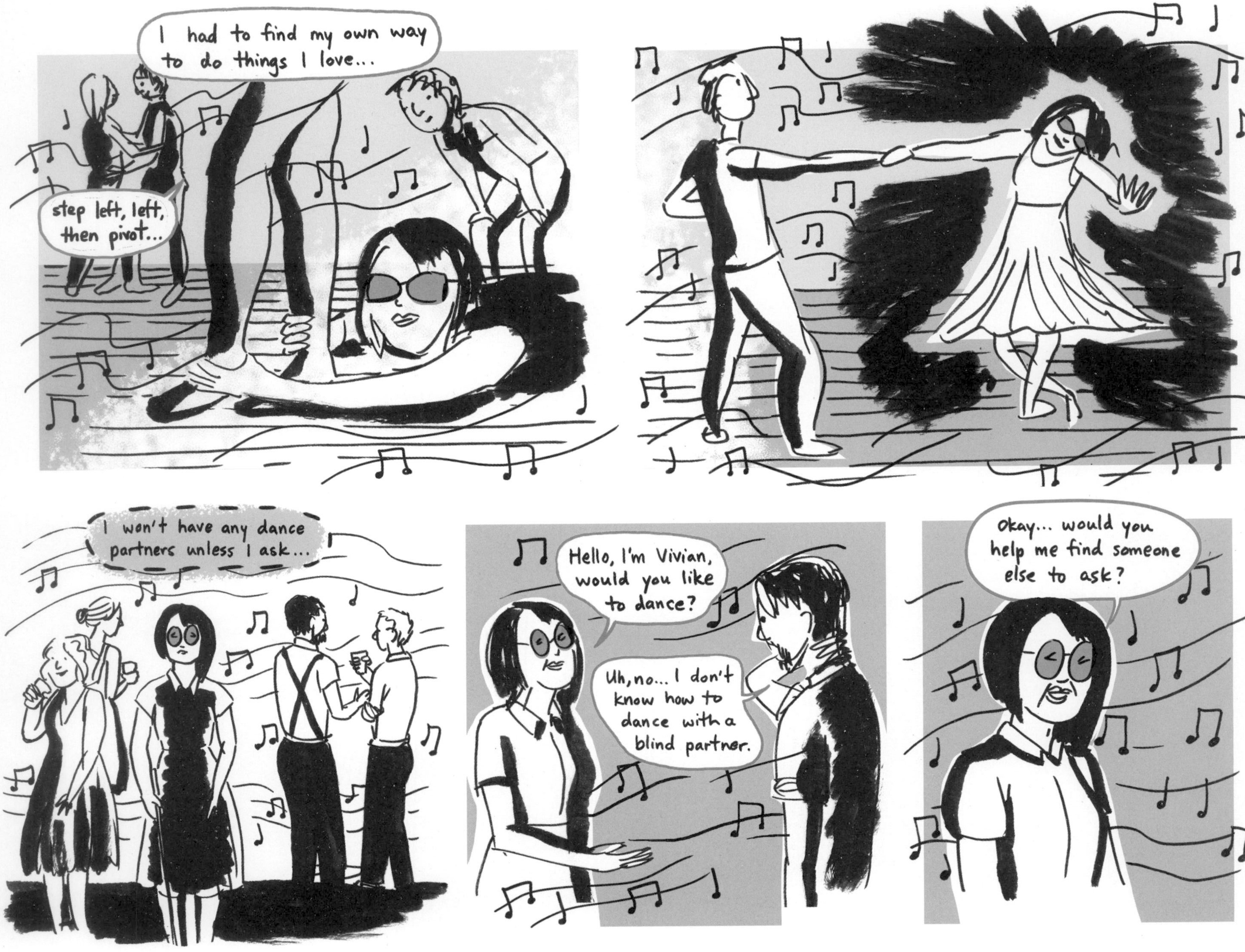
I had to find my own way to do things I love...
step left, left, then pivot...
I won't have any dance partners unless I ask...
Hello, I'm Vivian, would you like to dance?
Uh, no... I don't know how to dance with a blind partner.
Okay... would you help me find someone else to ask?

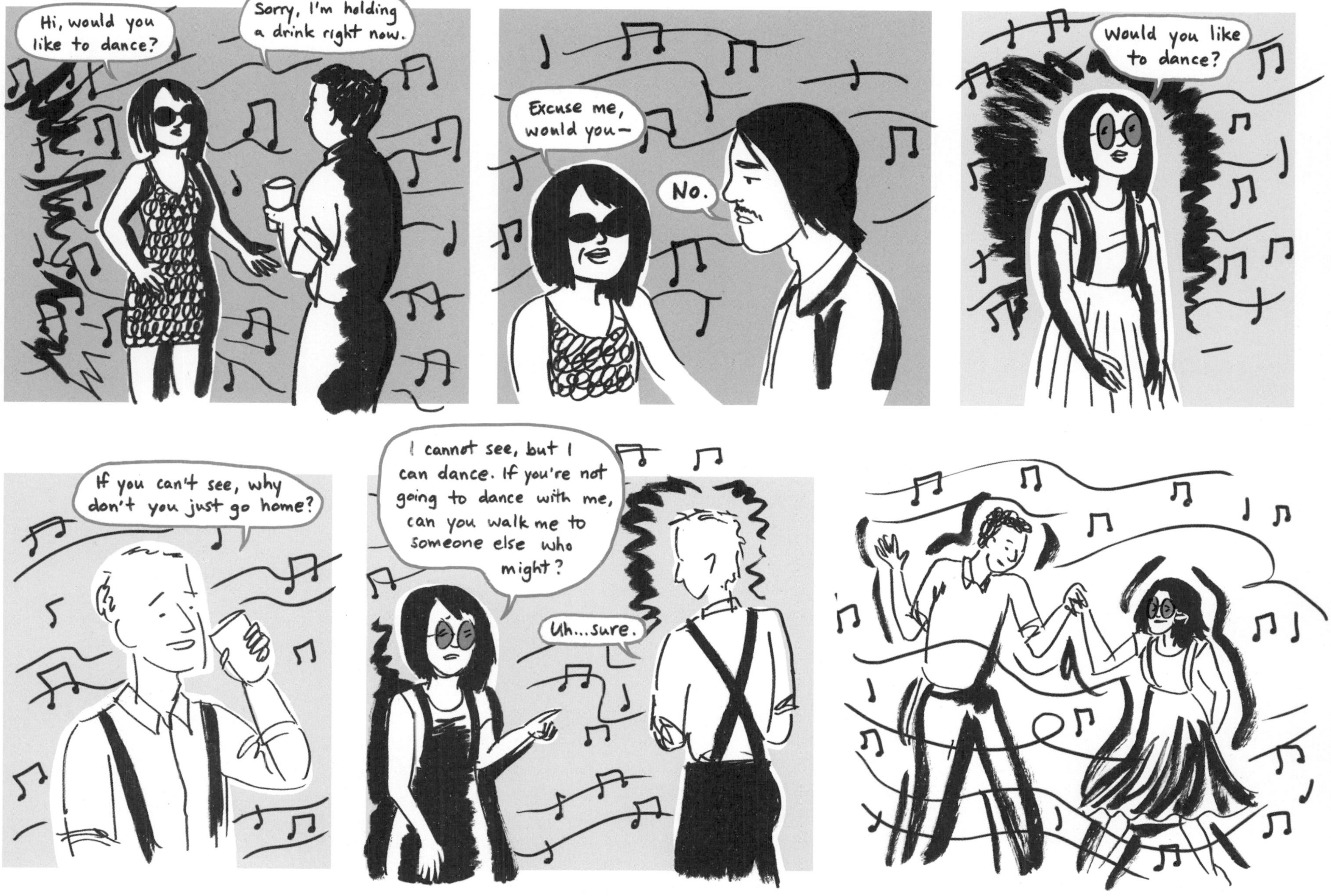
Hi, would you like to dance?
Sorry, I'm holding a drink right now.
Excuse me, would you—
No.
Would you like to dance?
If you can't see, why don't you just go home?
I cannot see, but I can dance. If you're not going to dance with me, can you walk me to someone else who might?
Uh...sure.

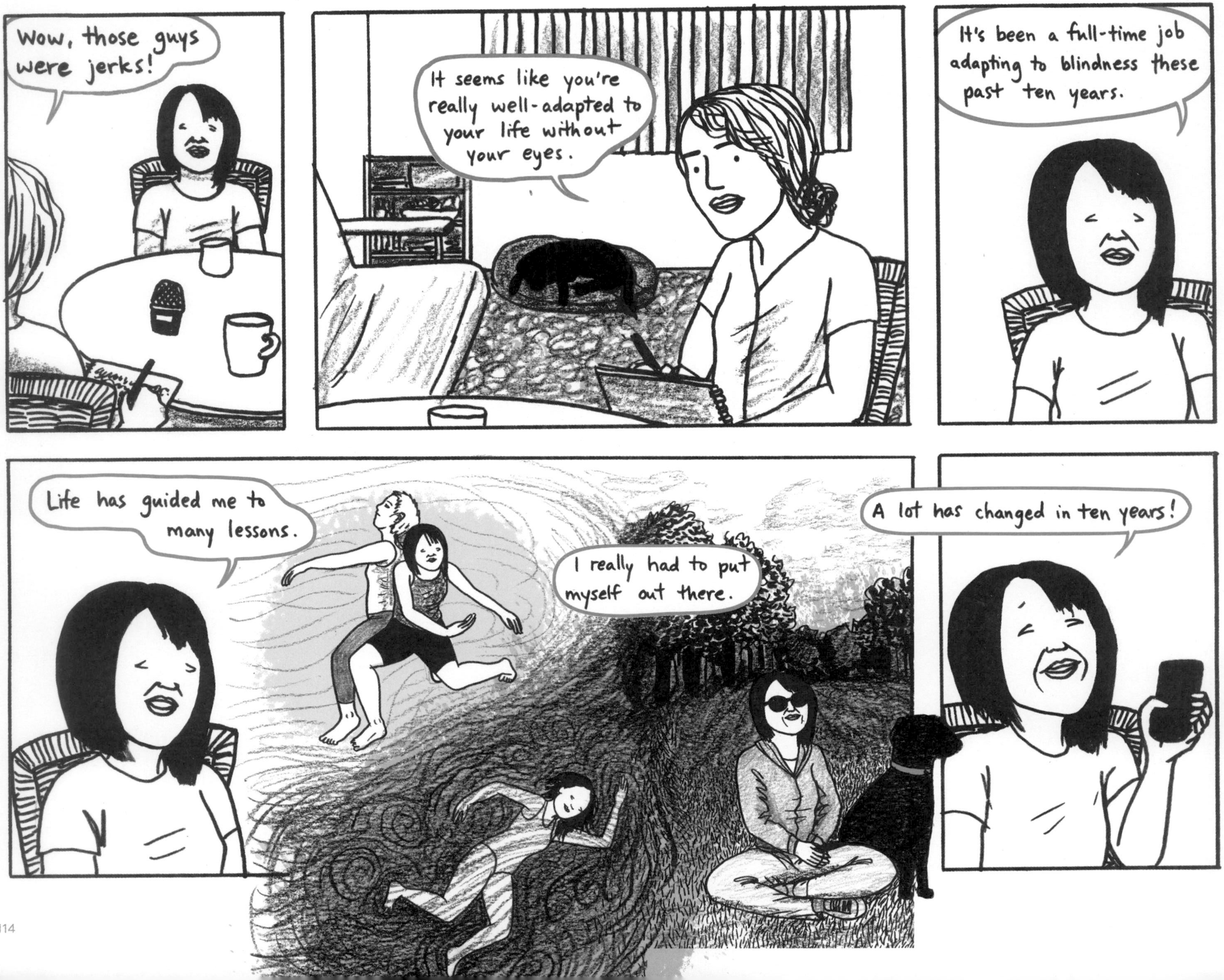
Wow, those guys were jerks!
It seems like you're really well-adapted to your life without your eyes.
It's been a full-time job adapting to blindness these past ten years.
Life has guided me to many lessons.
I really had to put myself out there.
A lot has changed in ten years!

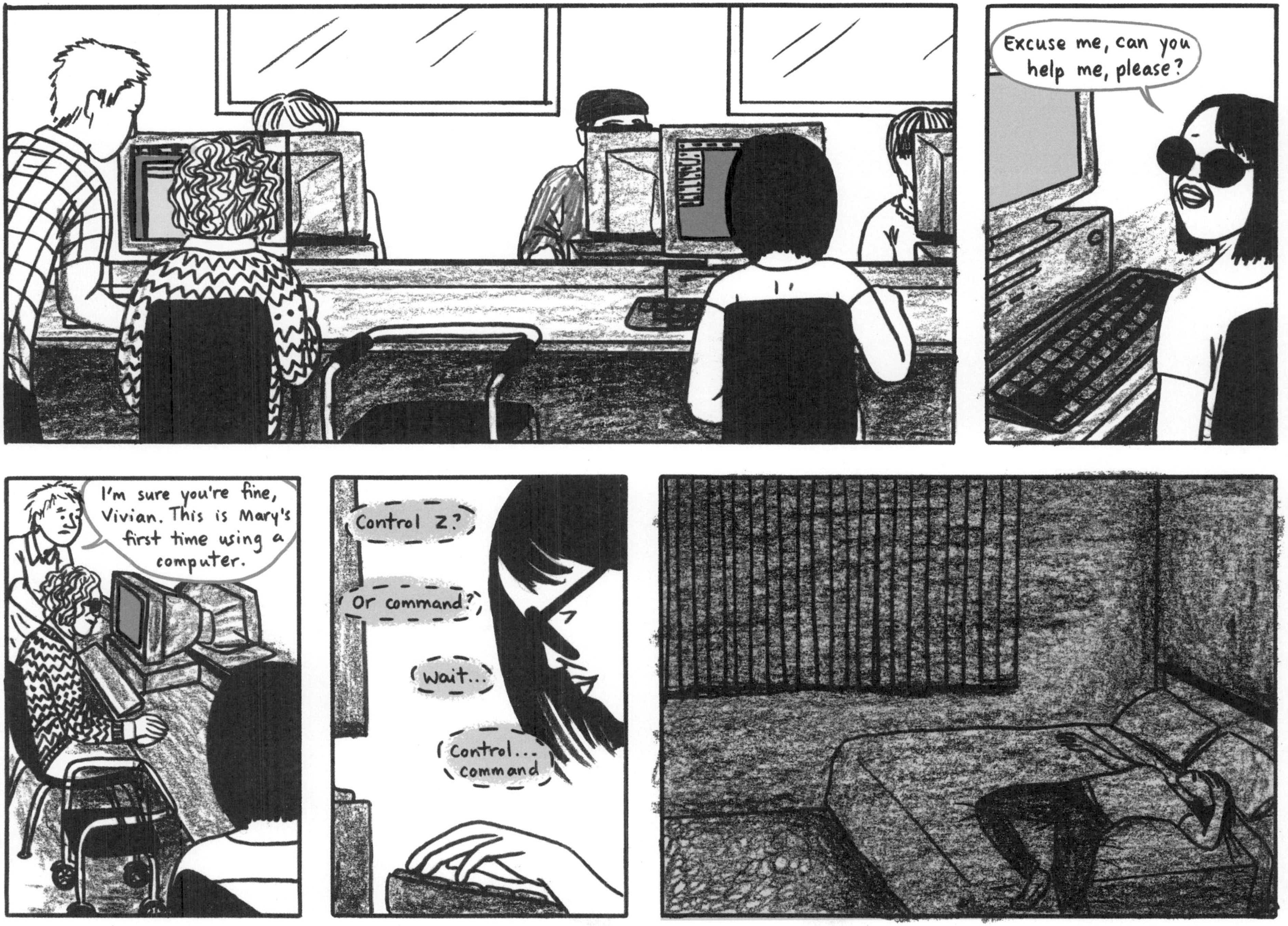
Excuse me, can you help me, please?
I'm sure you're fine, Vivian. This is Mary's first time using a computer.
Control Z?
Or command?
wait...
Control... command

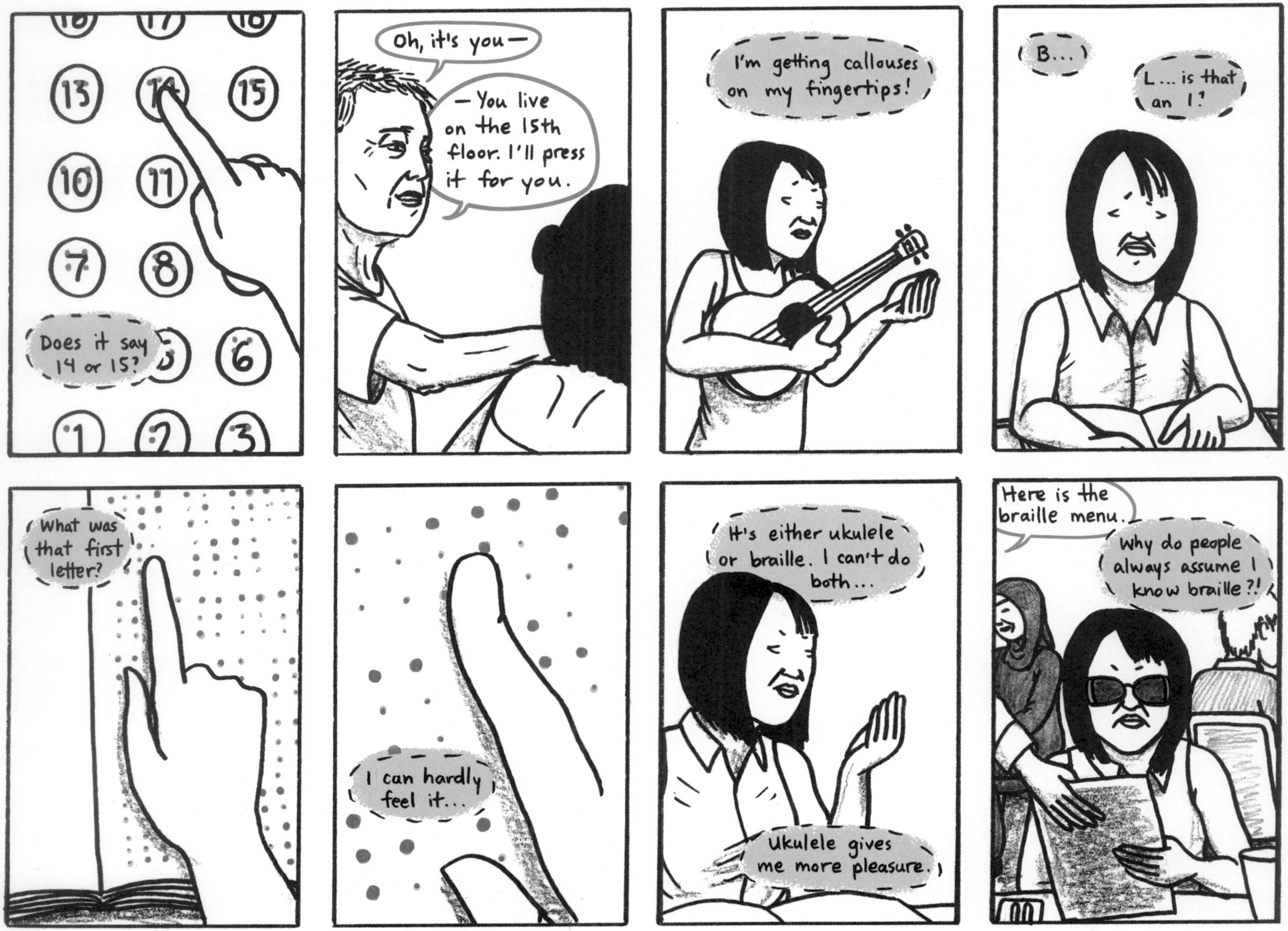

13
14
15
10
11
7
8
6
1
2
3
Does it say 14 or 15?
Oh, it's you—
—You live on the 15th floor. I'll press it for you.
I'm getting callouses on my fingertips!
B...
L... is that an l?
What was that first letter?
I can hardly feel it...
It's either ukulele or braille. I can't do both...
Ukulele gives me more pleasure.
Here is the braille menu.
Why do people always assume I know braille?!

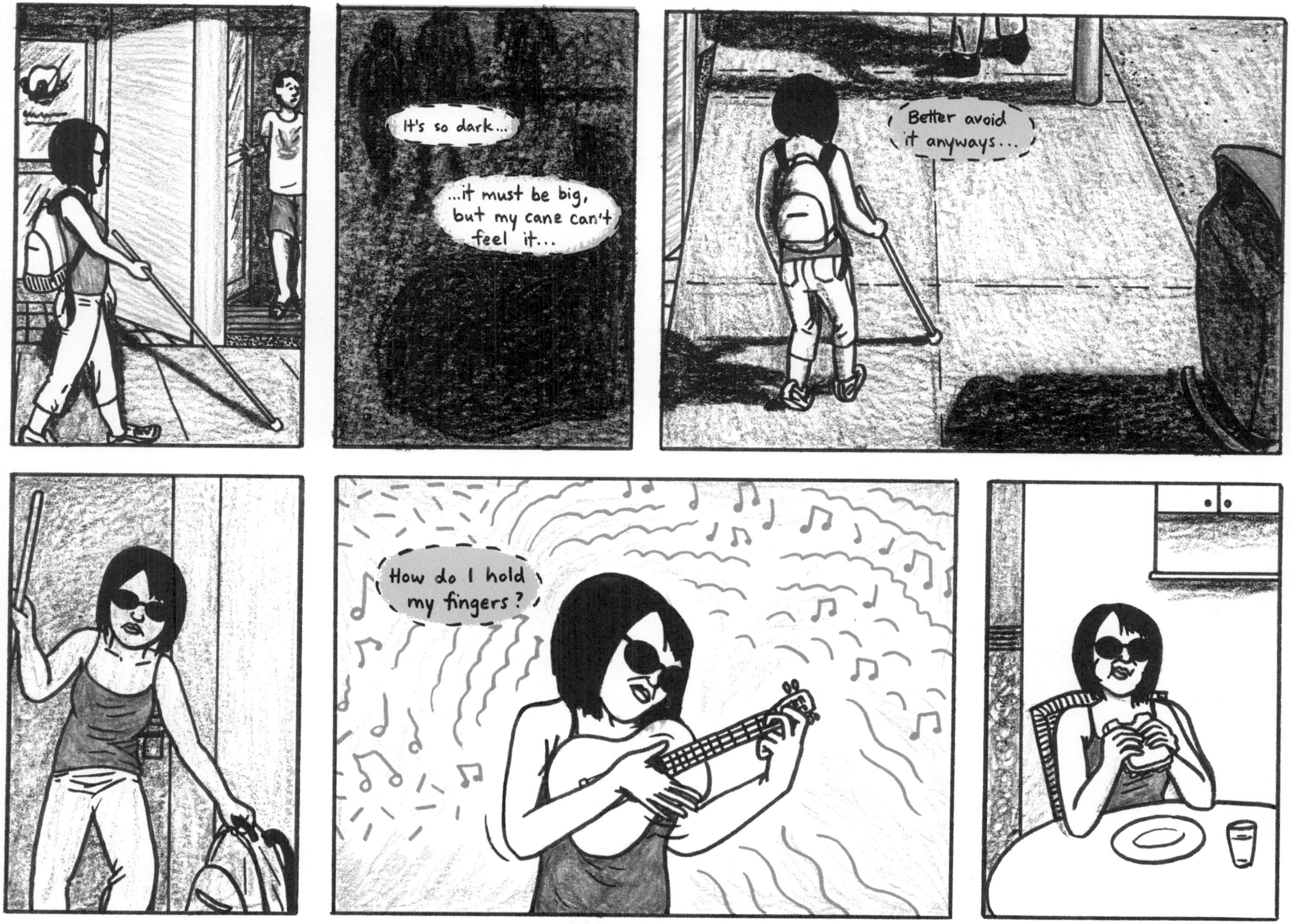
It's so dark...
...it must be big, but my cane can't feel it...
Better avoid it anyways...
How do I hold my fingers?

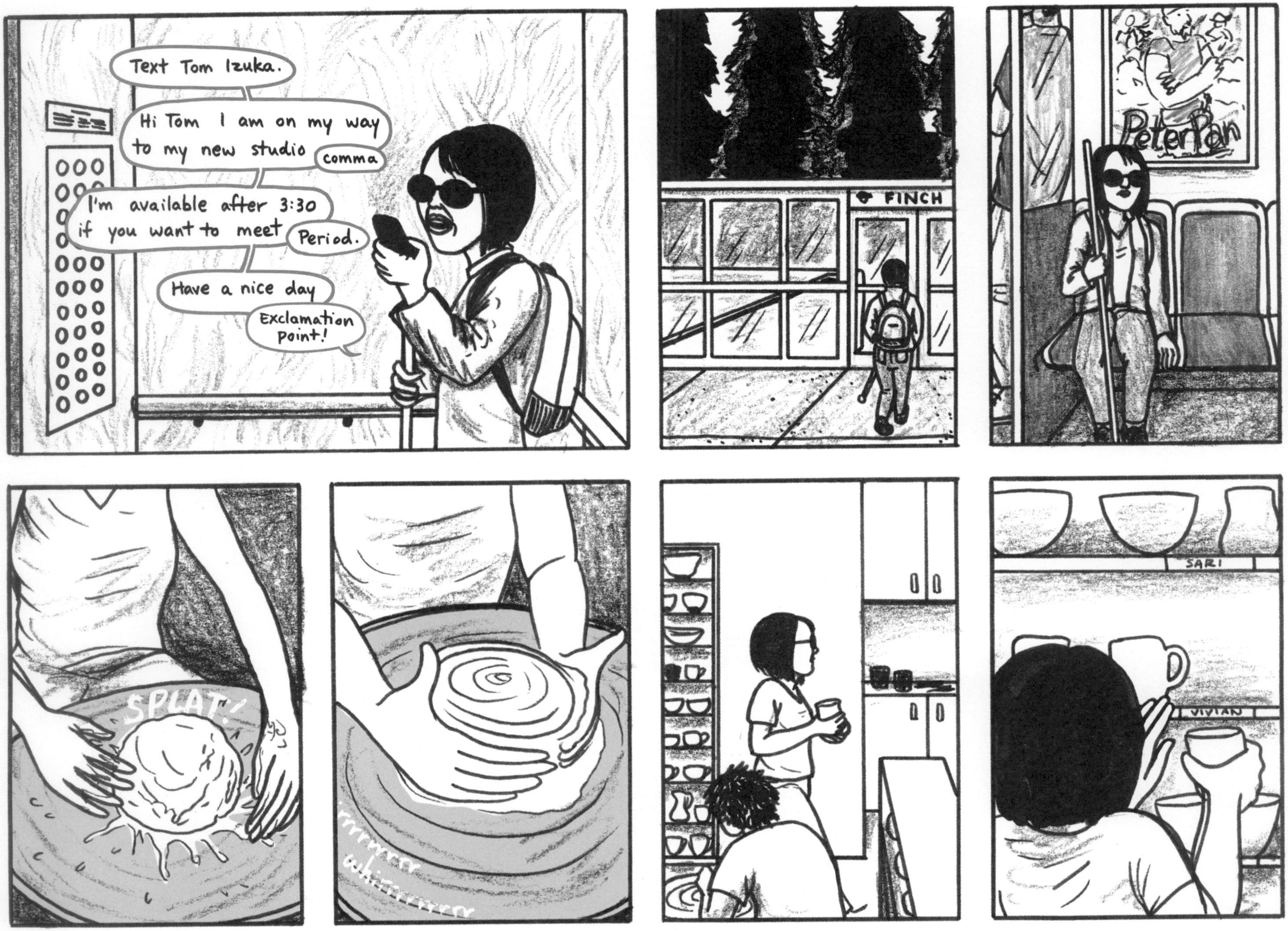
Text Tom Izuka.
Hi Tom I am on my way to my new studio
comma
I'm available after 3:30 if you want to meet
Period.
Have a nice day
Exclamation point!
FINCH
Peter Pan
SPLAT!
whirrrrrrrrrrrr
SARI
VIVIAN

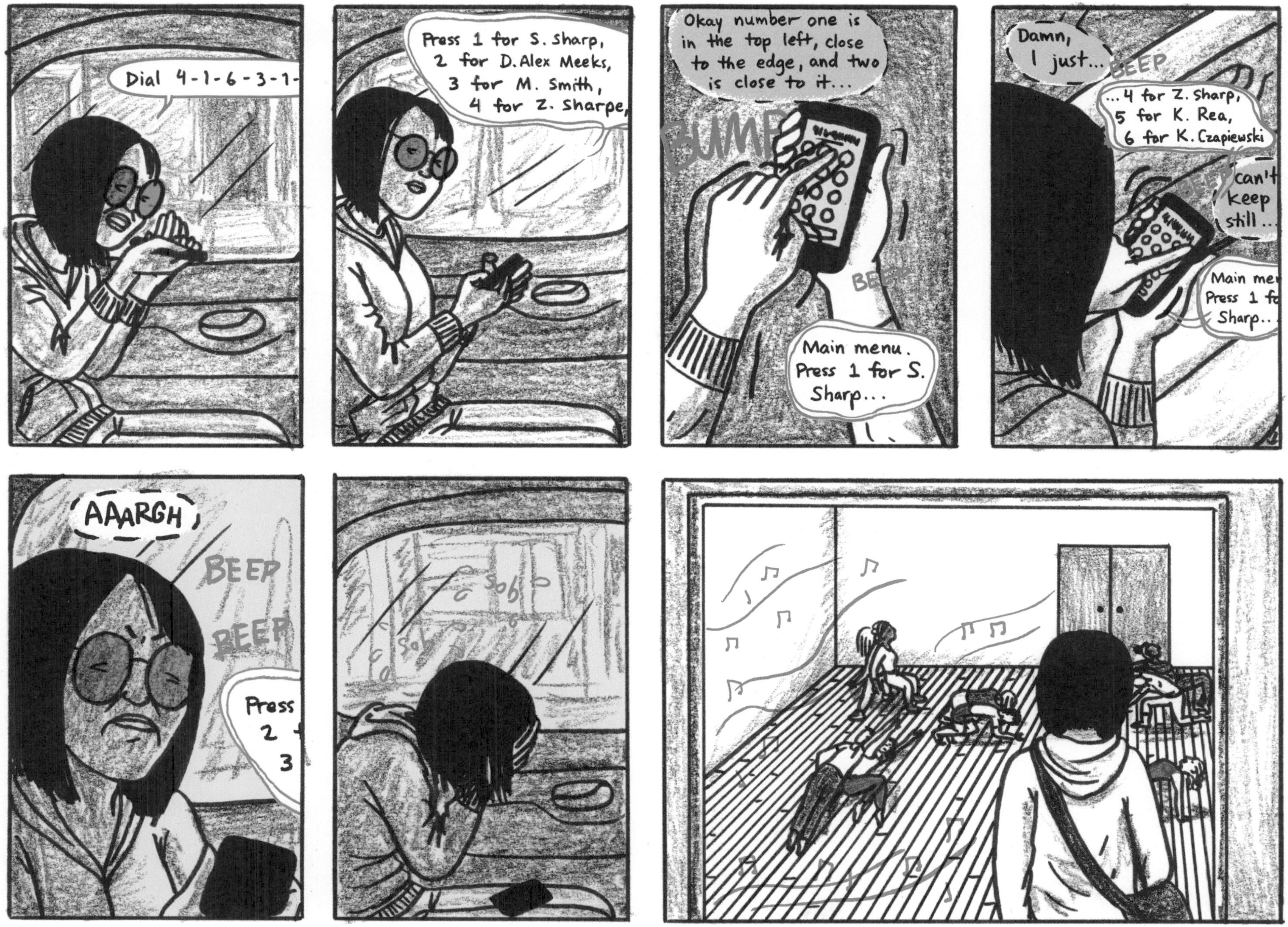
Dial 4-1-6-3-1-
Press 1 for S. sharp, 2 for D. Alex Meeks, 3 for M. Smith, 4 for Z. Sharpe,
Okay number one is in the top left, close to the edge, and two is close to it...
BUMP
BEEP
Main menu. Press 1 for S. Sharp...
Damn, I just...
BEEP
...4 for Z. Sharp, 5 for K. Rea, 6 for K. Czapiewski
can't keep still...
Main me
Press 1 f
Sharp...
AAARGH
BEEP
BEEP
Press
2
3
sob
sob

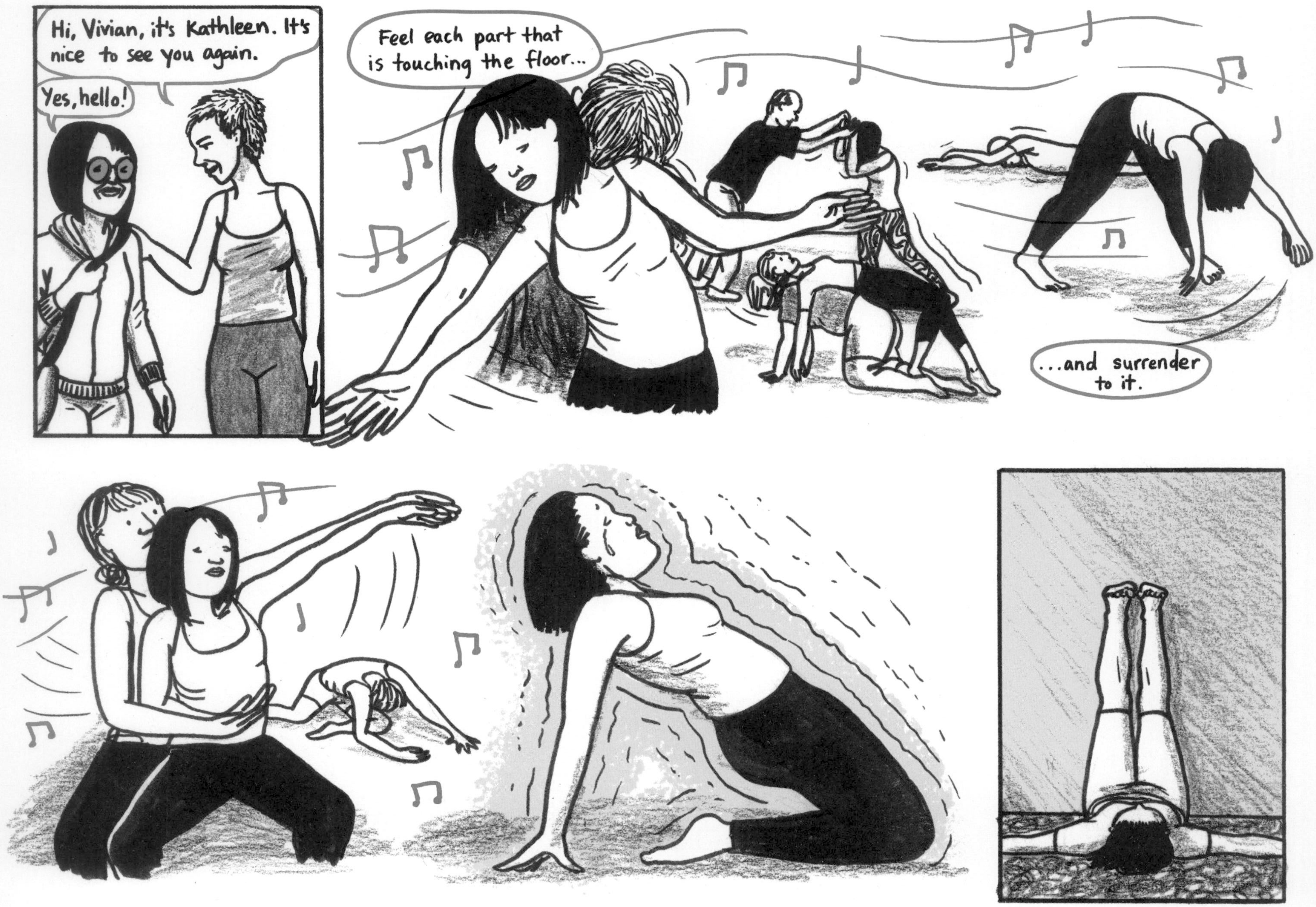
Hi, Vivian, it's Kathleen. It's nice to see you again.
Yes, hello!
Feel each part that is touching the floor...
...and surrender to it.

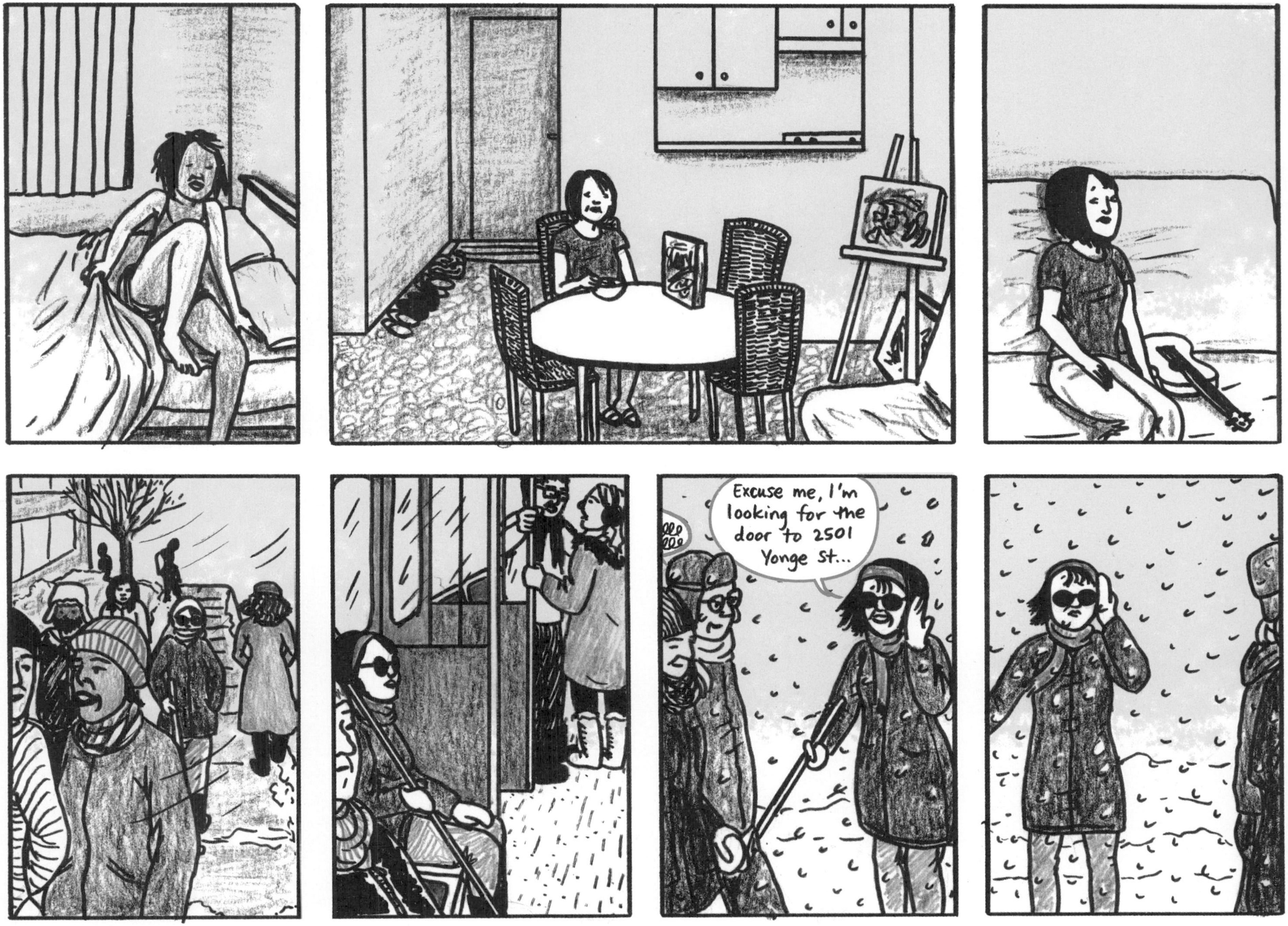
Excuse me, I'm looking for the door to 2501 Yonge st...

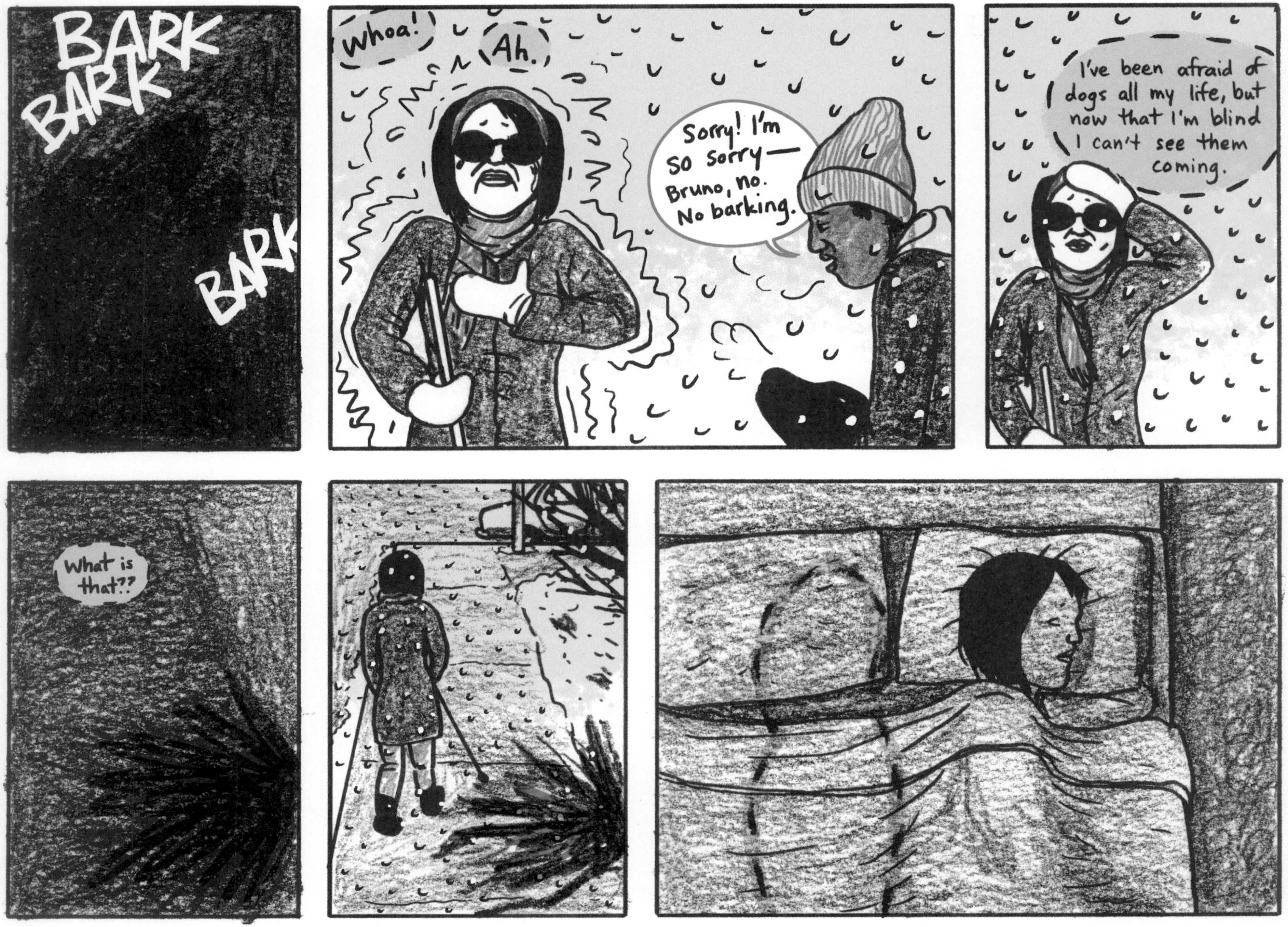
BARK
BARK
BARK
Whoa!
Ah.
Sorry! I'm so sorry— Bruno, no. No barking.
I've been afraid of dogs all my life, but now that I'm blind I can't see them coming.
What is that??

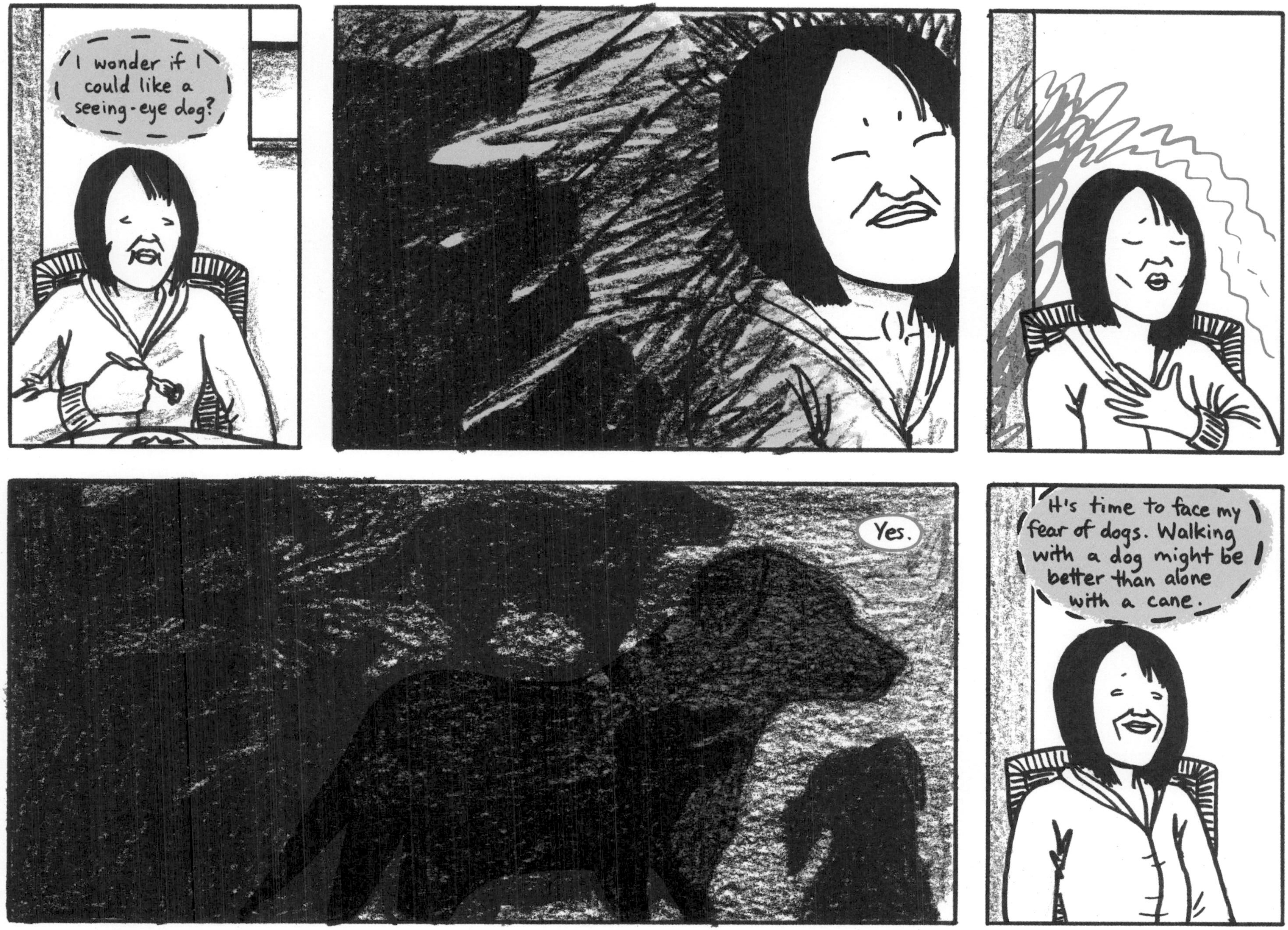
I wonder if I could like a seeing-eye dog?
It's time to face my fear of dogs. Walking with a dog might be better than alone with a cane.
Yes.

TEN

California, 2016

This is my decision. My trip. A dog will give me more freedom. This is going to work out.
Welcome to California

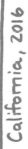

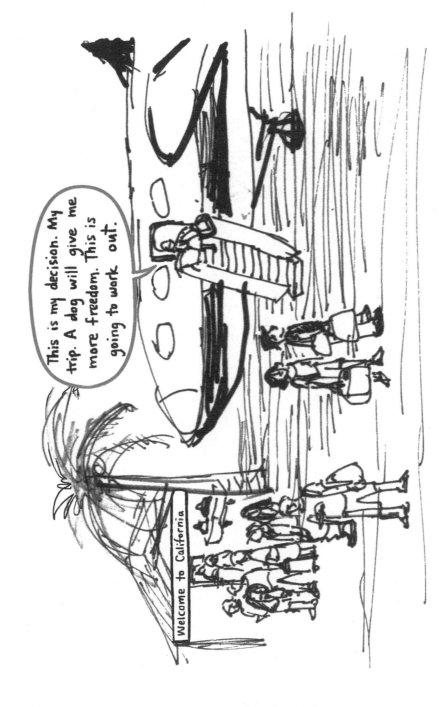

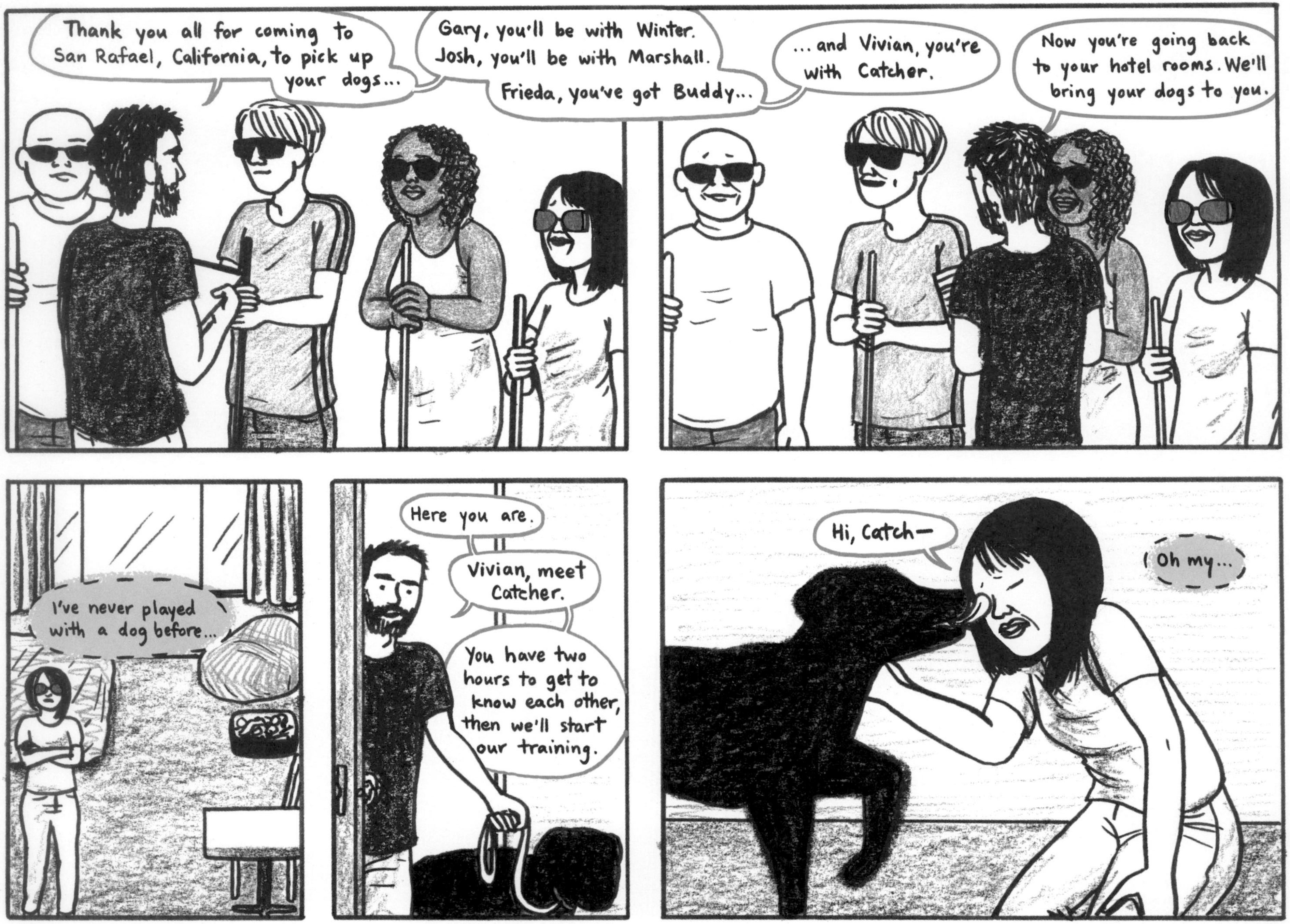
Thank you all for coming to San Rafael, California, to pick up your dogs...
Gary, you'll be with Winter. Josh, you'll be with Marshall.
Frieda, you've got Buddy...
...and Vivian, you're with Catcher.
Now you're going back to your hotel rooms. We'll bring your dogs to you.
I've never played with a dog before...
Here you are.
Vivian, meet Catcher.
You have two hours to get to know each other, then we'll start our training.
Hi, Catch—
Oh my...

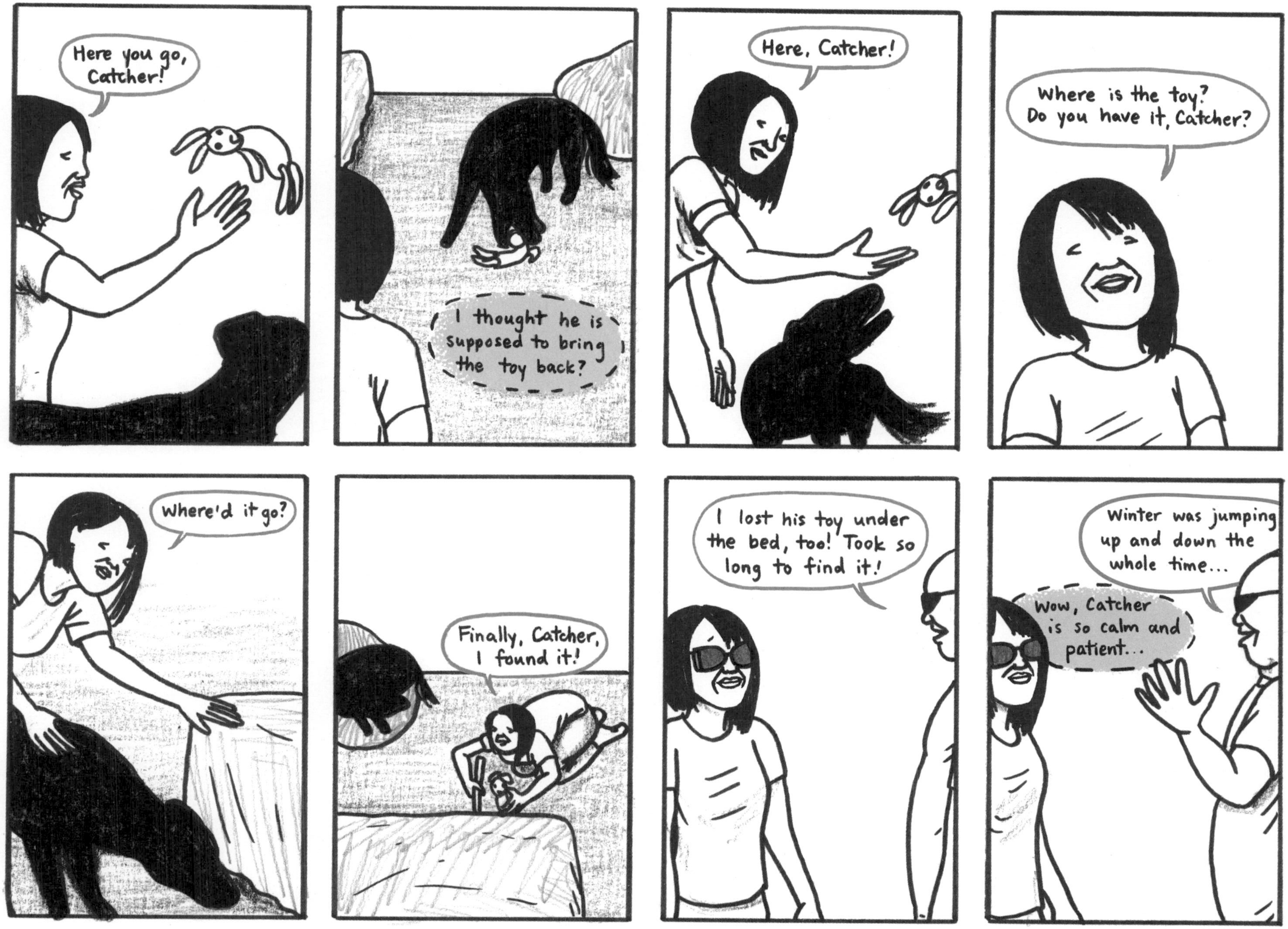
Here you go, Catcher!
I thought he is supposed to bring the toy back?
Here, Catcher!
Where is the toy? Do you have it, Catcher?
Where'd it go?
Finally, Catcher, I found it!
I lost his toy under the bed, too! Took so long to find it!
Winter was jumping up and down the whole time...
Wow, Catcher is so calm and patient...

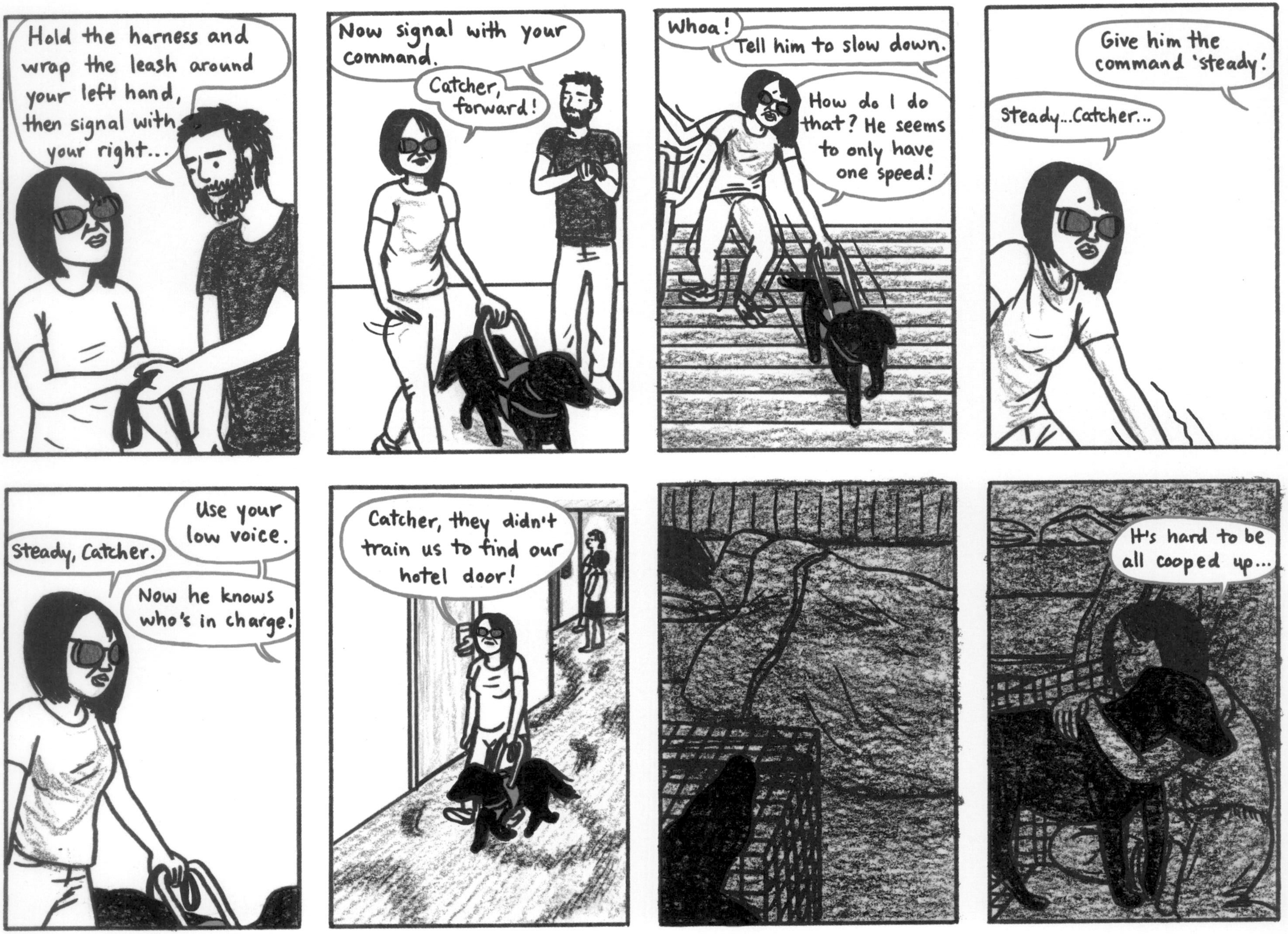
Hold the harness and wrap the leash around your left hand, then signal with your right...
Now signal with your command.
Catcher, forward!
Whoa!
Tell him to slow down.
How do I do that? He seems to only have one speed!
Give him the command 'steady.'
Steady...Catcher...
Steady, Catcher.
Use your low voice.
Now he knows who's in charge!
Catcher, they didn't train us to find our hotel door!
It's hard to be all cooped up...

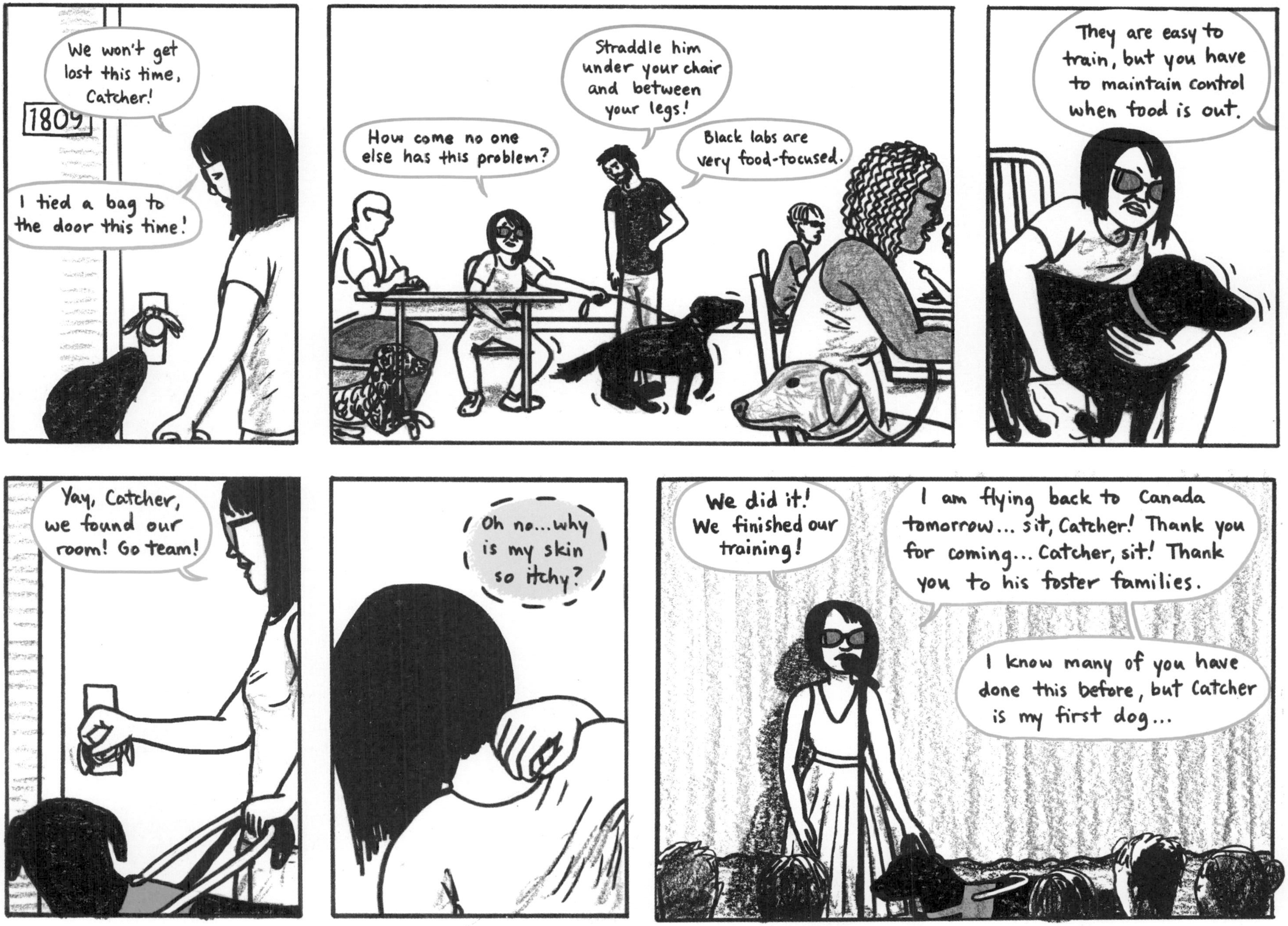
1809
We won't get lost this time, Catcher!
I tied a bag to the door this time!
How come no one else has this problem?
Straddle him under your chair and between your legs!
Black labs are very food-focused.
They are easy to train, but you have to maintain control when food is out.
Yay, Catcher, we found our room! Go team!
Oh no... why is my skin so itchy?
We did it! We finished our training!
I am flying back to Canada tomorrow... sit, Catcher! Thank you for coming... Catcher, sit! Thank you to his foster families.
I know many of you have done this before, but Catcher is my first dog...

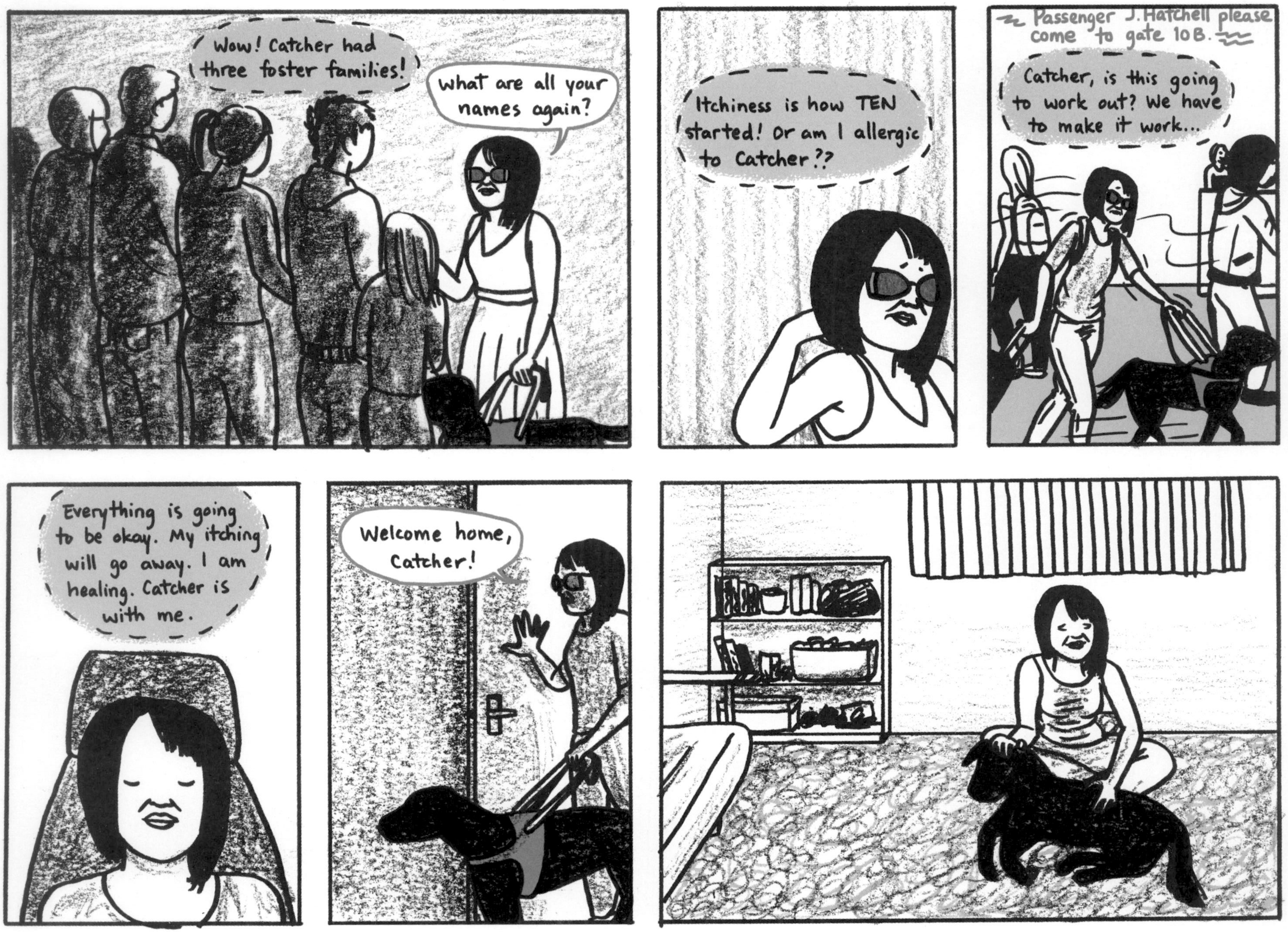
Wow! Catcher had three foster families!
What are all your names again?
Itchiness is how TEN started! Or am I allergic to Catcher??
Passenger J. Hatchell please come to gate 10B.
Catcher, is this going to work out? We have to make it work...
Everything is going to be okay. My itching will go away. I am healing. Catcher is with me.
Welcome home, Catcher!

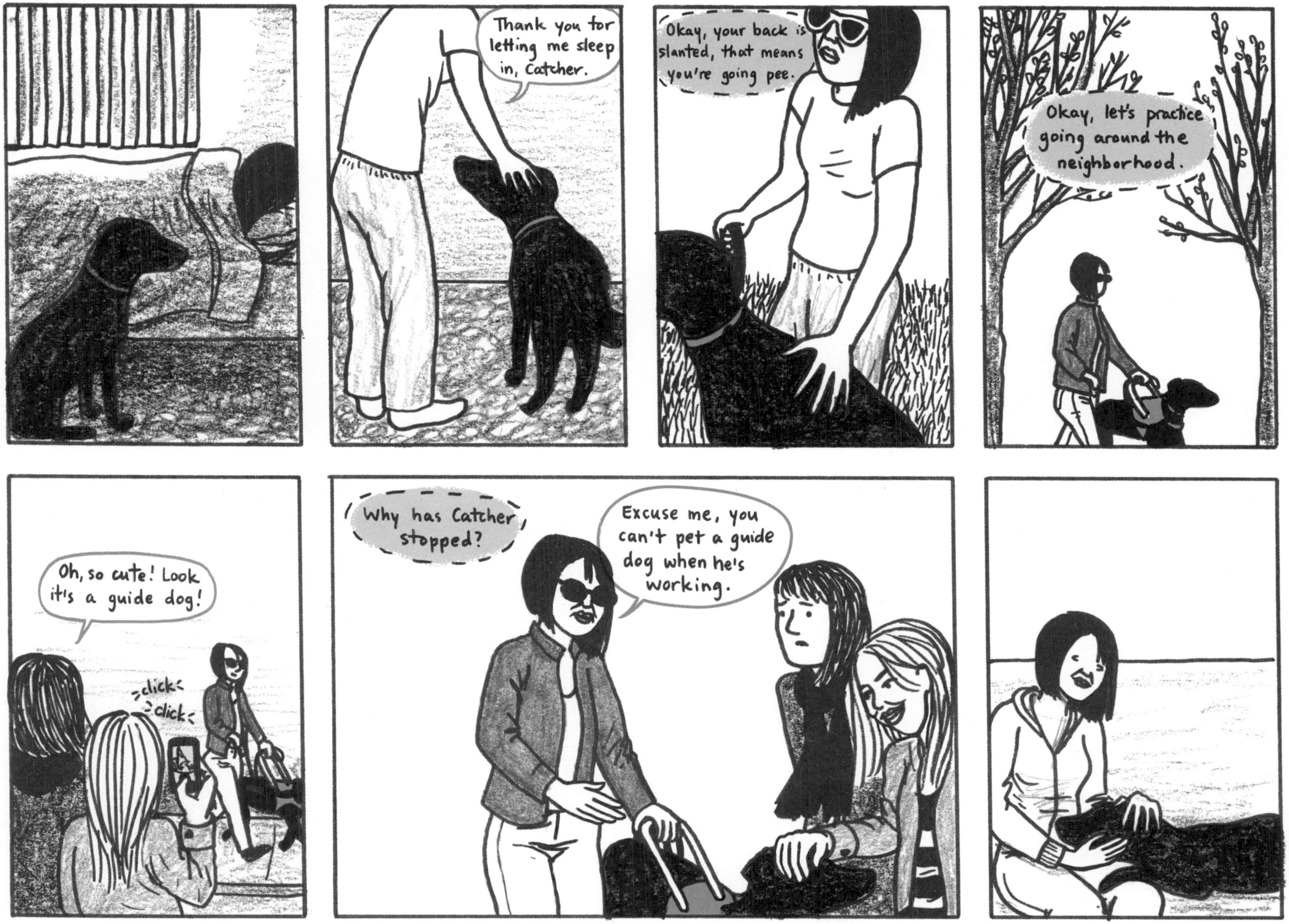
Thank you for letting me sleep in, Catcher.
Okay, your back is slanted, that means you're going pee.
Okay, let's practice going around the neighborhood.
Oh, so cute! Look it's a guide dog!
>click<
>click<
Why has Catcher stopped?
Excuse me, you can't pet a guide dog when he's working.

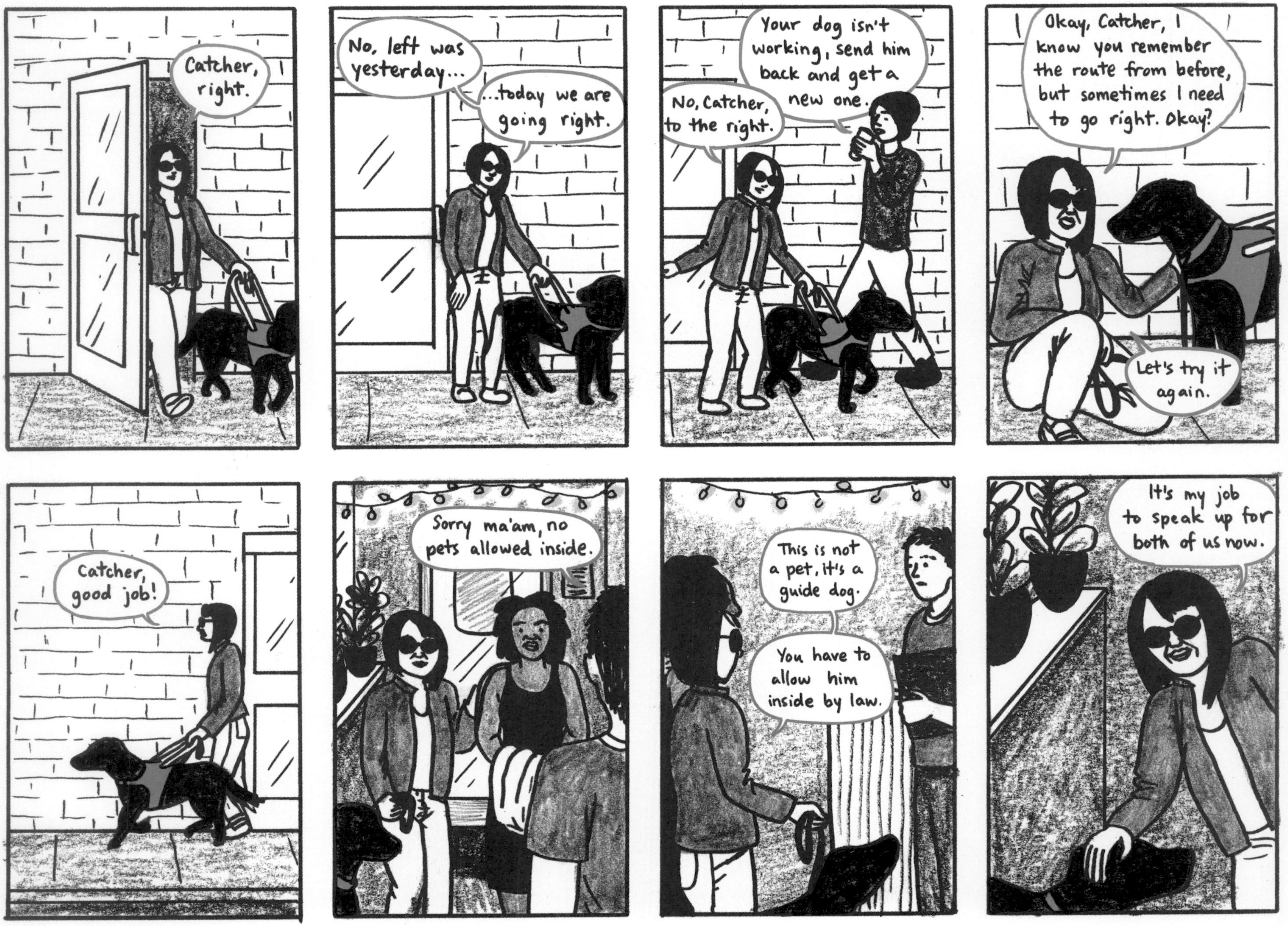
Catcher, right.
No, left was yesterday...
...today we are going right.
Your dog isn't working, send him back and get a new one.
No, Catcher, to the right.
Okay, Catcher, I know you remember the route from before, but sometimes I need to go right. Okay?
Let's try it again.
Catcher, good job!
Sorry ma'am, no pets allowed inside.
This is not a pet, it's a guide dog.
You have to allow him inside by law.
It's my job to speak up for both of us now.

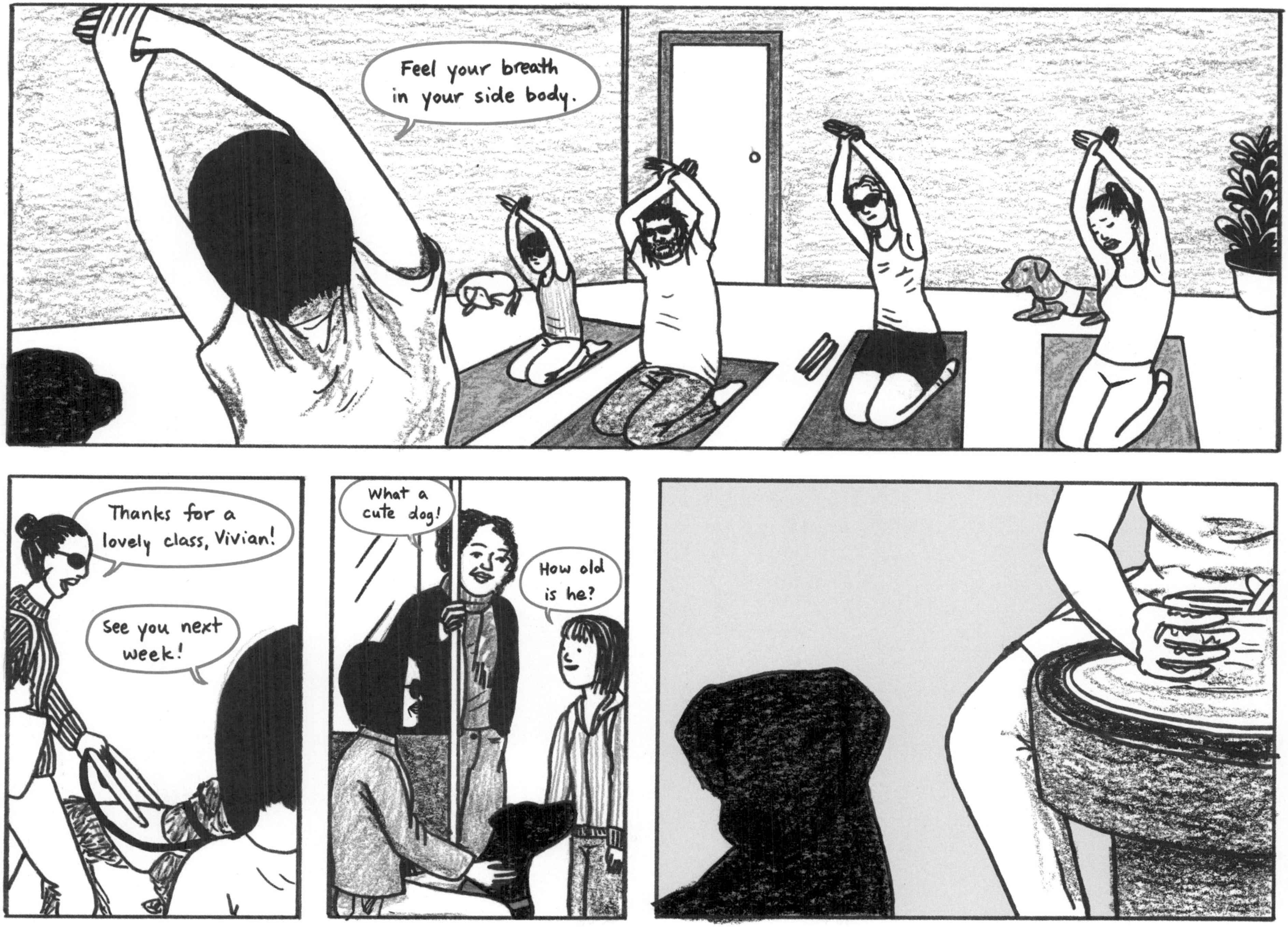
Feel your breath in your side body.
Thanks for a lovely class, Vivian!
See you next week!
What a cute dog!
How old is he?

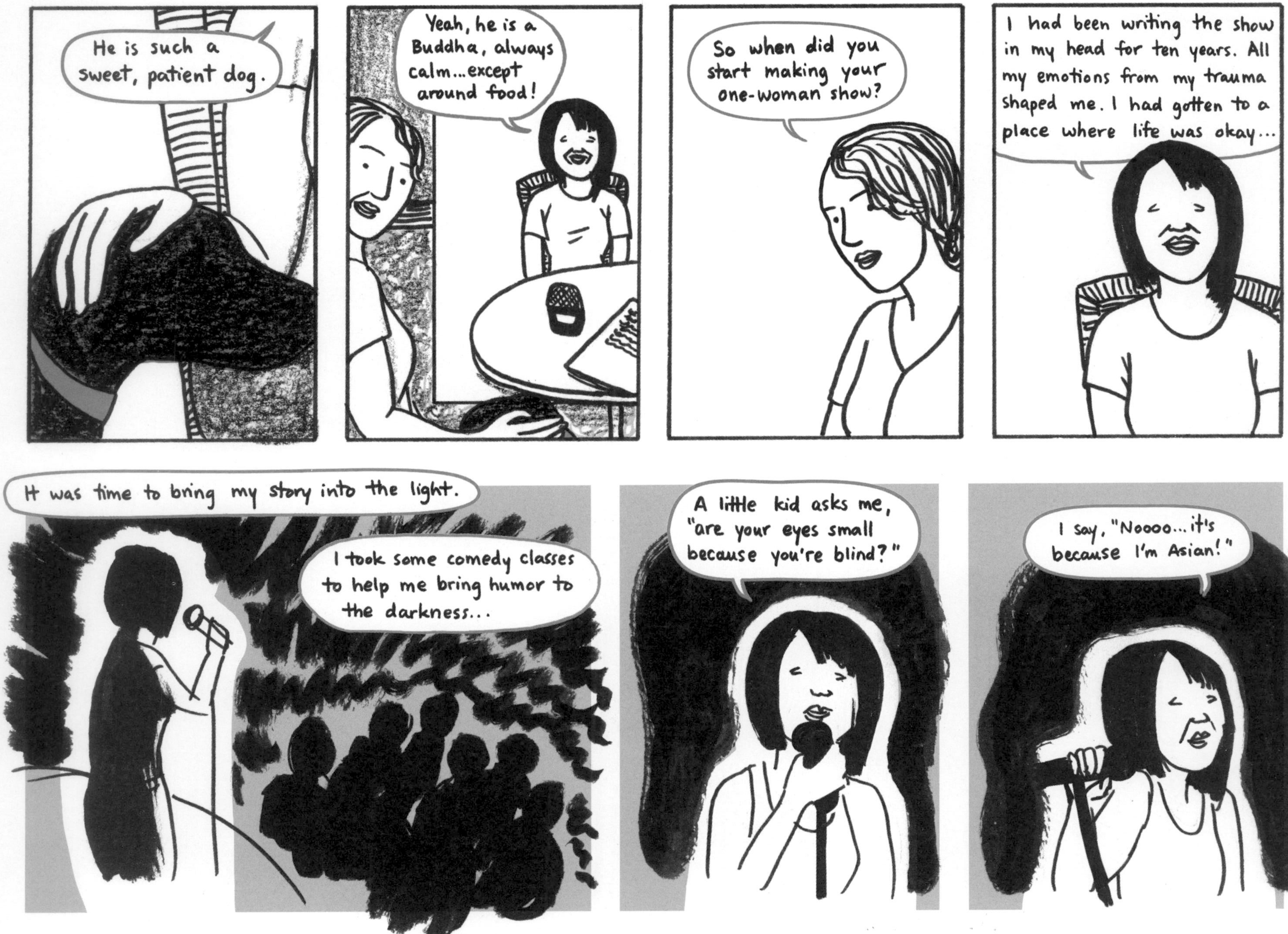
He is such a sweet, patient dog.
Yeah, he is a Buddha, always calm...except around food!
So when did you start making your one-woman show?
I had been writing the show in my head for ten years. All my emotions from my trauma shaped me. I had gotten to a place where life was okay...
It was time to bring my story into the light.
I took some comedy classes to help me bring humor to the darkness...
A little kid asks me, "are your eyes small because you're blind?"
I say, "Noooo... it's because I'm Asian!"

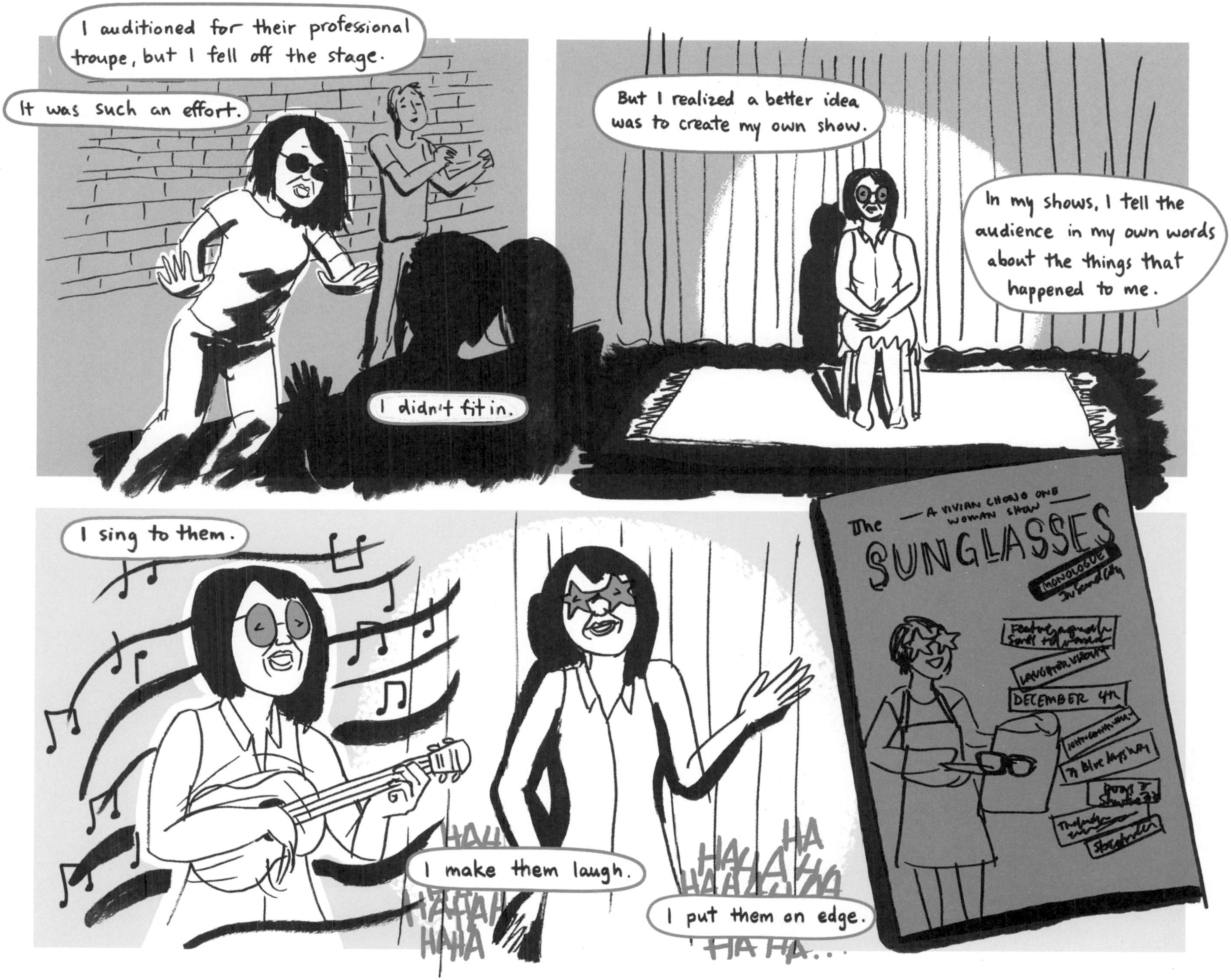
I auditioned for their professional troupe, but I fell off the stage.
It was such an effort.
I didn't fit in.
But I realized a better idea was to create my own show.
In my shows, I tell the audience in my own words about the things that happened to me.
I sing to them.
I make them laugh.
HAHA
I put them on edge.
HA HA...
The — A VIVIAN CHONG ONE WOMAN SHOW —
SUNGLASSES
MONOLOGUE
DECEMBER 4th

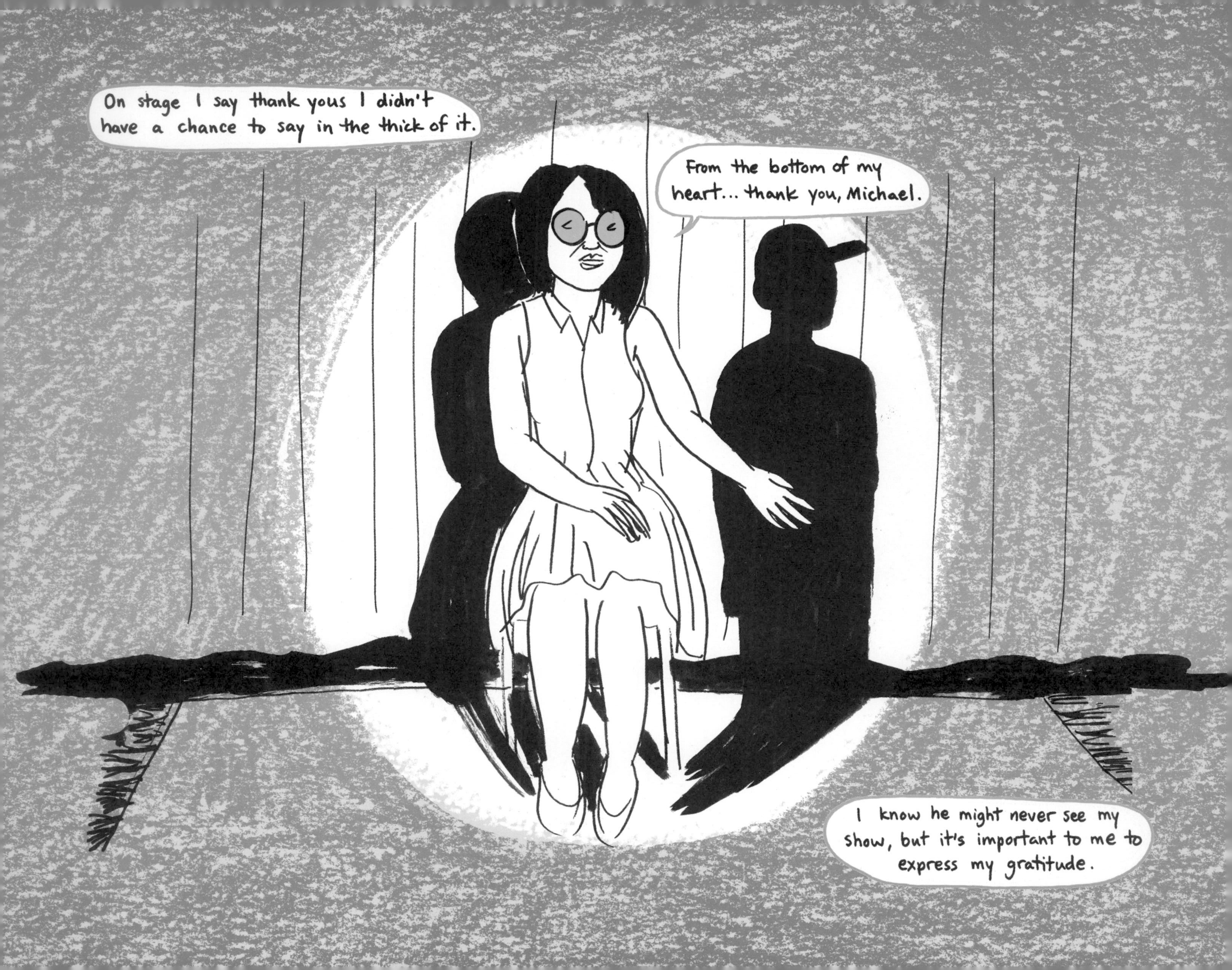
On stage I say thank yous I didn't have a chance to say in the thick of it.
From the bottom of my heart... thank you, Michael.
I know he might never see my show, but it's important to me to express my gratitude.

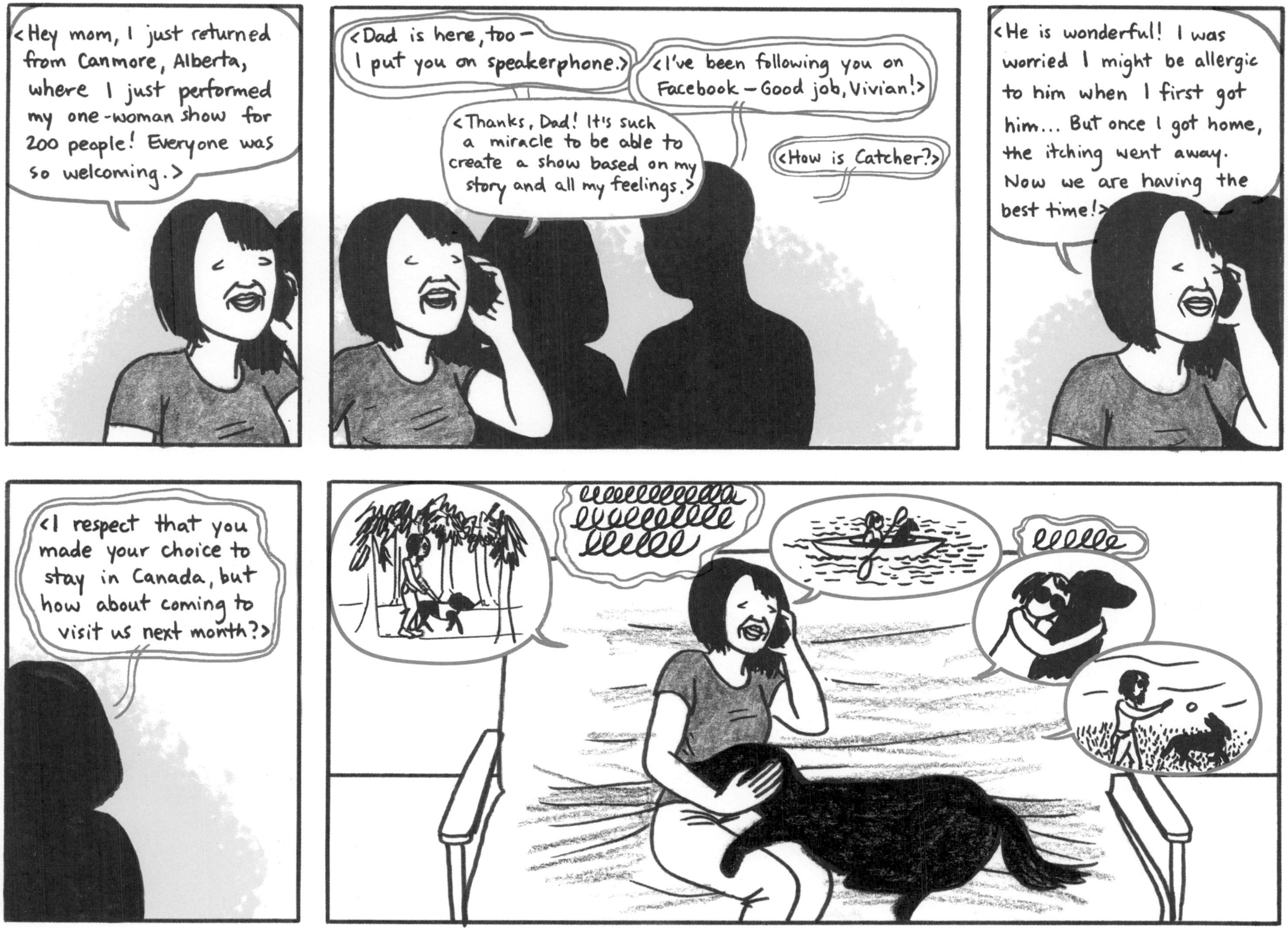
<Hey mom, I just returned from Canmore, Alberta, where I just performed my one-woman show for 200 people! Everyone was so welcoming.>
<Dad is here, too— I put you on speakerphone.>
<I've been following you on Facebook—Good job, Vivian!>
<Thanks, Dad! It's such a miracle to be able to create a show based on my story and all my feelings.>
<How is Catcher?>
<He is wonderful! I was worried I might be allergic to him when I first got him... But once I got home, the itching went away. Now we are having the best time!>
<I respect that you made your choice to stay in Canada, but how about coming to visit us next month?>
lllllllllla llllllllll lllll
lllle

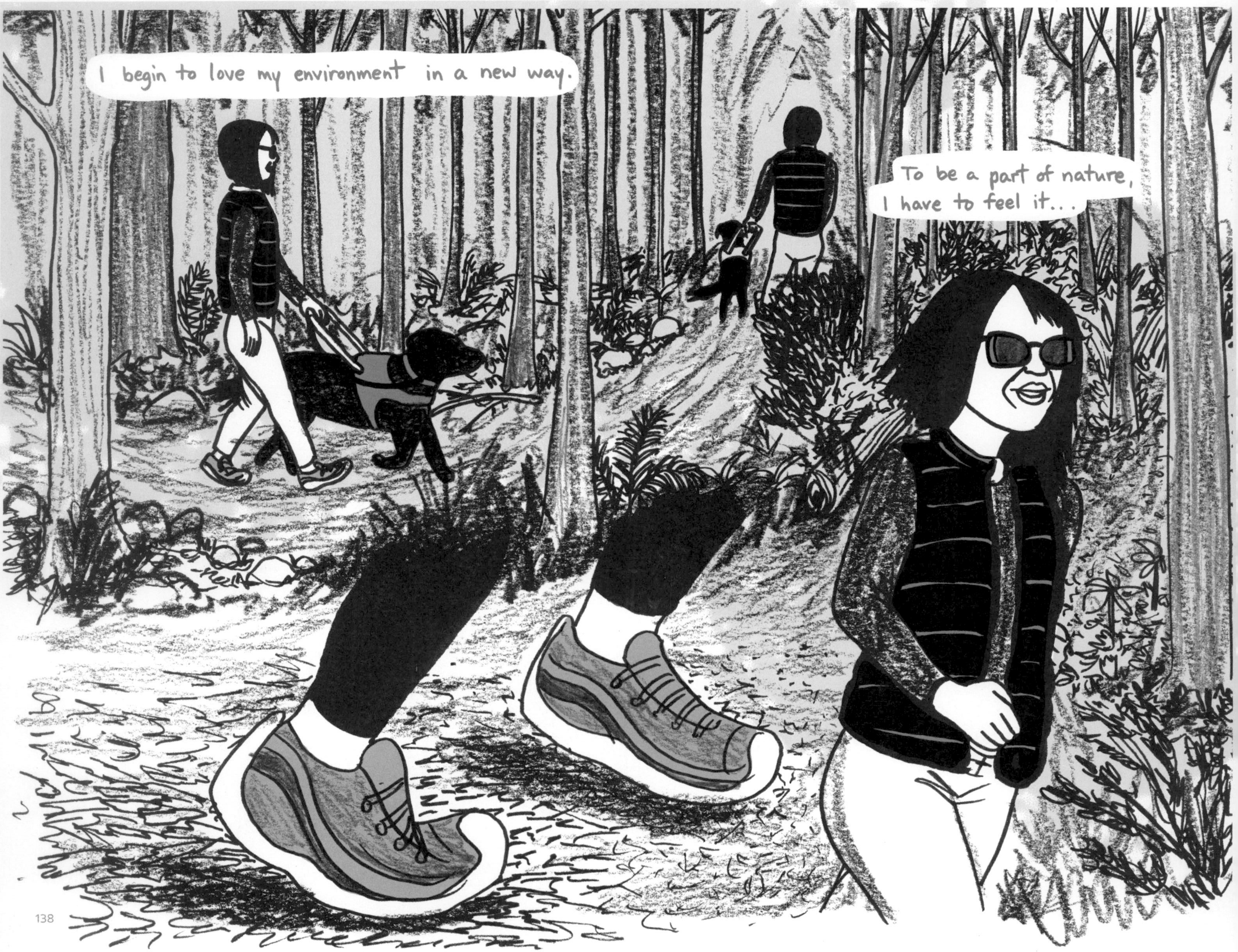
I begin to love my environment in a new way.
To be a part of nature, I have to feel it...

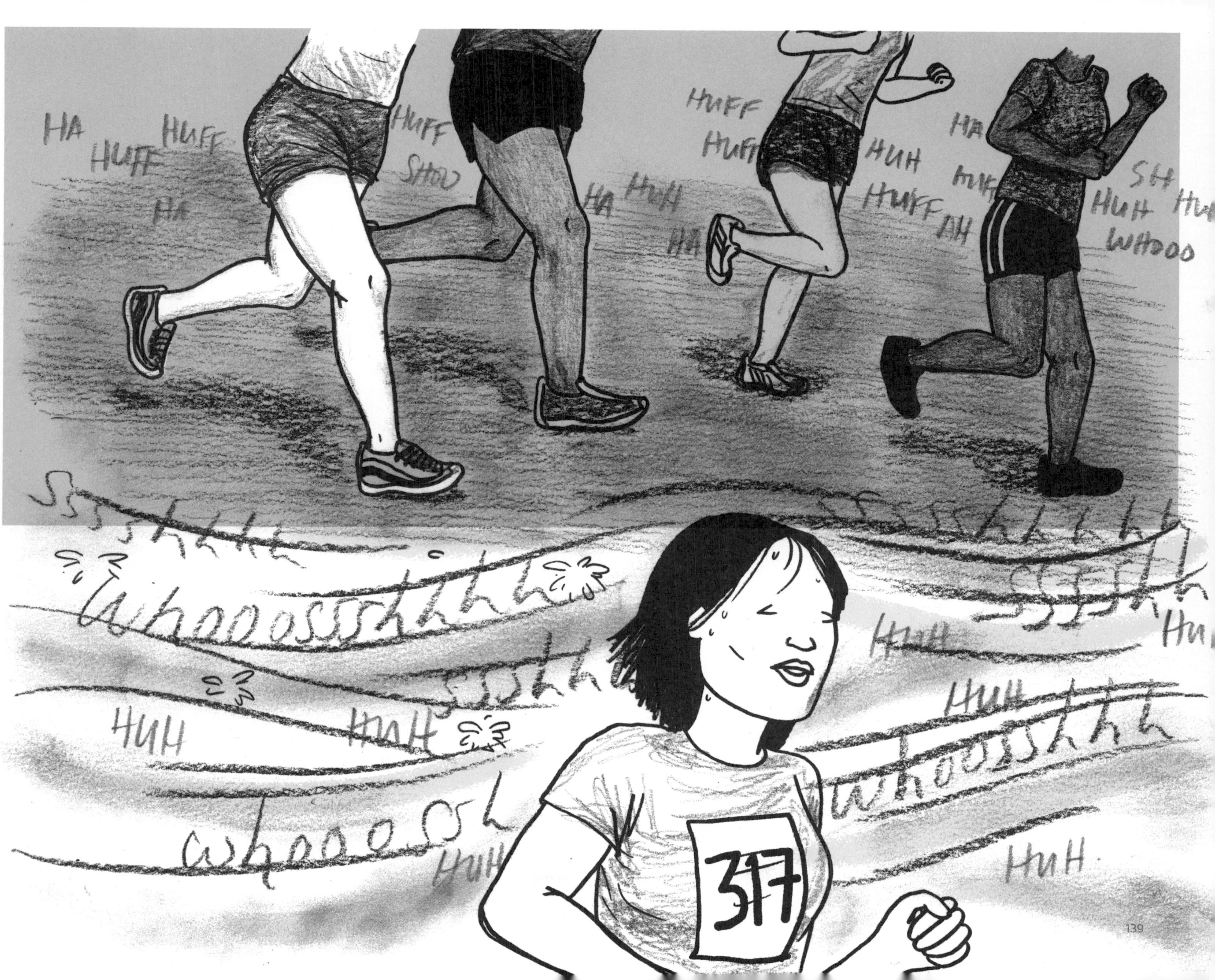
HA
HUFF
HUFF
HA
HUFF
SHOO
HA
HUH
HA
HUFF
HUFF
HUH
HUFF
AH
HA
HUFF
SH
HUH
WHOOO
ssshhhh
ssshhhhhh
whooosshhh
ssshhh
HUH
HUH
HUH
HUH
HUH
whooosshhh
whoooosh
HUH
HUH
317

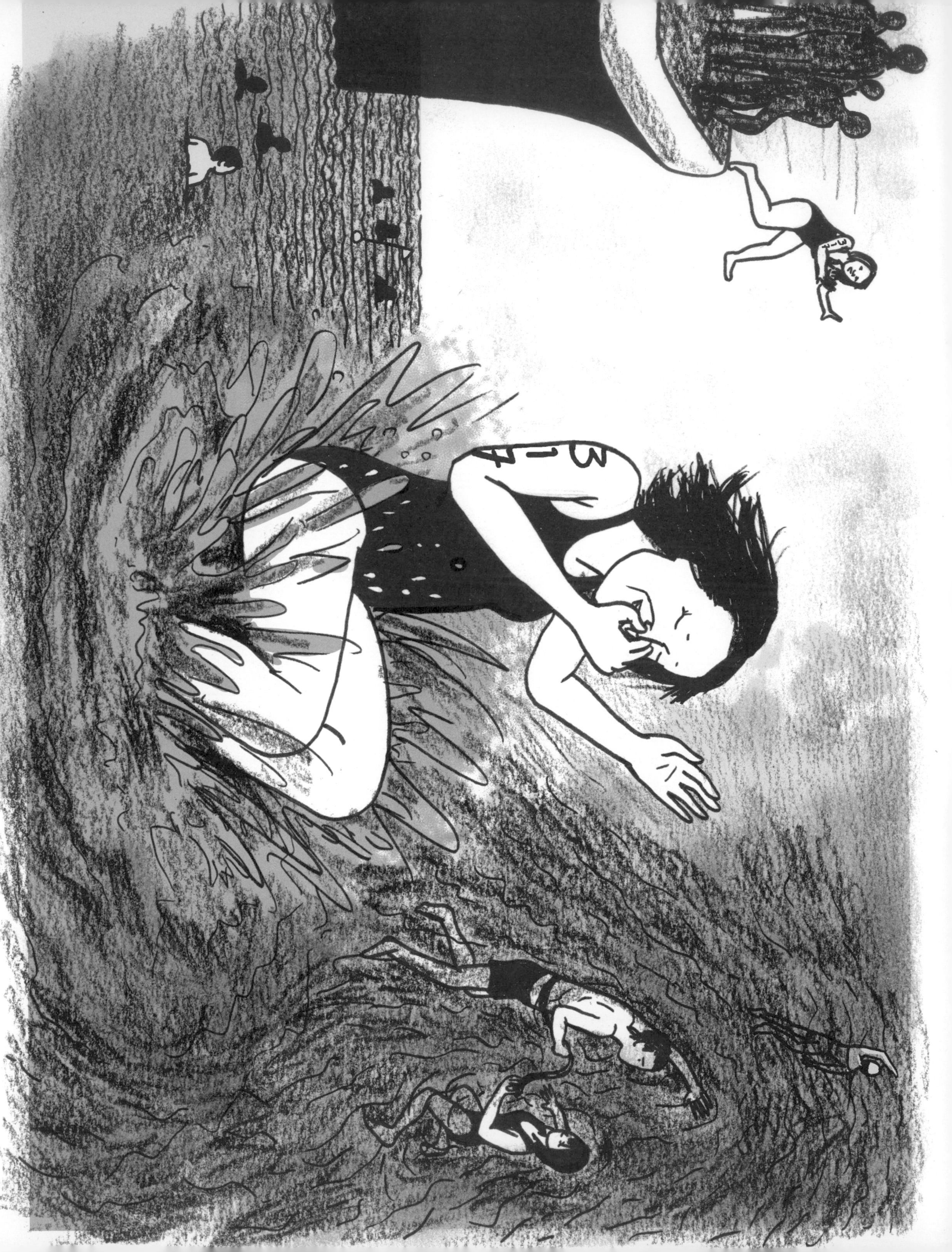

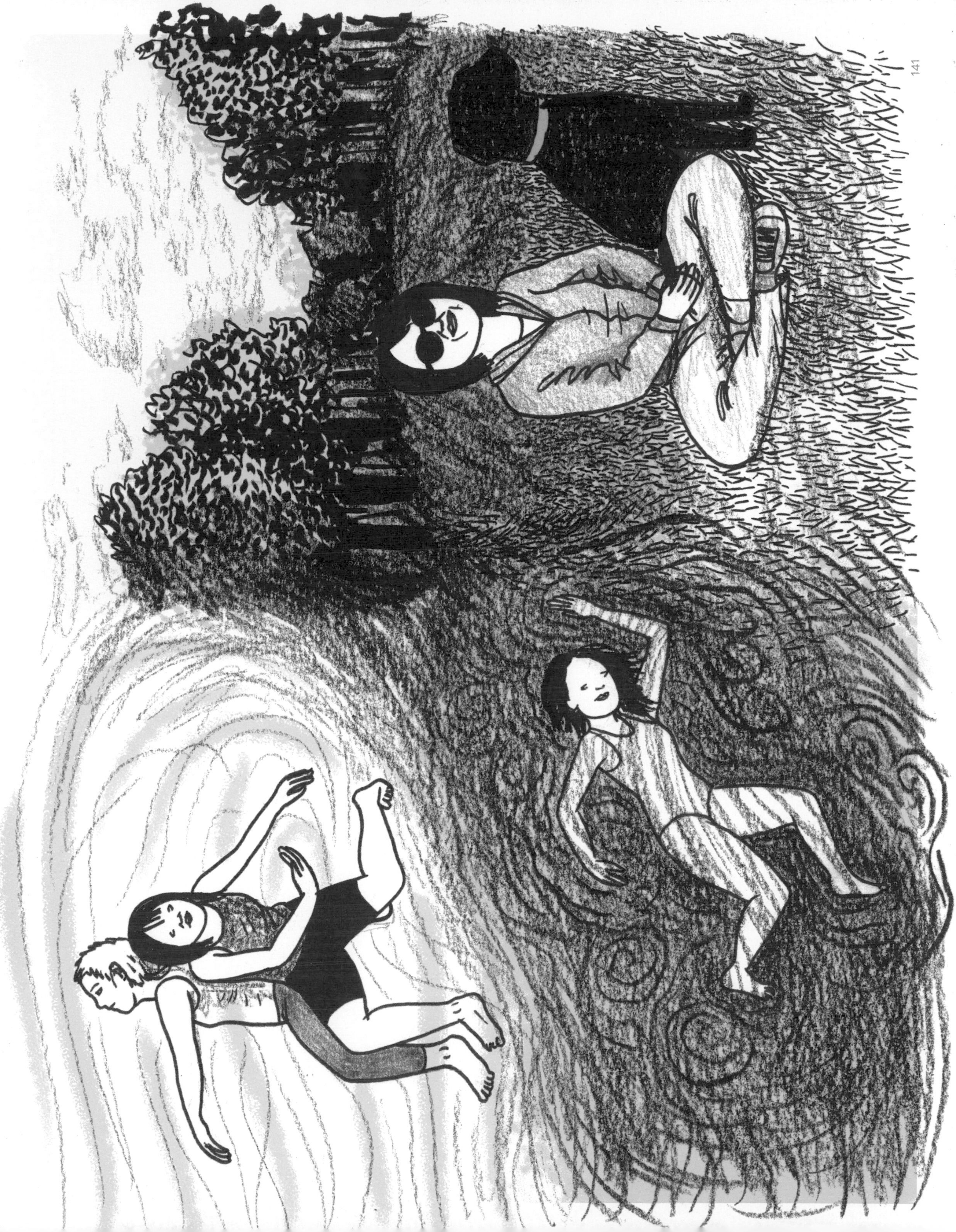

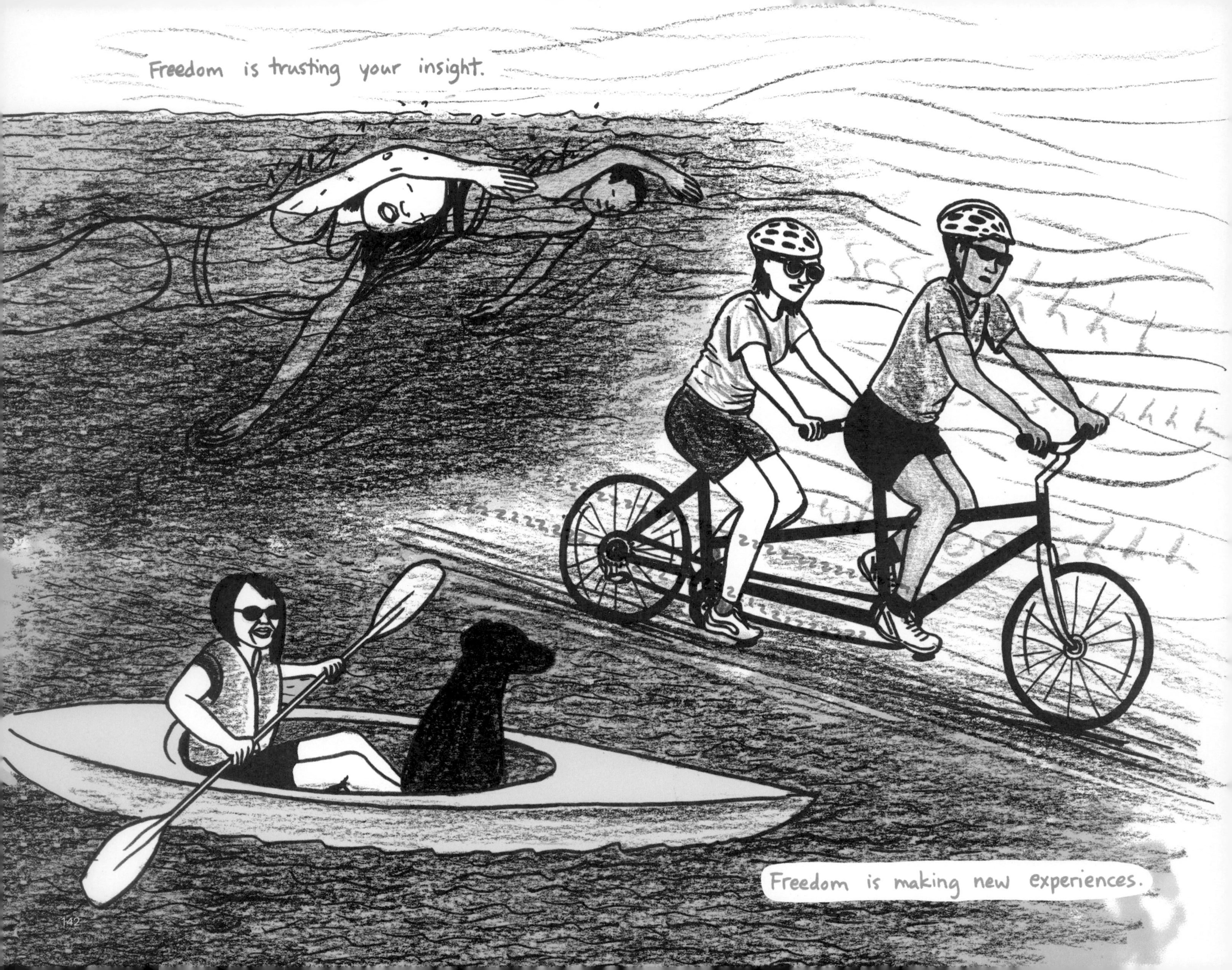

Freedom is trusting your insight.
Freedom is making new experiences.

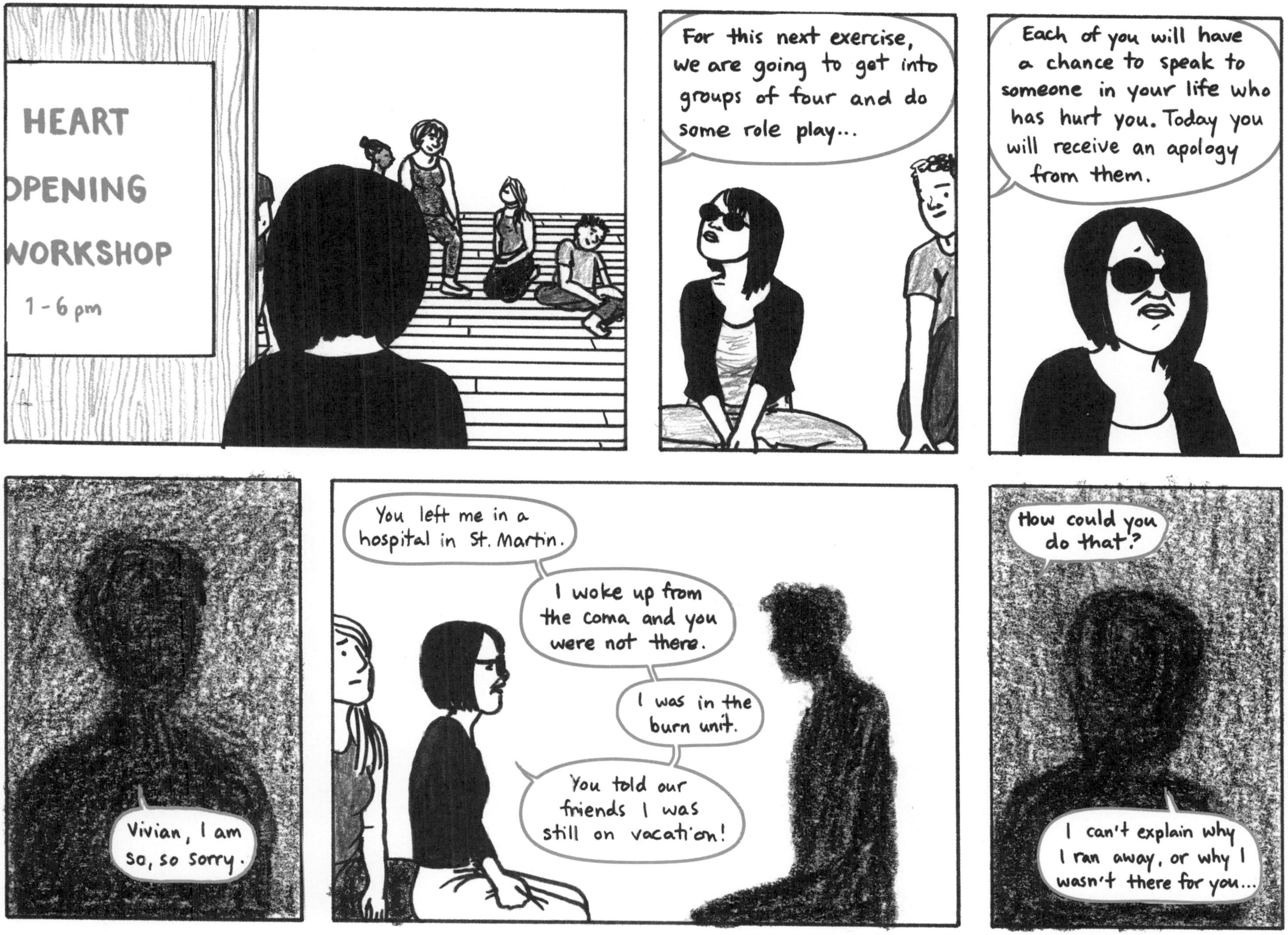
HEART
OPENING
WORKSHOP
1 - 6 pm
For this next exercise, we are going to get into groups of four and do some role play...
Each of you will have a chance to speak to someone in your life who has hurt you. Today you will receive an apology from them.
Vivian, I am so, so sorry.
You left me in a hospital in St. Martin.
I woke up from the coma and you were not there.
I was in the burn unit.
You told our friends I was still on vacation!
How could you do that?
I can't explain why I ran away, or why I wasn't there for you...

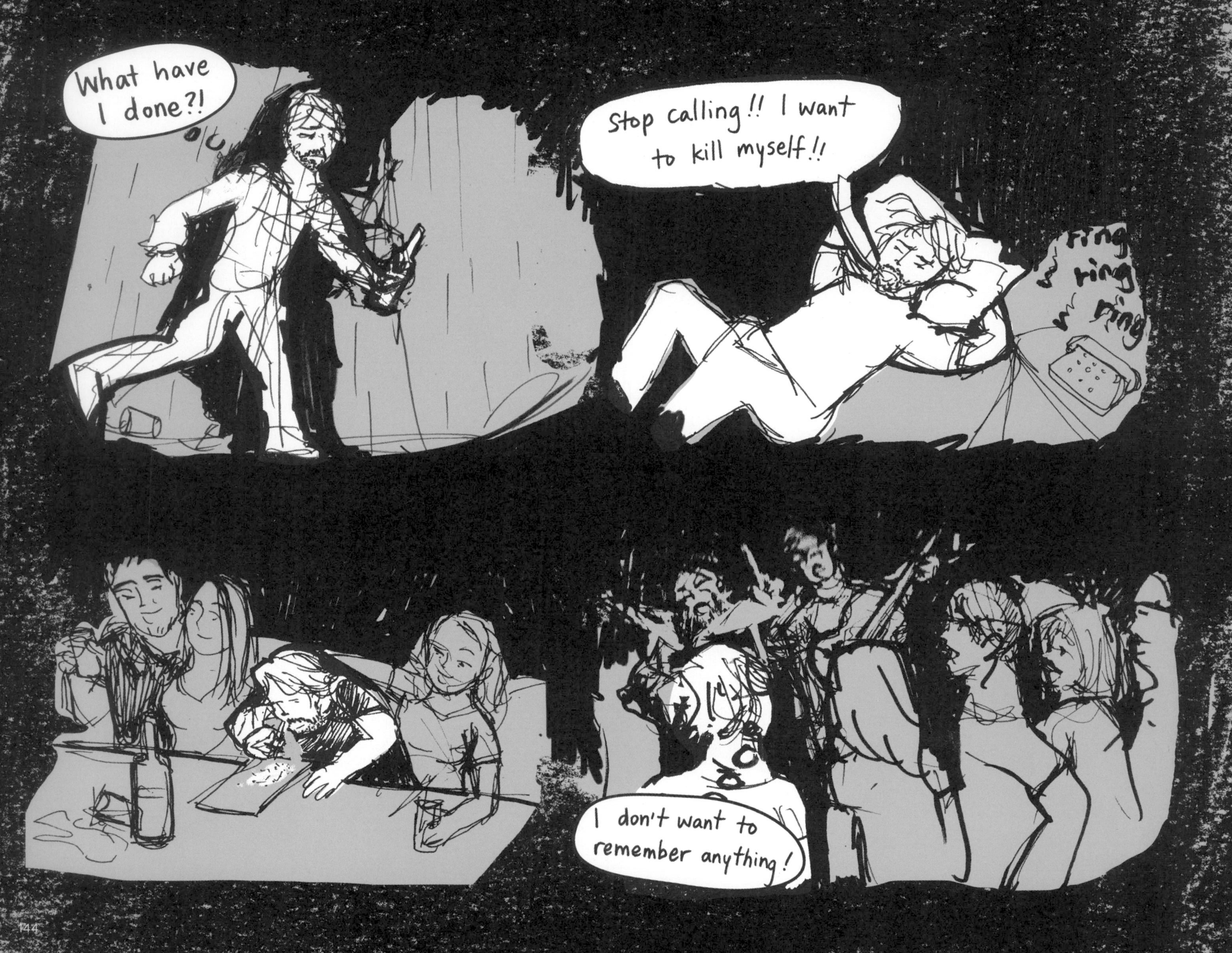
What have I done?!
Stop calling!! I want to kill myself!!
ring ring ring
I don't want to remember anything!

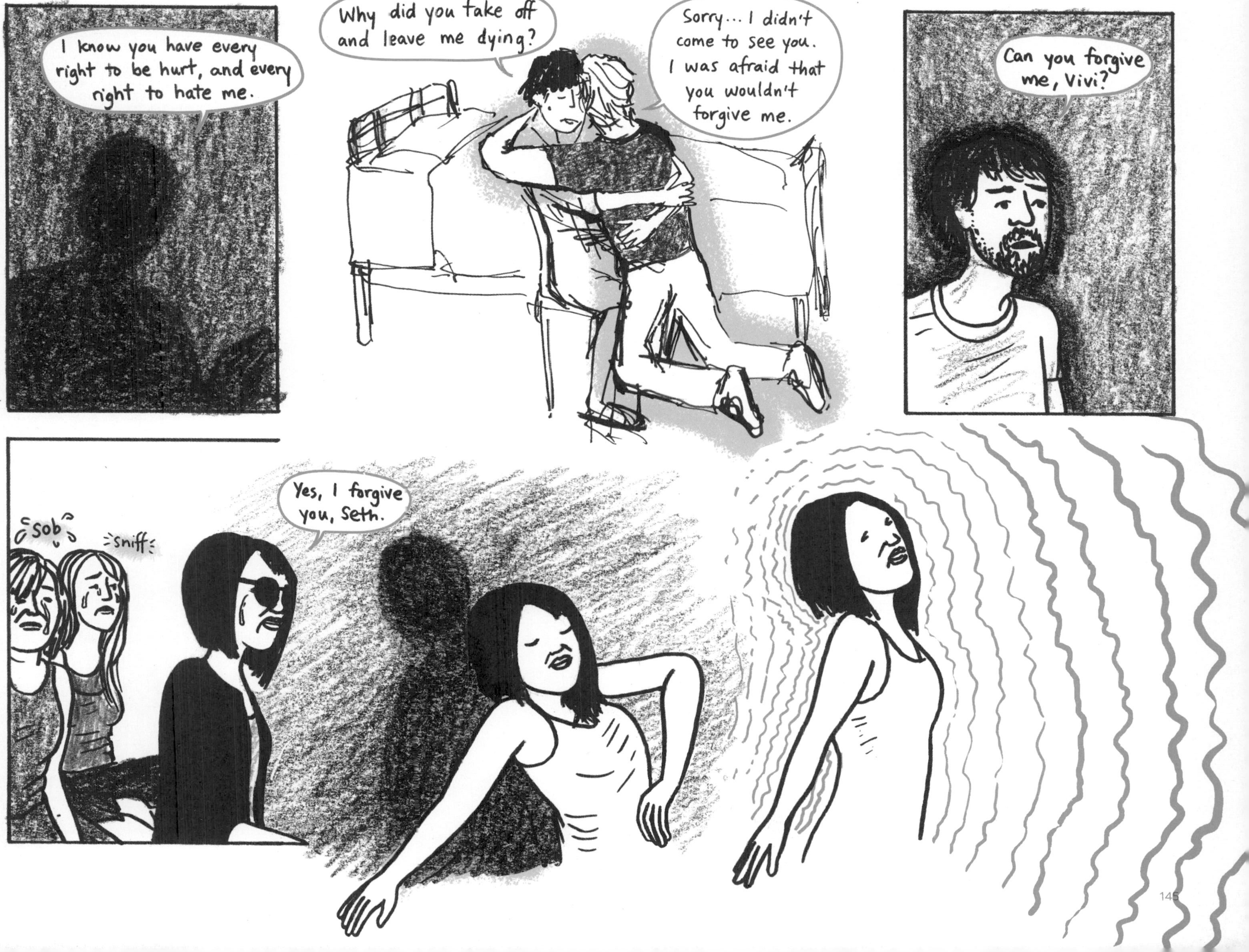
I know you have every right to be hurt, and every right to hate me.
Why did you take off and leave me dying?
Sorry... I didn't come to see you. I was afraid that you wouldn't forgive me.
Can you forgive me, Vivi?
sob
sniff
Yes, I forgive you, Seth.

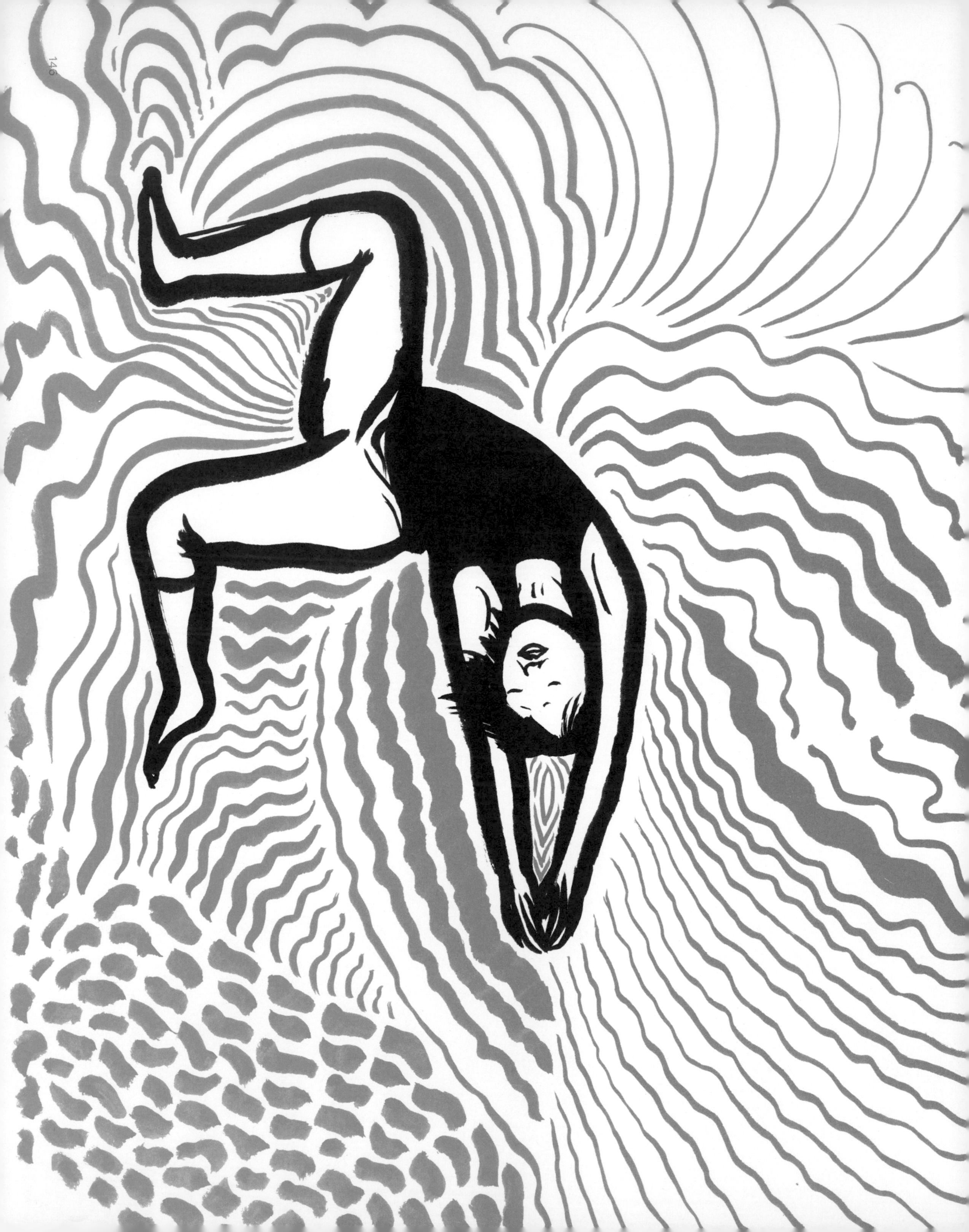

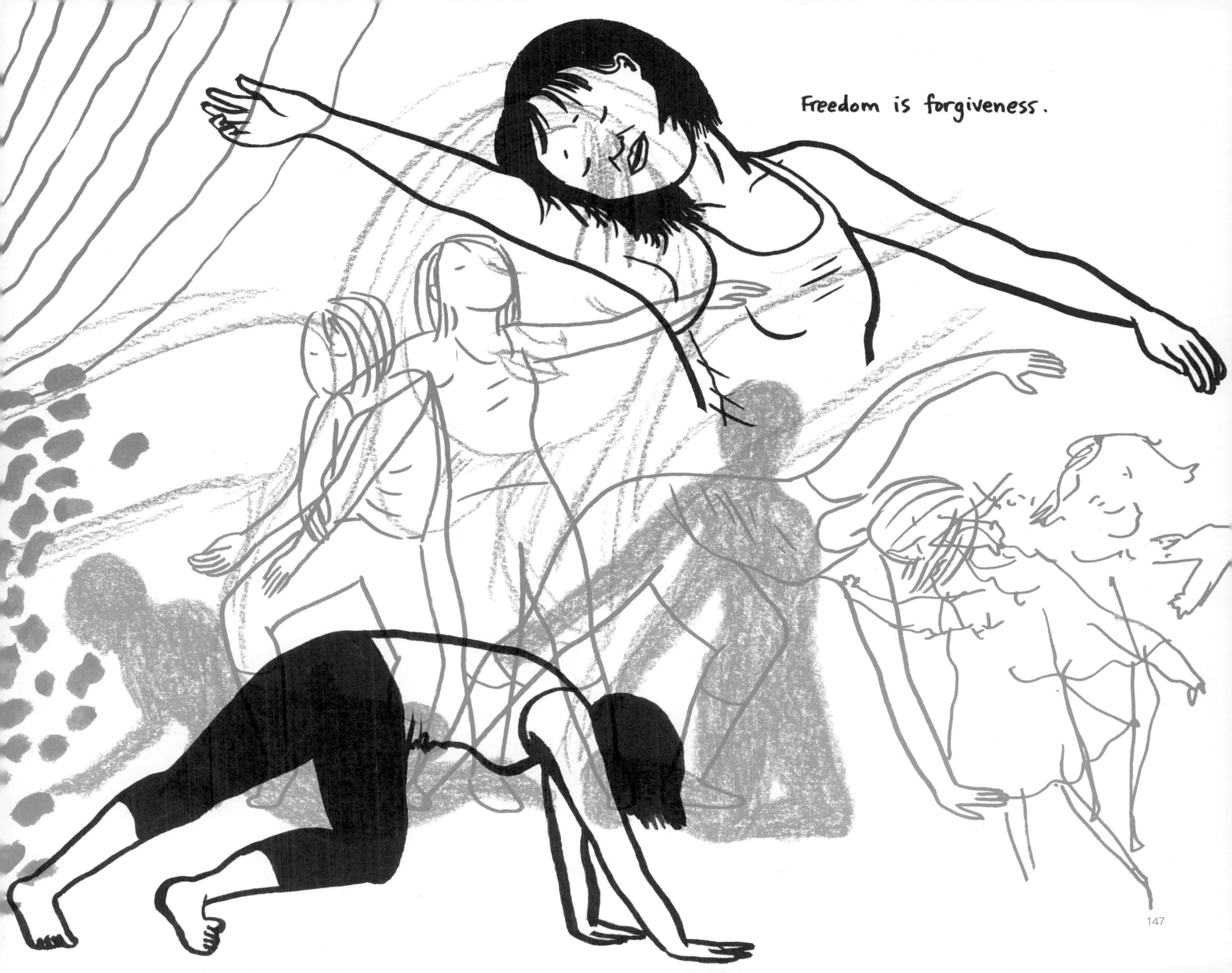
Freedom is forgiveness.

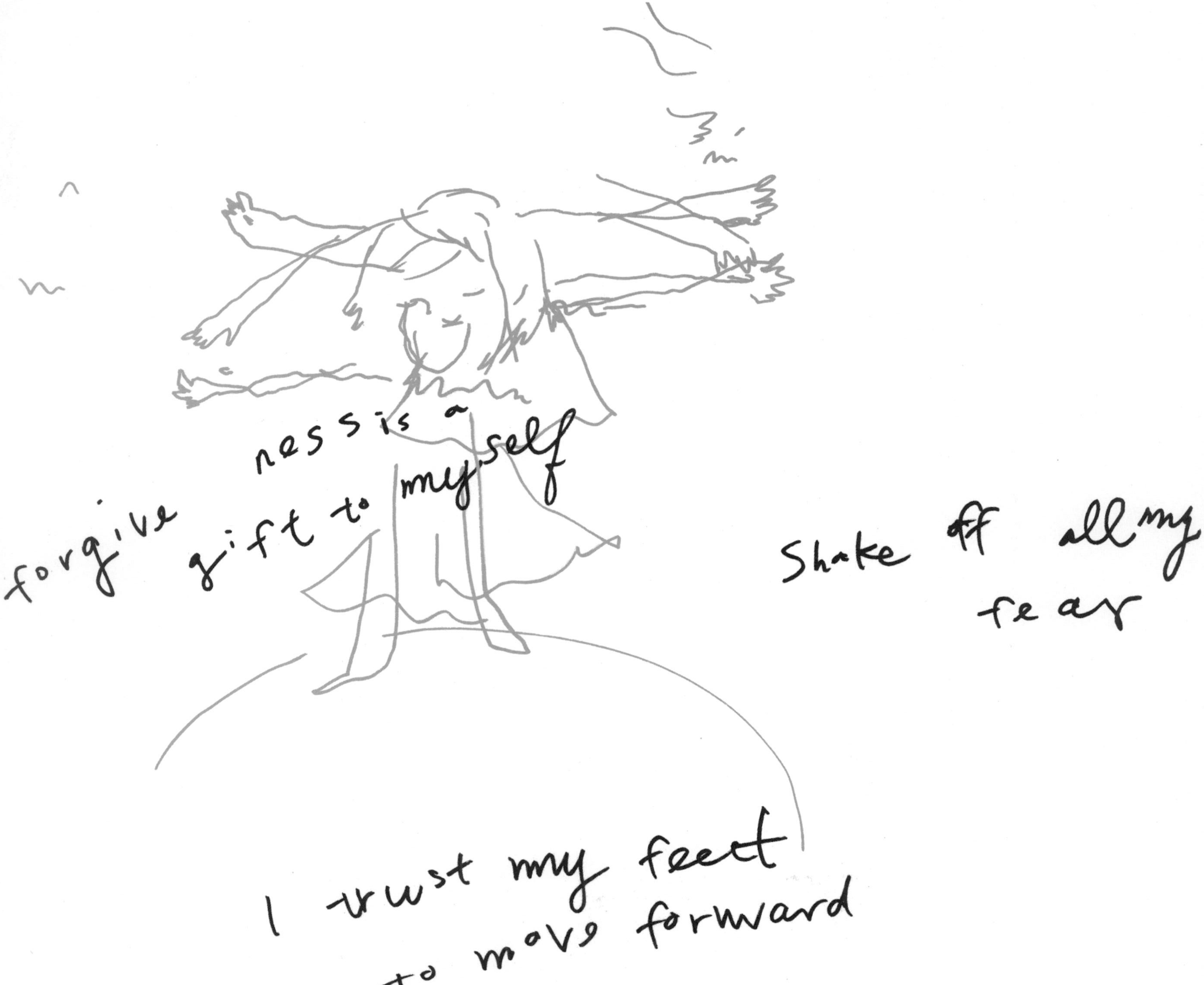
forgiveness is a
gift to myself
Shake off all my
fear
I trust my feet
to move forward

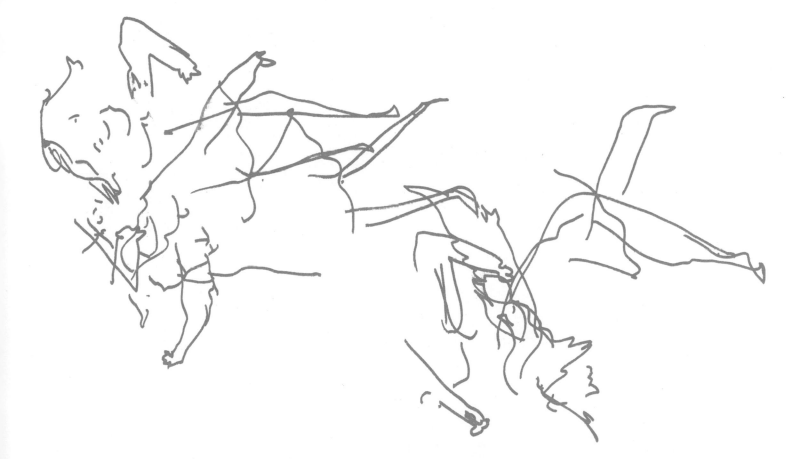

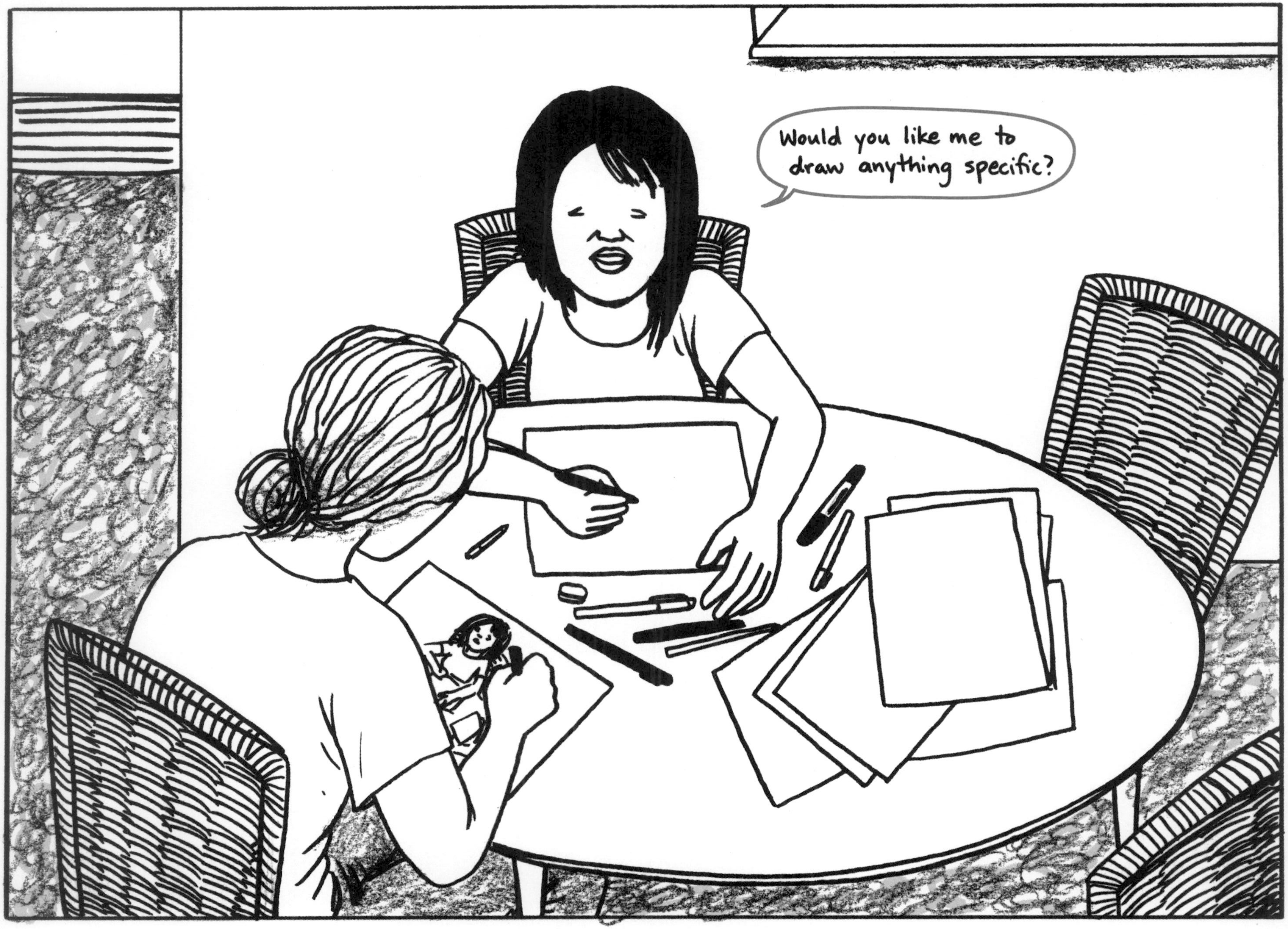
Would you like me to draw anything specific?

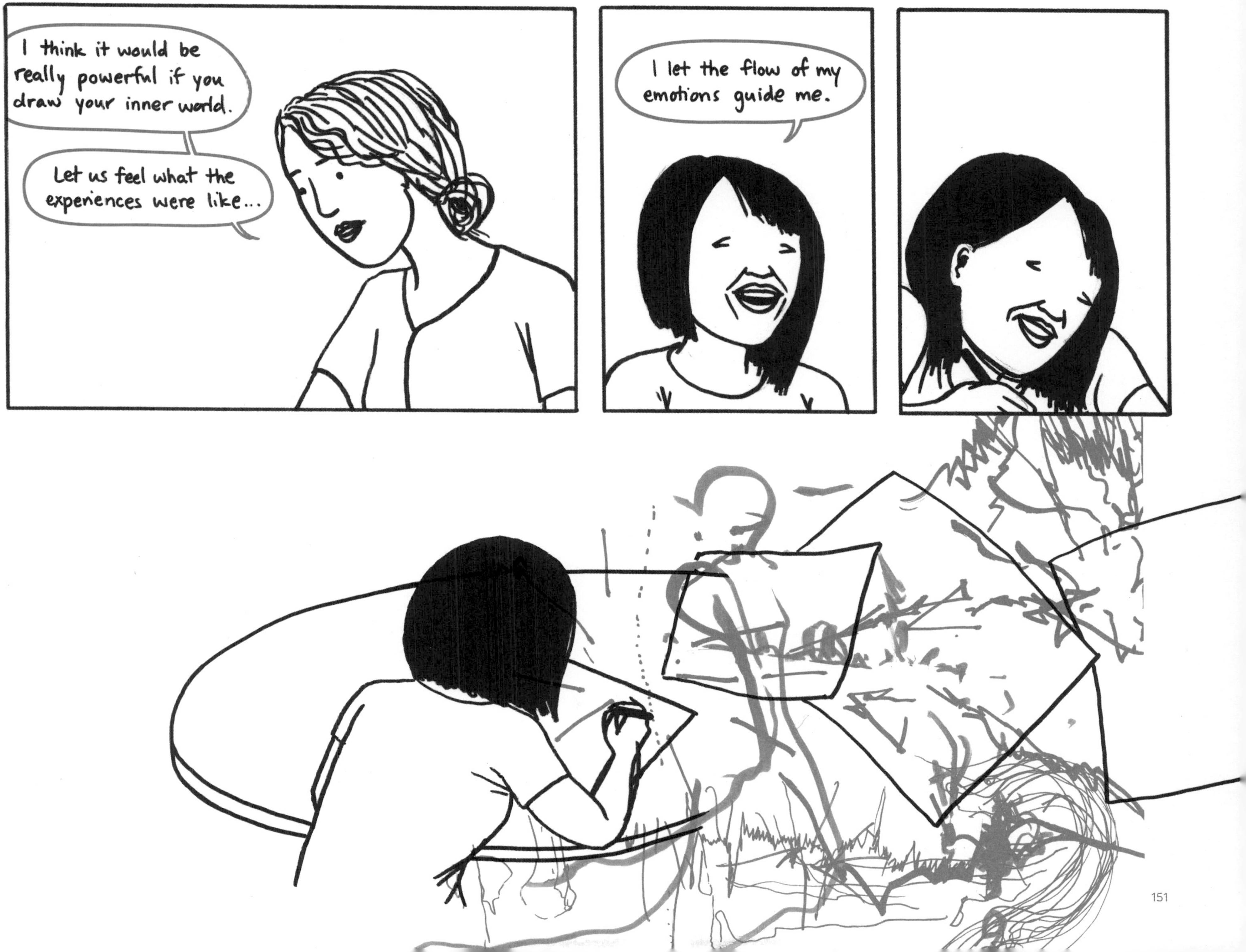
I think it would be really powerful if you draw your inner world.
Let us feel what the experiences were like...
I let the flow of my emotions guide me.

Inside a dog is pure joy.

Listening patiently
with awareness.

Mindfully living in
the moment.

Leash tug,

arched back.

Bag in hand.

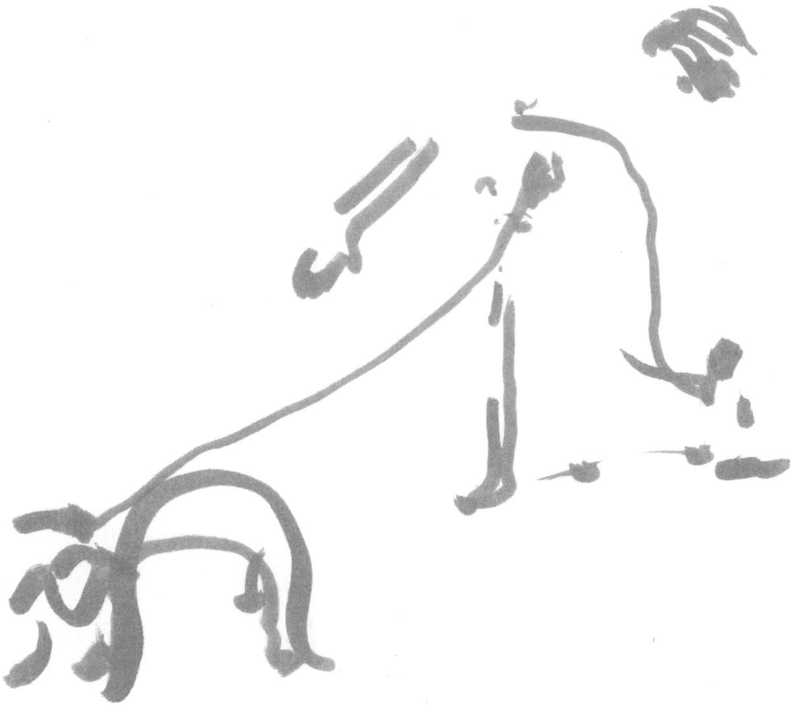

Squish.

Sometimes life is messy.
I can handle it.

154

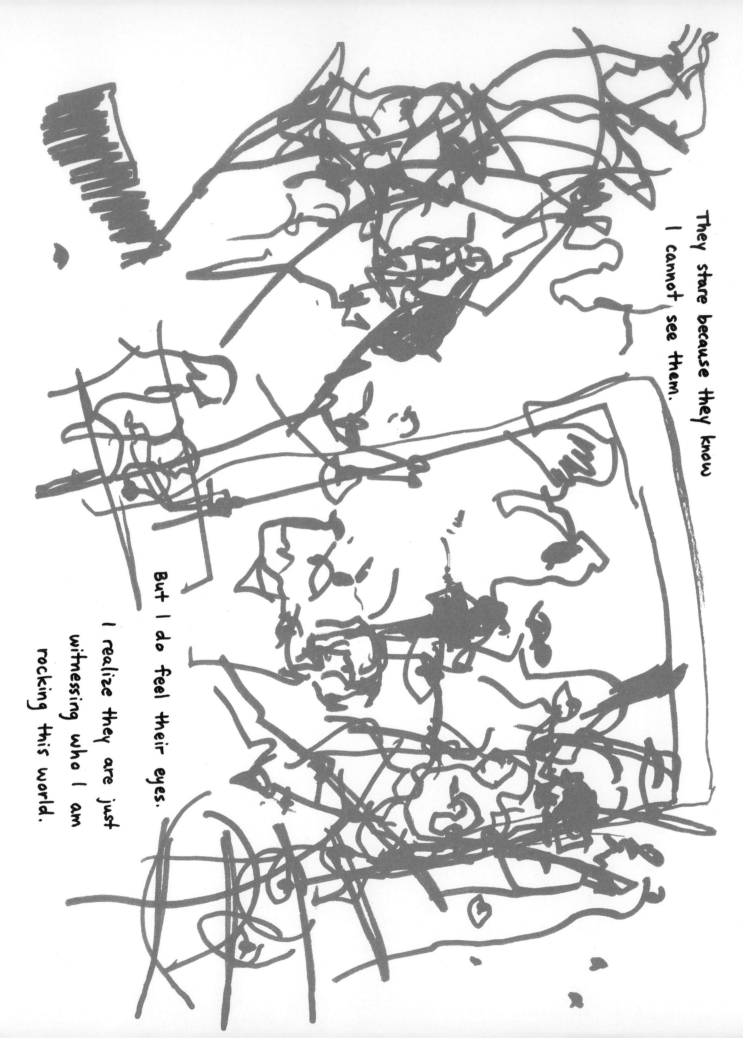

They stare because they know
I cannot see them.

But I do feel their eyes.

I realize they are just
witnessing who I am
rocking this world.

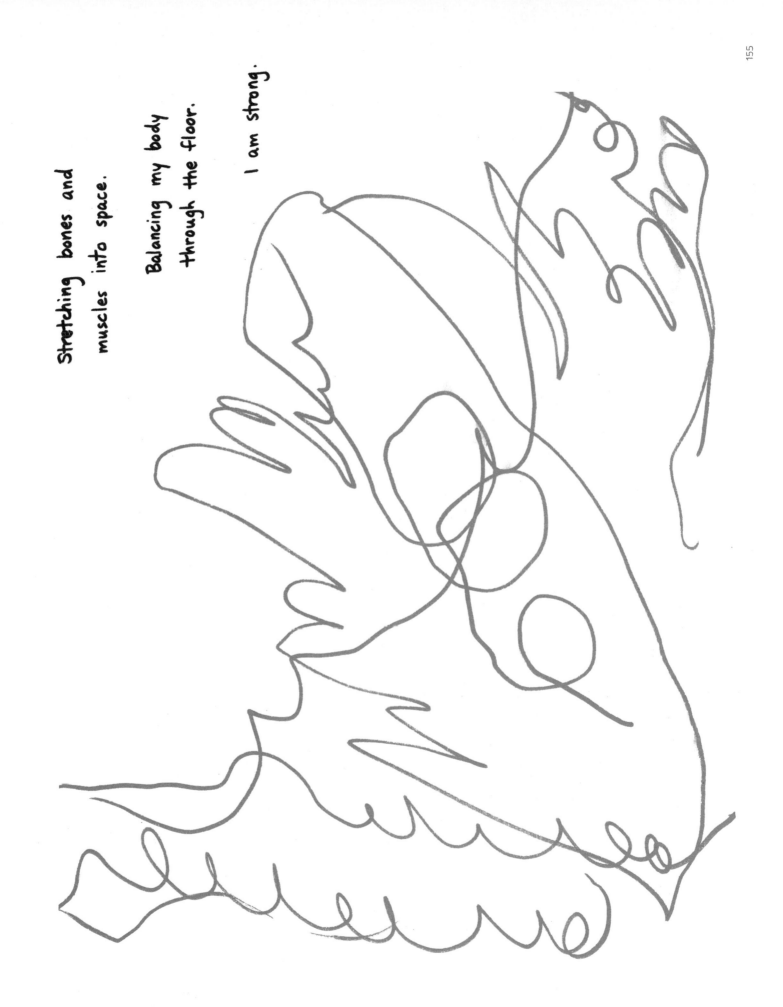

Stretching bones and
muscles into space.

Balancing my body
through the floor.

I am strong.

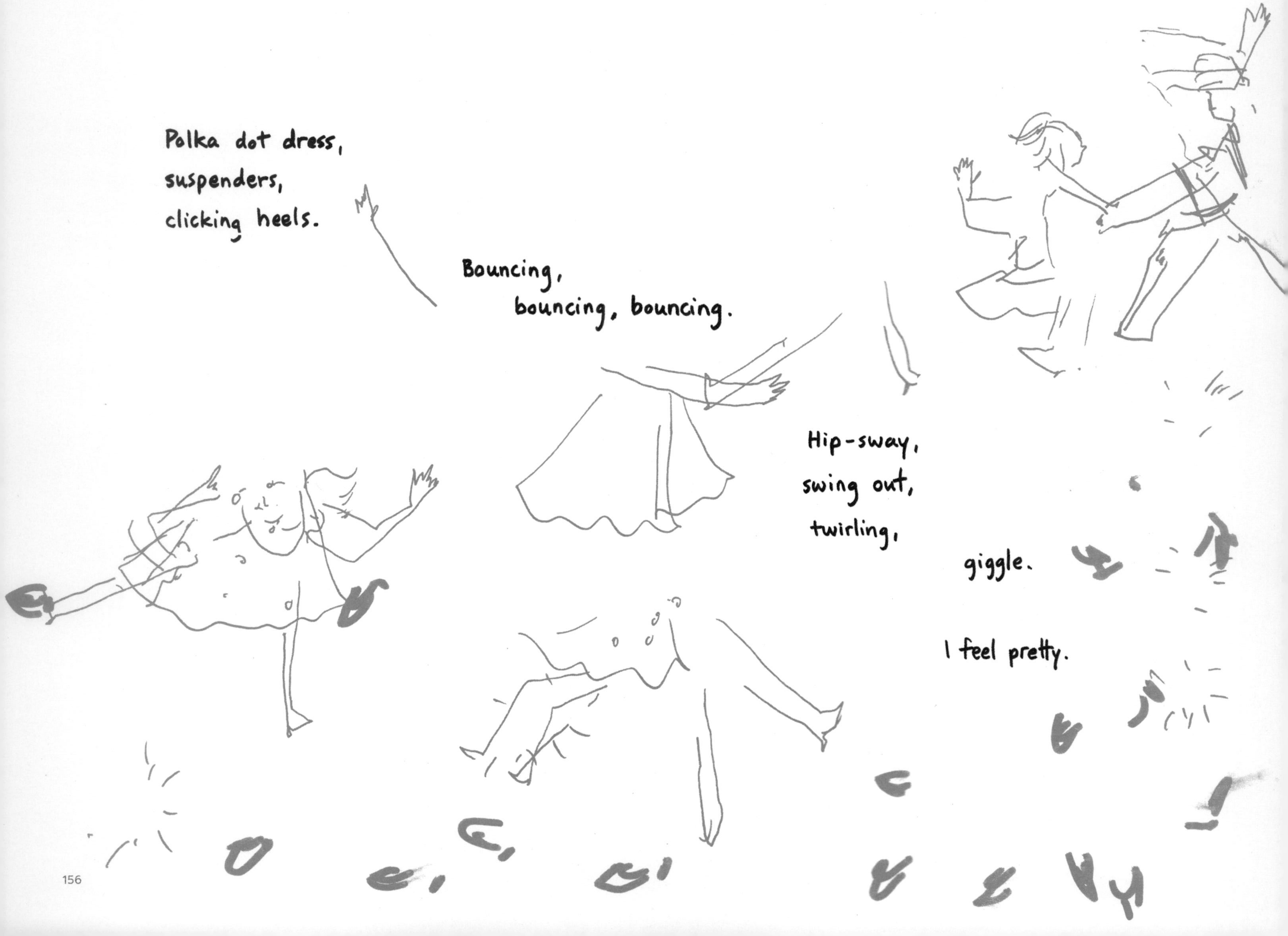

Polka dot dress,
suspenders,
clicking heels.

Bouncing,
bouncing, bouncing.

Hip-sway,
swing out,
twirling,

giggle.

I feel pretty.

The unknown is in front.
Impact of coolness.

Bubbles around me.

Kicking, flip, cut
through water.

Floating. Relax.

Water supports me.

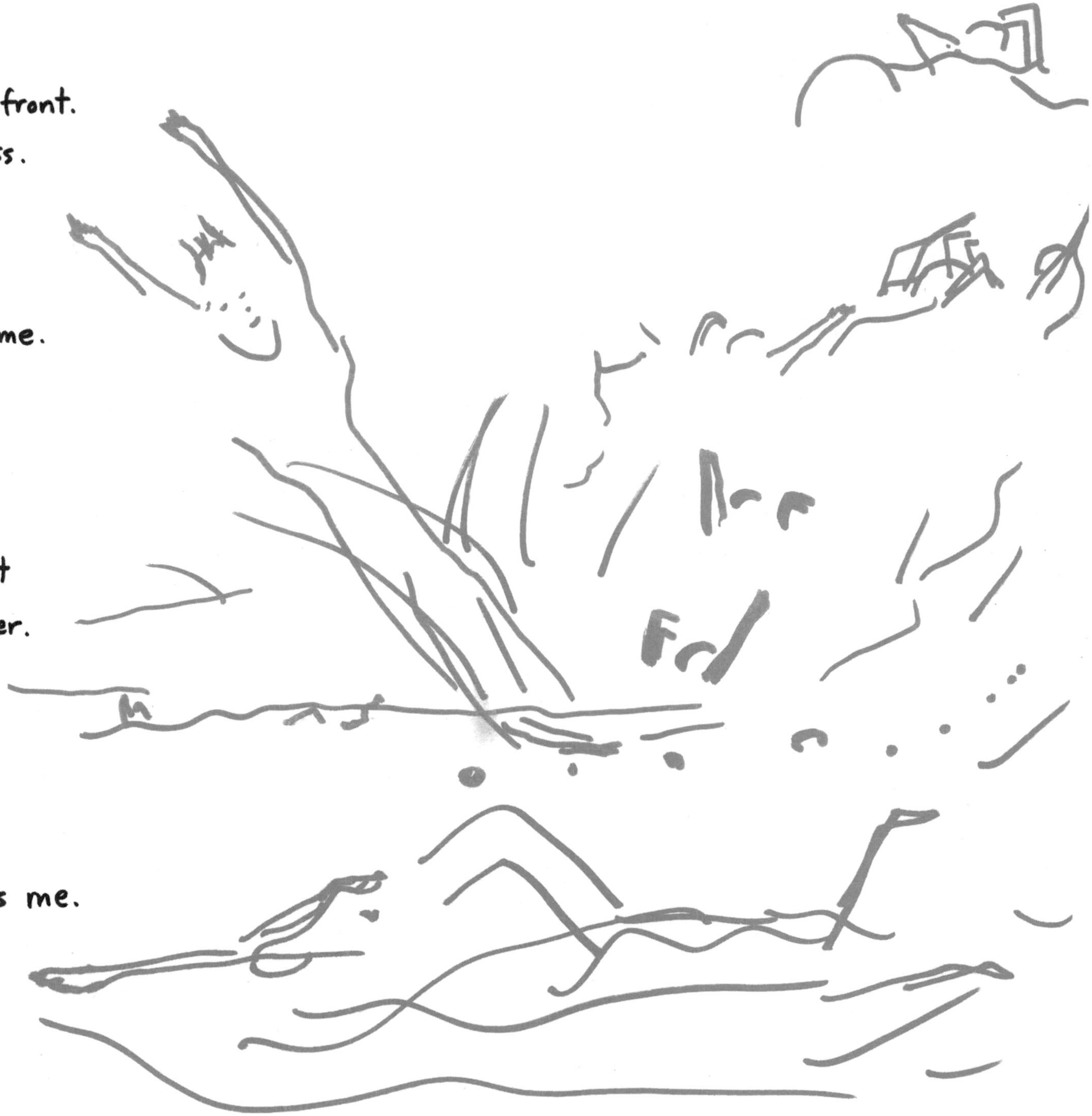

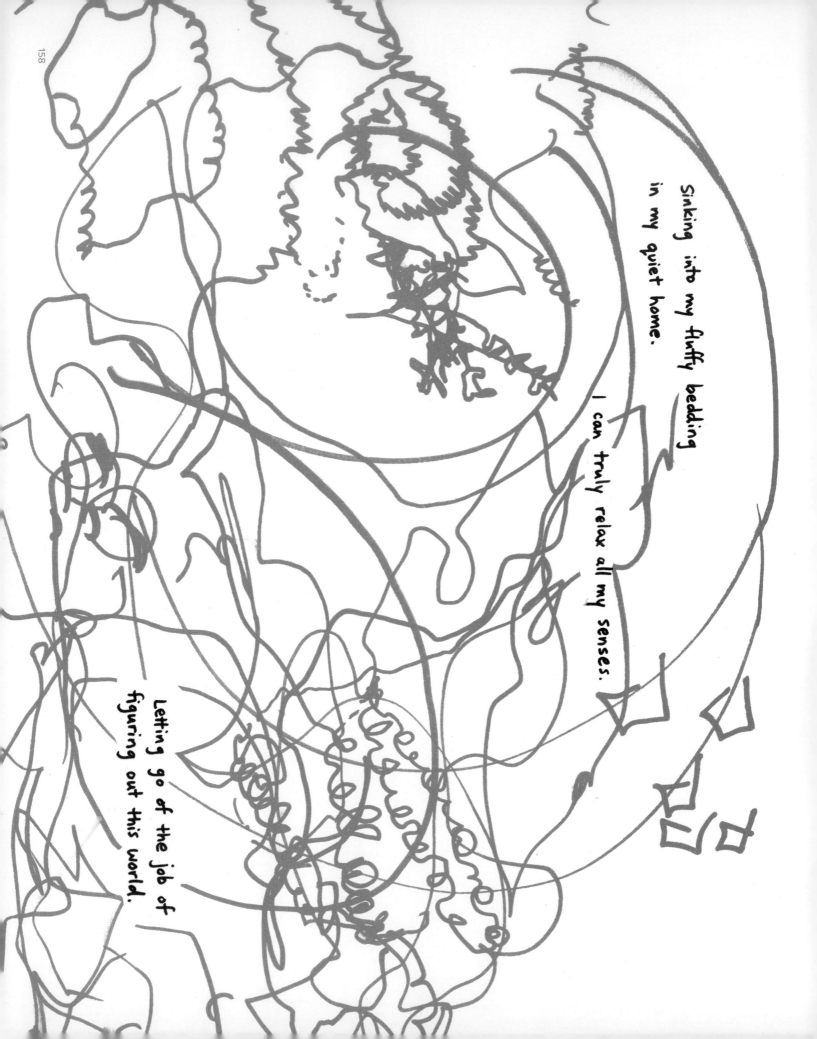

Sinking into my fluffy bedding
in my quiet home.

I can truly relax all my senses.

Letting go of the job of
figuring out this world.

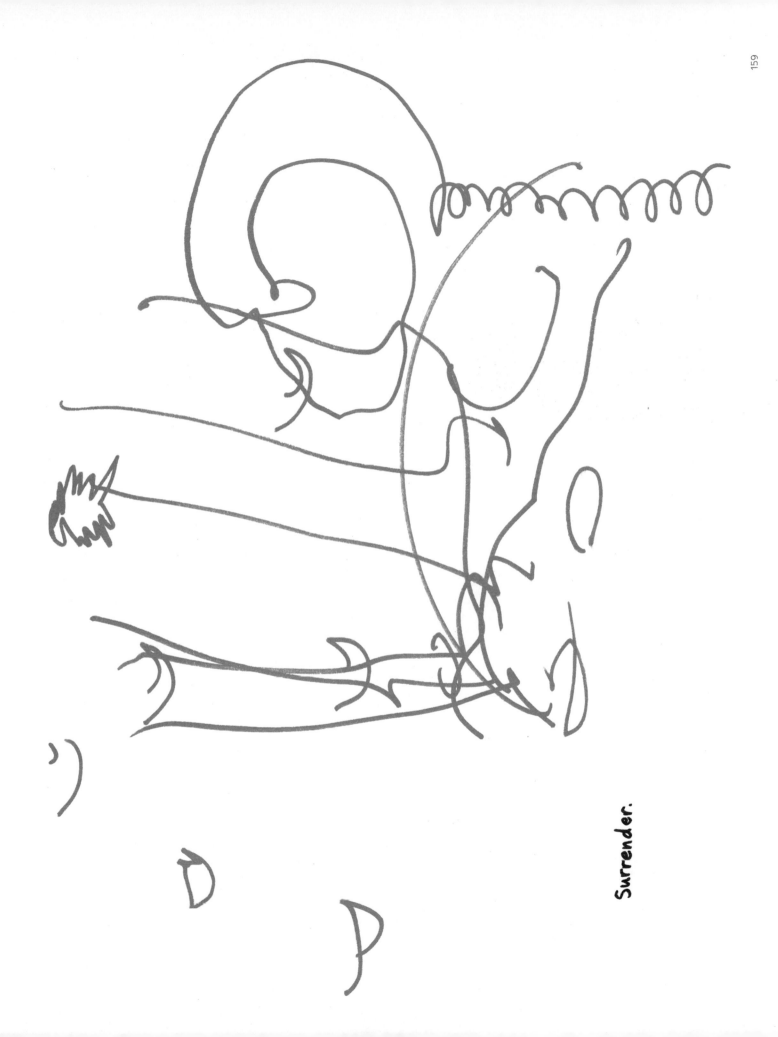

Surrender.

You can't add more time to your life, but you can add more life to your time.
Enjoy the ride!

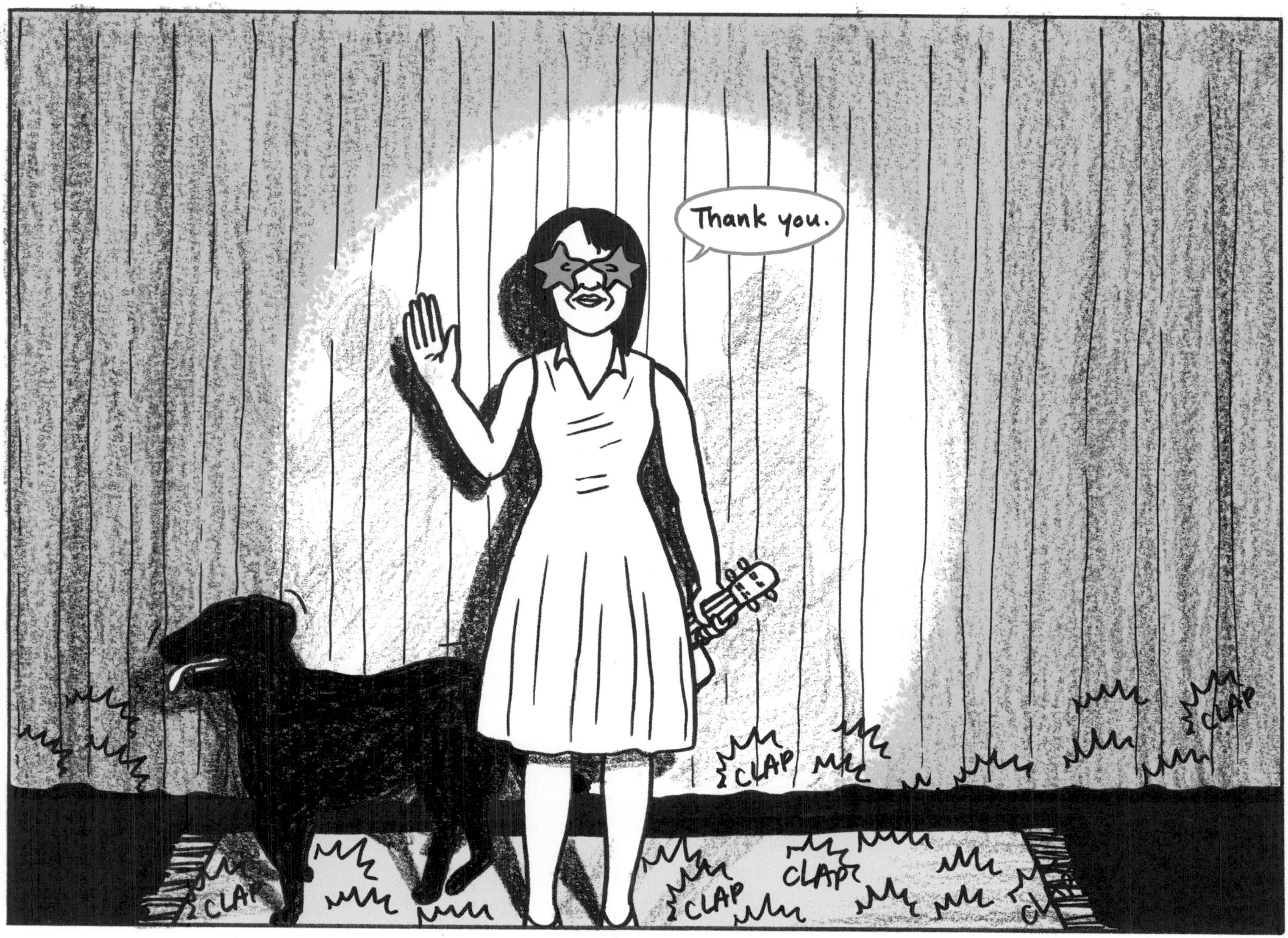
Thank you.
CLAP
CLAP
CLAP
CLAP
CLAP

Bringing My Story to the Page: Drawing as a Team

Vivian Chong

This book is my gift to the ever-curious sighted world, my answer to the ongoing questions about how I lost my sight and how blindness has affected my daily life. Let me tell you about how my graphic memoir came together.

Two years after I lost my sight, a cornea transplant restored 20% of my vision. I immediately started drawing. I was driven to tell the story of my medical journey, when due to a rare reaction to medication (Toxic epidermal necrolysis syndrome, or TEN) I suffered burns to the entire surface of my skin, fell into a coma, and lost my sight and hearing. The sight gains from my cornea transplant were short lived, lasting only a few weeks. As scar tissue grew over my corneas, I could see less and less; I drew with my face an inch away from the paper. The rough, chaotic feeling of my drawings reflects the mental and physical state of going blind and running out of time to draw. I drew on paper of various sizes—whatever I could find—and then taped my draw-ings into a large sketchbook to protect them. (In *Dancing After TEN*, I decided to include tape marks on some pages because they reflect the process of trying to preserve my art when I could no longer see.) I drew for as long as I could until my vision once again faded. What I had in my hands but could no longer see was the first draft of my graphic memoir.

This rough draft languished on the shelf for 12 years, until I met dance-theatre director Kathleen Rea and we started working together on a dance-theatre production about my life story. As part of our research I shared my drawings with her. Kathleen was moved by the images and encouraged me to tell the whole story. Together we sought out a comics artist who could collaborate with me to bring the rest of my story to the page—and found Georgia Webber, whose drawing style and experience with the graphic medicine genre made her a great fit for the project.

I began this project by relaying to Georgia all the important memories that shaped who I am today. We exchanged audio recordings, emails, and phone calls, she visited me in person, and I gave her access to my original drawings; she then organ-ized this information using her cartooning skills to create a plan that integrated both of our styles. She wrote panel-by-panel image descriptions, which I reviewed using adaptive technology. Kathleen and I would then discuss these descriptions, and I would add, remove, or adjust each panel or sequence of draw-ings. I would then write the dialogue so that my voice, sense of humor, and the emotional value of each interaction came through.

Once I approved the plan for the book, we began the drawing phase. Georgia crafted pages that filled the gaps in my first draft, while I worked on new drawings that expressed my emotional state within the story. TEN did not take away my ability to draw, just my ability to see my drawings. After the comics pages were completed, Kathleen described the art, panel by panel, so that I could picture it in my head. Acting as my "eyes," Kathleen gave me her impressions of how our different drawing styles synched together and helped me keep track of story continuity. She then sent Georgia my drawing revision notes. We repeated this process until a final round of describing confirmed that the all pages of the book were complete.

Once we were finished, Kathleen recorded a rough audio descrip-tion of the entire book so that I had access to it. In the near future, I plan to create a professional audio described version of *Dancing After TEN* to provide access to my story to those who cannot see. Recently, my journey has been interpreted through another med-ium as well. April 2020 marks the world premiere of *Dancing with the Universe*, a dance-theatre production co-directed by Kathleen and I that tells my life story. In this production, I look forward to acting and dancing as myself.

Acknowledgements

Whenever things do not go your way, just remember that you are the author of your life. You can write the chapter of your tragedy, but don't forget to turn the page and cast new characters to take your story in a new direction. In this process there are always many people to thank along the way. I want to give a big thank you to Kathleen Rea for recognizing my talent for drawing upon seeing my first draft of *Dancing After TEN*. Her faith in me as an artist is the pillar of this project. She stepped in as my "eyes" and helped me with the editing process, and through this we have become friends. Thank you to comics artist Georgia Webber for your drawings and for trusting in my story and my vision for the project. Together we show how collaboration makes a kinder world. Thank you to Kathleen, Georgia, and all the donors for fundraising efforts that made this project possible. Thank you to Fantagraphics for having the foresight to hire a comic artist who cannot see. Thank you to Gary Groth from Fantagraphics for taking a personal interest in this project. Thank you to mom and dad for buying me many Etch-A-Sketches over the years, which supported my love of drawing and taught me not to be attached to the image. This showed me that the essence of artistic expression is the act of creation itself. Most of all, thank you to Catcher for being my devoted silent partner. You remind me that love comes in many forms.

— VIVIAN CHONG

This book was an enormous learning process for me. There is a river of gratitude flowing through to these wonderful people: Vivian was an insightful artistic force, putting her trust in me to bring her story to the world. Kathleen was a steady hand guiding both of us through creative collaboration with equity, accessibility, and grace. Kevin Czapiewski provided extraordinary editing help and support. Sid Sharp and Mike Smith were the best production assistants I could ask for, and Sid provided a beautiful background drawing on page 33. Zoe Sharpe was my writing buddy, making the process less lonely and lots more fun. My parents were the emergency dinner team, providing home-cooked nourishment when I was drawing too much to cook. And D Alex Meeks, the ever-patient, ever-loving presence that he is, provided support that I can't describe and don't ever want to live without.

— GEORGIA WEBBER

Vivian Chong's first love is drawing. Ever since she could hold a pencil, she drew day and night and, after formal training, eventually worked as a graphic designer, video editor, and 3-D animator. After a rare medical reaction to ibuprofen left her without sight, she experienced a creative rebirth and became a medal-winning triathlete, an access-focused yoga instructor, a motivational speaker, a musician, a dancer, and performer. She is part of the Brazilian percussion ensemble Samba Elégua and performs regularly with them in community events in Toronto. In 2016, she created and performed a one-woman show, *The Sunglasses Monologue*, which toured throughout Canada. In 2020, she collaborated with choreographer Kathleen Rea to create *Dancing with the Universe*, a dance-theatre production starring Chong along with a cast of five dancers and a musician. She was featured in the documentary *A Whole New Light*, profiled in CBC Arts, and appears — with her guide dog, Catcher — in the children's book *Claire Wants A Boxing Name*. Chong and Catcher often hike together, and have, over the last two years, trekked the entire 275 kilometers of the Oak Ridges Trail through rain and shine.

Georgia Webber is a comics artist, writer, and editor living in southern Ontario. She is best known for her debut graphic memoir, *Dumb: Living Without a Voice* (Fantagraphics, 2018), the chronicle of her severe vocal injury and sustained vocal condition which causes her pain from using her voice. This difficult experience led her to work as a cranial sacral therapist, a meditation facilitator, and as an improvising musician, blending elements of healthcare, body awareness, and creative expression within constraints. She has extended her love of the voice into a community arts organization, called MAW Vocal Arts, that celebrates the diversity, creativity, and power of the voice with live showcase-style events several times a year. Webber is an active member of the Graphic Medicine community of artists who make comics that relate to health, speaking and giving work-shops at conferences across North America. Follow her exploits at www.georgiawebber.com.

Kathleen Rea was the project manager, access support, fundraiser, and one of the copyeditors for *Dancing After TEN*. Rea has danced with Canada's Ballet Jorgen, National Ballet of Canada, and Tiroler Landestheater (Austria). She has choreographed over 40 dance works and been nominated for five DORA awards. She is a recipient of a K.M. Hunter Choreographic Award and is a published author (*The Healing Dance*, Charles C. Thomas, 2012). She has a Master's in Expressive Arts Therapy through the Create Institute and the European Graduate School and teaches dance at George Brown College. She is the director of REAson d'etre dance productions, which produces dance-theatre productions and films.